"The Old Lady Trill, the
Victory Yell"

Native Americans
Interdisciplinary Perspectives
Edited by John R. Wunder and Cynthia Willis Esqueda

Other Books in this Series:

The Power of the Land
Identity, Ethnicity, and Class Among the Oglala Lakota
Paul Robertson

Political Principles and Indian Sovereignty
Thurman Lee Hester, Jr.

Dance Lodges of the Omaha People
Building From Memory
Mark Awakuni-Swetland

Blood Matters
*The Five Civilized Tribes and the Search
for Unity in the 20th Century*
Erik March Zissu

Three Nations, One Place
*Comparative Analyses of Comanche and Caddo
Social Change During the Spanish Colonial Era*
Martha McCollough

"The Old Lady Trill, the Victory Yell"
The Power of Women in Native American Literature

Patrice E. M. Hollrah

LONDON AND NEW YORK

First published 2004 by Routledge

2 Park Square, Milton Park, Abingdon, Oxon OX14 4RN
711 Third Avenue, New York, NY 10017, USA

Routledge is an imprint of the Taylor & Francis Group, an informa business

First issued in paperback 2016

Copyright © 2004 Taylor & Francis

Transferred to Digital Printing 2011

Contributions from the author's profits of this book will be made to the American Indian College Fund.

All rights reserved. No part of this book may be reprinted or reproduced or utilised in any form or by any electronic, mechanical, or other means, now known or hereafter invented, including photocopying and recording, or in any information storage or retrieval system, without permission in writing from the publishers.

Notice:
Product or corporate names may be trademarks or registered trademarks, and are used only for identification and explanation without intent to infringe.

Publisher's Note
The publisher has gone to great lengths to ensure the quality of this reprint but points out that some imperfections in the original may be apparent.

Library of Congress Cataloging-in-Publication Data

Hollrah, Patrice E. M., 1949–
    "The old lady Trill, the victory yell" : the power of women in Native American literature / Patrice E. M. Hollrah.
        p.   cm.
    ISBN 0-415-94697-2 (hardback : alk. paper)
    1. American literature—Indian authors—History and criticism.
    2. Women and literature—United States.   3. Indian women in literature.
    4. Women in literature.   5. Indian women.   I. Title.
        PS153.I52H65   2003
        813.009′352042—dc21
                                                                2003009692

ISBN 978-0-415-94697-1 (hbk)
ISBN 978-1-138-97744-0 (pbk)

Portions of this book appeared in slightly altered form in the following publications:

"Stretching Sexual Boundaries in Sherman Alexie's 'Indian Country,'" *Proceedings of Maple Leaf and Eagle Conference on North American Studies, Renvall Institute, University of Helsinki, Helsinki, Finland, September 3–6, 2002.* New York: Routledge, 2003.

"'The Men in the Bar Feared Her': The Power of Ayah in Leslie Marmon Silko's 'Lullaby.'" *Studies in American Indian Literatures* 15.2 (Summer 2003).

"'Size Matters: Humor and Death in Sherman Alexie's *The Lone Ranger and Tonto Fistfight in Heaven*," *Thalia: Studies in Literary Humor* 22.1-2 (Fall 2003).

"'This Ain't Real Estate': Intellectual Sovereignty and Economics in Louise Erdrich's *The Bingo Palace.*" *Native American Literary Strategies for the New Millennium. Proceedings of Conference,* Nov. 11–14, 1999, Puerto Vallarta, Mexico. Ed. Gwen Griffen (Sisseton Dakota) and Jane Hafen (Taos Pueblo). Las Vegas: U of Nevada P, 2004.

"Sherman Alexie's Challenge to the Academy's Teaching of Native American Literature, Non-Native Writers, and Critics," *Studies in American Indian Literatures* 13.3 (Summer/Fall 2001): 23–35.

To
Eva Virginius Falk,
My Grandmother,
and
Joseph Avery Falk,
My Uncle

CONTENTS

Acknowledgments		xi
Chapter 1	Introduction: "Writing Is Different from Tribe to Tribe": Historical and Cultural Contexts	1
Chapter 2	"The Old Lady Trill, the Victory Yell": Why Feminist Theory Does Not Apply to Native American Literature	17
Chapter 3	"We Must Be Masters of Our Circumstances": Rhetorical Sovereignty as Political Resistance in the Life and Works of Zitkala-Ša	27
Chapter 4	"The Men in the Bar Feared Her": The Power of Ayah in Leslie Marmon Silko's "Lullaby"	53
Chapter 5	"Women Are Strong, Strong, Terribly Strong": Female Intellectual Sovereignty in the Works of Louise Erdrich	89
Chapter 6	"'I'm Talking Like a Twentieth-Century Indian Woman'": Contemporary Female Warriors in the Works of Sherman Alexie	133
Chapter 7	Conclusion: "Indian Women Were and Are Powerful": Intellectual Sovereignty and the Strength of Female Warriors	171
Notes		177
Bibliography		183
Index		191

Acknowledgments

I want to express my gratitude to P. Jane Hafen (Taos Pueblo), without whose patience and willingness to work with me in Native American literature this book would not have been possible. I am indebted to her and her gentle lion roars. I also would like to thank faculty members at the University of Nevada, Las Vegas—Joseph B. McCullough, Jr., Sharon R. Moore, and Joanne L. Goodwin—for their thoughtful feedback on early drafts.

I would like to extend my deepest appreciation to my family, friends, and colleagues, who continuously offered their encouragement. There are many who deserve recognition for their support in one way or another, but they are too numerous to mention and know who they are. Special mention, however, must go to Gwen Griffin (Sisseton Dakota), Minnesota State University, Mankato, and John Wunder, University of Nebraska, Lincoln, whose generous gift of reading an early draft was invaluable.

I never could have accomplished my successes without my mother, Carmecita Muñoz-Daignault, who was the first to instill in me a love of learning, and my husband, Gary J. Hollrah, who managed our lives so I could concentrate on this book. Finally, I want to thank the staff members of the University of Nevada, Las Vegas, Library for all their assistance throughout my research. Of those mentioned and many more whom I have not noted by name, I am most appreciative.

CHAPTER 1

Introduction: "Writing Is Different from Tribe to Tribe"
Historical and Cultural Contexts

The political ramifications of gender complementarity for women in Native American literature result in strong female characters in the works of Zitkala-Ša (Yankton Sioux), Leslie Marmon Silko (Laguna Pueblo), Louise Erdrich (Ojibwe), and Sherman Alexie (Spokane/Coeur d'Alene).[1] These authors create powerful females who live autonomous lives. Considering the tribal constructs of gender relations when examining the female characters helps explain why these women are politically empowered, whereas using a Western theoretical framework, for example, white feminism, will not produce the same kind of reading or explain as well why these female figures are so impressive.

The scholar/author Michael Dorris (Modoc) relates the story about his mailman, who was a Scout leader. The troop wanted to be as authentic Iroquois as possible during a week-long stay in the woods, so the mailman asked Dorris to recommend items to take along. Dorris told him they should take their mothers along because "Iroquois were matrilineal, and these little fourteen-year-old kids wouldn't know what to do without their mothers telling them what to do" (Moyers 145). Unfortunately, the mailman was not interested in this information because he was focused on the popular stereotyped image of the Native American male, which included "hatchets or something" (145). In addition to not understanding the importance of the Native woman in the life of the Iroquois, perhaps the mailman also had a popular stereotyped image of the Native woman based on erroneous images of figures like Princess Pocahontas and Sacajawea. Because Native women have not always received the critical attention that they deserve, these misrepresentations have not been rectified in popular culture.

Looking at popular and scholarly writings about Native American women, American Indian studies scholar Rayna Green (Cherokee) reviews "work done since the seventeenth century in the United States and Canada which [...] spans several academic and professional fields—anthropology, history, psychology, literature, medicine, law, and journalism" (248–49). Her comments on the increase of anthropologists' contributions in the seventies to the study of Native American women are relevant to the works of the authors discussed in this book:

> Discarding views of powerless slaves to warriors, children, and subsistence life, these authors portray the pervasiveness of powerful roles for women, ones complementary to those of men. Challenging feminist scholars' insistence on the pervasiveness of male dominance in Native American cultures, these writers insist on tribal rather than Western definitions of role and status. (260)

Within the writings of Zitkala-Ša, Silko, Erdrich, and Alexie, evidence of gender complementarity in both traditional tribal communities and contemporary urban settings can be seen at work in the roles of powerful female characters.

Gender complementarity within tribal constructs arose out of the gendered division of labor. Because women were responsible for the bearing of and usually the caring for children, their work involved tasks that could be done close to the home. The men were responsible for protection of the community and also were able to travel farther away from the home to secure food and other necessities. Men and women had their assigned roles in tribal life, and women could be involved in numerous areas, such as decision making and landownership. The important aspects of men and women's roles is that they complemented each other, and they were equally valued for the contributions they made to the community; one role did not have more importance than another. This general description of gender complementarity allows for many variations, as gender roles are social constructs, more importantly tribal constructs. Often, females could also perform tasks that normally would be considered male behaviors within the tribe, and because of special circumstances, such as widowhood or merely living as a single person, they would not seem unusual. Additionally, because people could act with autonomy, making decisions about their own conduct, women could choose to engage in male-gendered behaviors, for example, as warrior women, and not seem atypical. Although contemporary Native female women have survived the impact of colonization and the changes it has brought, gender complementarity continues to the present day, and examples can be found in the construction of literary female characters. In the works of Zitkala-Ša, Silko, Erdrich, and Alexie, gender complementarity is seen in the political, religious, economic, educational, and social areas of Native life.

In the political arena, Zitkala-Ša works for the Indian cause—tribal sovereignty and self-determination—through her writing, lectures, and political activism. For example, she establishes a new Pan-Indian organization in 1926, the National Council of American Indians (NCAI), and is the self-appointed president, and her husband, Raymond T. Bonnin (Yankton Sioux), is the secretary-treasurer. Zitkala-Ša sees men and women working together, sharing positions of power that complement each other, and knows that she is as capable as any Native man working in an organization of improving the lives of American Indians. As she states in her personal correspondence of May 2, 1901, to Carlos Montezuma (Yavapai), "Am I not an Indian woman as capable to think in serious matters and as thoroughly interested in the race as any one or two of you men put together?" Clearly, Zitkala-Ša sees her work and contribution as equally valuable and as complementary to that of any male. The same is true of the contemporary figure Marie Polatkin in Alexie's mystery novel *Indian Killer,* a college student who pursues political activism for Indian rights as a way of survival.

Similar to the gender complementarity in the political arena, Native spirituality also represents both men and women. Unlike the monotheism of Christianity, Native spirituality incorporates male and female deities that complement one another, as in the case of Mother Earth and Father Sky. In Silko's short story "Lullaby," there is the unspoken presence of an important Navajo female deity, Changing Woman, who symbolizes nature and the mystery of birth. She is significant in determining the high standing that Navajo women have in their community. Despite colonization's legacy of missionaries' putting an end to Native ceremonies and converting Natives to Christianity, many tribes embrace both their Native practices and Christianity. In Erdrich's novel *The Last Report on the Miracles at Little No Horse,* she imagines what could have been a more positive outcome for the work of missionaries when a woman disguised as a Catholic priest begins to accept some of the Ojibwe spiritual beliefs, as the Ojibwe have Catholicism. In like fashion, Alexie shows in his novel *Reservation Blues* how Big Mom handles the traditional Spokane part of the funeral for Junior Polatkin while Father Arnold attends to the Catholic ritual. Big Mom tells Father Arnold, "'[Y]ou cover all the Christian stuff; I'll do the traditional Indian stuff. We'll make a great team'" (280). Native female figures participate in and complement other aspects of the religious life of Native communities.

In the same way that gender complementarity plays a key role in Native spirituality, in the area of economics, women and men contribute equally to the production and distribution of goods and services. In Silko's "Lullaby," the female protagonist, Ayah, is from a matriarchal and matrilineal tribe, so although she is married, she owns her hogan (Navajo home) and livestock. In Erdrich's fiction, the women engage in numerous occupations: In *The Birchbark House,* for example, Old Tallow hunts, fishes, dresses the animals, and shares her catch with Omakayas's family, and in *The Bingo Palace,* Shawnee Ray Toose designs clothing to sell that is steeped in the style of her Chippewa heritage. In the same novel, Albertine Johnson studies to become a doctor, and in *Love Medicine* Margaret Kashpaw and Fleur are traditional Ojibwe midwives, performing services that pregnant women would have to pay for in a mainstream hospital. Most importantly, Fleur manages her resources in such a way that she is able to buy back Pillager land, one of the most significant and empowering economic acts in *The Bingo Palace* and *The Last Report on the Miracles at Little No Horse.* These female characters complement the labor performed by the male characters, who work as tribal chairmen (Nanapush), as businessmen in bingo halls and casinos (Lyman Lamartine), and as healers (Lipsha Morrisey). The women's economic activities are as necessary to and valued by the community as the work done by the men.

Native men and women are both portrayed in the area of education. In Alexie's fiction, characters such as Roman Gabriel Fury and his wife, Grace Atwater, are college graduates who manage to finish their education by relying on their intellectual sovereignty and each other. When the couple returns to the Spokane Reservation, Grace teaches at the elementary school. Alexie also uses the female character Marie Polatkin to critique higher education and the content of Native American literature courses. As a powerful Spokane female, Marie challenges her white male professor and by extension the patriarchal academic institution. In a critical discourse, Marie provides an important Native viewpoint, one that balances the dominant academic culture's male voice.

In the social realm of Native life, gender complementarity plays out in the husband-wife relationships seen in Ayah and Chato of Silko's "Lullaby," Roman Gabriel Fury and Grace Atwater in Alexie's "Saint Junior," James and Norma Many Horses in Alexie's "The Approximate Size of My Favorite Tumor," and Sid and Estelle Polatkin of Alexie's "Indian Country," to name just a few of the intimate male-female relationships, which are dealt with in later chapters of this book. Erdrich and Alexie go further and explore same-sex relationships in their writing; however, the concept of each partner's making a valued and equally regarded contribution to the relationship remains the same. In "Saint Junior," Alexie accurately assesses the work required by both partners in marriage: "Damn, marriage was hard work, was manual labor, and *unpaid* manual labor at that. Yet, year after year, Grace and Roman had pressed their shoulders against the stone and rolled it up the hill *together*" (emphasis added, *Toughest* 177–78). In comparing the effort and energy necessary in a good marriage to the unending labor of Sisyphus, repeatedly rolling the stone up the hill, Alexie correctly captures the teamwork involved in the marriage relationship, an example of gender complementarity at work.

Native women who use "their power to become agents of change for their communities" are described in the preceding examples of gender complementarity (Green 259). Female characters who make autonomous decisions based on their intellectual sovereignty affect the welfare of their community and are politically empowered by their acts. For example, Zitkala-Ša manages to mediate between Native cultures and the dominant mainstream society, a maneuver that groups of marginalized peoples often adopt. Being able to function in both worlds does not mean that the Native woman is any less Indian when in the mainstream culture; nor does it mean that she gives up her sense of gender complementarity. She knows that Indian women might be treated differently by mainstream culture because of their race and gender, but knowing the cultural codes of both worlds only adds to her intellectual sovereignty and the ways she chooses to use that information. In contemporary Native American literary theory, James Ruppert defines mediation:

> By mediation, I mean an artistic and conceptual standpoint, constantly flexible, which uses the epistemological frameworks of Native American and Western cultural traditions to illuminate and enrich each other. In working toward an understanding of Native American writers' texts, it is more useful to see them not as between two cultures (a romantic and victimist perspective) but as participants in two rich cultural traditions. While some may say these writers are apologists for one side or the other, or that their texts inhabit a no-man's-land, a mediational approach explores how their texts create a dynamic that brings differing cultural codes into confluence to reinforce and re-create the structures of human life: the self, community, spirit, and the world we perceive. (*Mediation* 3)

Ruppert's definition of mediation stops short of pointing out how it is a necessary and pragmatic survival tool for Native Americans, not just a tool for literary analysis. His concept of mediation, however, helps illuminate how a Native woman like Zitkala-Ša functions as a participant in "two rich cultural traditions." She can embrace the values of white women in a patriarchal culture if they will help attain her objectives for American Indians and at the same time maintain her Native worldview of gender complementarity. Exercising this kind of intellectual sovereignty empowers Native women such as Zitkala-Ša. According to Joseph Bruchac (Abenaki), Bonnin knew the expectations of her predominantly white audiences better than they knew themselves: "Bonnin, in fact, knew how to communicate to the white world so well that she would abandon literature after only two books and quite effectively devote her life to working as an activist and lobbyist for Indian rights" (xliii).

The idea of gender complementarity in this discussion is inherently linked to the ideas of autonomy, intellectual sovereignty, and political empowerment. In view of a history of conquest, war, disease, sterilization, and cultural genocide, author and literary critic Gloria Bird (Spokane) observes the obvious political implications of Native survival on the North American continent: "That we are still here as native women in itself is a political statement" (Harjo 30). Survival for Native peoples in the face of continued racism, oppression, marginalization, and challenges to tribal sovereignty is a political issue that touches all aspects of Native life. The construct of these connected ideas might be represented best as points on a circle that lead to and from one another: Because women are able to make autonomous choices about their lives based on their own intellectual sovereignty within the context of gender complementarity, they are politically empowered.

Critics also must take into account the history and culture of specific Native American tribes in question when discussing literatures. Often, current literary theories alone do not account for these factors that must be considered. Feminist theory, for example, does not always provide a broad enough lens through which critics can view Native American literature because it often focuses on political inequality between genders. Ignoring the broader cultural context of specific tribes frequently renders the feminist view of the literature incomplete and, therefore, inaccurate. In this book, I explore how a tribal construct of gender relations—gender complementarity— functions in the works of Zitkala-Ša, Leslie Marmon Silko, Louise Erdrich, and Sherman Alexie. Gender complementarity, or balanced reciprocity, acknowledges that the worlds of men and women are "distinctly different but not generally perceived as hierarchical" (Klein and Ackerman 14). If gender roles are not seen as unequal but as simply "different," the resulting political relationships do not necessarily result in power struggles for equality. Examining the political ramifications of gender complementarity for women in Native American literature is approached through the historical and cultural contexts of each specific tribe. The research focuses primarily on evidence that proves how the female characters are empowered by the very nature of their tribal social structure of gender complementarity. In addition, focusing on gender complementarity without accounting for the holistic nature of tribal worldviews could result in the same error as using feminist criticism. In other words, gender complementarity alone cannot account for a specific political result; the structure of gender roles is part of a connected whole. By examining the concept of gender complementarity within the tribal context, the critical readings should more fully illuminate the role of Native American women as politically empowered.

As anthropologists and historians have begun to rethink the images of Native American women promoted by popular culture and to search for an understanding that involves new concepts of gender, so too do literary scholars need to evaluate Native American literary female characters in a cultural paradigm that is less European-American and more closely situated in a specific tribal context. In *Decolonizing Methodologies: Research and Indigenous Peoples*, Linda Tuhiwai Smith (Ngati Awa/Ngati Porou) writes about the assumptions that non-Natives impose on research about indigenous peoples:

> Research 'through imperial eyes' describes an approach which assumes that Western ideas about the most fundamental things are the only ideas possible to hold, certainly the only rational ideas, and the only ideas which can make sense of the world, of reality, of social life and of human beings. It is an approach to indigenous peoples which still conveys a sense of innate superiority and an overabundance of desire to bring progress into the lives of indigenous peoples—spiritually, intellectually, socially and economically. It is research which from indigenous perspectives 'steals' knowledge from others and then uses it to benefit the people who 'stole' it. Some indigenous and minority group researchers would call this approach simply racist. It is research which is imbued with an 'attitude' and a 'spirit' which assumes a certain ownership of the entire world, and which has established systems and forms of governance which embed that attitude in institutional practices. These practices determine what counts as legitimate research and who count as legitimate researchers. (56)

Tuhiwai Smith rightly acknowledges the concern that Native scholars have when people from outside the indigenous peoples' cultures carry on research and then dictate what the "real" history and culture are of those people.

Similarly, when non-Native critics write about Native American literature, they can be met with resistance to them as cultural outsiders who claim authority about material of which they have no personal knowledge. Admittedly, white people can rarely speak as cultural insiders about Native American literature; however, to compensate for this lack of personal experience, they can acknowledge their limited perspective and focus on the sovereignty, history, and culture of the specific tribe in question, whether that of the author and/or of the text. Beginning with this caveat should help create a context that allows for a less European-American focus by the critic and one closer to that of a Native American worldview. Tuhiwai Smith recommends that nonindigenous researchers become more culturally sensitive and address the issues that will make a difference for indigenous peoples' lives (176–77). Writing about Native American literature in a way that promotes the understanding that the literature is about the people's lives—not a fiction in the usual sense—works toward that end.

For example, in *Tribal Secrets: Recovering American Indian Intellectual Traditions*, American Indian studies theorist Robert Allen Warrior (Osage) discusses the importance of American Indians' establishing a criticism based on a framework of intellectual sovereignty to examine their own culture. Intellectual sovereignty is an individual manifestation of the worldview of tribal sovereignty, the inherent right of a nation to rule itself, "conduct its own affairs, in its own place, in its own way," without any outside interference (Lyons 450). In the same way that Scott Richard Lyons (Ojibwe/Mdewakanton Dakota) defines rhetorical sovereignty as "the inherent right and ability of *peoples* to determine their own communicative needs," intellectual sovereignty implies the inherent right and ability of peoples to determine that their own knowledge systems are valid, useful, and applicable to their lives and their survival (449). Warrior argues that a criticism based in intellectual sovereignty must be open-ended with connections to the land and community, and capable of flexibility, much like an ongoing process, in order to accommodate the many different kinds of American Indian writing being produced today (44). Warrior calls for a criticism that arises within the tribal community rather than one from without, which often results in a layering of non-Native ideology onto the Native American discourse, a skewed perspective at best. By examining the perspectives of American Indian intellectuals John Joseph Matthews (Osage) and Vine Deloria, Jr. (Standing Rock Sioux), Warrior moves "toward a cultural criticism that is grounded in American Indian experiences but which can draw on the insights and experiences of others who have faced similar struggles" (xxiii).

Correspondingly, author Leslie Marmon Silko (Laguna Pueblo) has the same opinion that readers need a better understanding of place, or of the land. When asked during a 1977 interview what she thought people needed to know about context before reading her stories, she responded:

> I would wish that people would have a little better understanding of place, that in geography classes they would teach how people live in Bethel, Alaska, and Laguna, New Mexico, or Iowa City, etc.... What I would ideally wish for is that people had just a general familiarity, a sense of the history, when the Spaniards came in, just American history, for Christ's sake, but they don't.... Included in geography should be the way people live, some of their attitudes, their point of view, so if you have even just a smattering of Pueblo point of view, that helps. It's not much. (Fisher 21)

Although possibly not as emphatically as Warrior, Silko still calls for close attention to the land and the community when discussing Native American literature. However, in order to understand the relevance of the land and the community to a Native American tribe, one must begin with its history and culture.

In his essay "Native American Literature in an Ethnohistorical Context," Dorris supports this approach when he writes that knowledge of any national literature is improved with recognition of the larger cultural context: "Without some knowledge of language, of history, of inflection, of the position of the storyteller within the group, without a hint of the social roles played by males and females in the culture, without a sense of the society's humor or priorities—without such knowledge, how can we, as reader or listener, penetrate to the core of meaning in an expression of art? (237).[2] Dorris notes that because there are several hundred Native cultures, there is no true concept of "American Indian literature," and therefore, readers must have an awareness of the nature of the specific tribe in question. Author Louise Erdrich (Ojibwe) agrees: "Writing is different from tribe to tribe, the images are different from tribe to tribe" (Coltelli 48). Thus, the critic needs to look at the specific history and culture of the tribe in question.

In *Studies in Native American Literature,* Gunn Allen concurs with this premise when she states, "Simply put, the teachers and critics of American Indian literature must place the document within a context that allows readers and students to understand it in terms that do not distort it" (x). Her assumption presupposes that history and culture are the context for that understanding. Gunn Allen goes on to say,

> [T]he critic in American Indian literature becomes important—not as a scholarly adjunct to the creating and re-creating that are always the component parts of the synergy between teller and listener, but as a mediator who allows teller and listener to share a particular understanding even though they come from widely divergent traditions. (xi–xii)

In other words, Gunn Allen calls for the non-Native critic to be familiar with different Native cultures in order to help readers move beyond their ethnocentric positions and to have a better understanding of the Native literatures, to move between them, much as Native Americans have had to do for the last five hundred years in mediating between their cultures and the dominant one. In fact, the trend in Native literary theories continues to emphasize history and culture, while moving closer to theories growing out of tribal literatures themselves.

Most recently, in *Red on Red: Native American Literary Separatism,* Craig Womack (Muskogee Creek/Cherokee) argues for self-determination in discussing Native American literature, a Native perspective that allows Indian people to speak for themselves:

> [S]uch a viewpoint exists and has been silenced throughout U.S. history to the degree that it finally needs to be heard. [...] there is the legal reality of tribal sovereignty, recognized by the U.S. Constitution and defined over the last 160 years by the Supreme Court, that affects the everyday lives of individuals and tribal nations and, therefore, has something to do with tribal literatures. (6)

Womack notes the legal relationship that tribal nations have with the U.S. government, a fact of life that cannot be ignored when reading Native American literature. He sees tribal literatures not only as "the oldest literatures in the Americas, the most American of American literatures," but also as separate from the academic American canon, not as a branch of American literature (6–7). In other words, Womack views Native American literature as its own canon; therefore, it deserves no less than its own criticism. He believes that this criticism should grow out of the intellectual history of the tribes' literature, and he focuses on

> the idea that Native literary aesthetics must be politicized and that autonomy, self-determination, and sovereignty serve as useful literary concepts. [...] a literary criticism that emphasizes Native resistance movements against colonialism, confronts racism, discusses sovereignty and Native nationalism, seeks connections between literature and liberation struggles, and, finally, roots literature in land and culture. (11)

Clearly, Womack privileges the Native voice in Native American literary criticism, illustrating that any other Western theoretical approach is simply another act of colonization. Womack's position presents one more reason for non-Native scholars to rely on the critical works of Native scholars. As he says, "Native literature, and Native literary criticism, written by Native authors, is part of sovereignty: Indian people exercising the right to present images of themselves and to discuss those images" (14).

Non-Native scholars of Native American literature join ranks with Native scholars in choosing to focus on history and culture for their critical approach. In discussing the problems associated with interpreting Native American literature, Gregory Salyer argues that readers must pay particular attention, so they do not fall into the trap of their own ethnocentric viewpoint:

> Crossing cultural boundaries, even literary ones, is a difficult and sometimes painful process, and without a willingness to adjust our expectations, reading across cultures can trivialize or exaggerate the distinctiveness of the other culture and simply reinforce our own beliefs about the world. It is crucial that we allow Native American literature to teach us and that we read in order to learn how to read. Otherwise, we will end up simply projecting our own cultural assumptions onto a body of work by people who do not share these assumptions, and in the end we will not have learned anything but how to drive our assumptions deeper into the background while a whole other world passes before our eyes. (12)

Although Salyer highlights the importance of critical self-reflection when reading Native American literature, he does so in a context of cultural assumptions. To offset the limitations of being trapped in one's own cultural

Introduction: "Writing Is Different from Tribe to Tribe" • 11

circle, the critic needs to examine the historical and cultural contexts of the Native American author and/or tribe in the text.

The importance of the historical and cultural contexts in this book might signal to the reader a new historicist approach. However, the desires to "relate literature to history, to treat texts as indivisible from contexts, and to do so from a politically charged perspective forged in the present" are not new concepts to the Native American worldview (Ryan x–xi). Gunn Allen distinguishes between Native and non-Native cultures in their perception of time and space:

> Another difference between these two ways of perceiving reality lies in the tendency of the American Indian to view space as spherical and time as cyclical, whereas the non-Indian tends to view space as linear and time as sequential. The circular concept requires all "points" that make up the sphere of being to have a significant identity and function, while the linear model assumes that some "points" are more significant than others. In the one, significance is a necessary factor of being in itself, whereas in the other, significance is a function of placement on an absolute scale that is fixed in time and space. (*Sacred* 59)

Because all events carry equal importance in the Native worldview, when they happen does not diminish nor increase their importance. In fact, mythic time conflates the past, present, and future, reinforcing the notion of a fluid cyclical time in which all events are of equal significance. In other words, the past always carries meaning for the present that distance and time cannot attenuate.

Much of the current historical criticism deals with English Renaissance literature in two camps: in Britain, cultural materialism, and in the United States, new historicism. Jonathan Culler succinctly summarizes a major preoccupation of this criticism: "A key question for the new historicists has been the dialectic of 'subversion and containment': how far do Renaissance texts offer a genuinely radical critique of the religious and political ideologies of their day and how far is the discursive practice of literature, in its apparent subversiveness, a way of containing subversive energies?" (130). This book does not deal with the Native American texts in the same way. Rather, in examining the political ramifications of gender complementarity for women, the concern lies with demonstrating how women are already empowered in their communities and in mainstream society. Because European Americans have impacted Native American cultures since the time of contact, changes have occurred in how those cultures have adapted to external pressures. In that sense, the following chapters examine how women in the selected texts have responded to those changes. As legal scholar Rebecca Tsosie (Pascua Yaqui) states, "For many Indian groups, the traditional worldviews which emphasize a holistic, balanced universe continue to counter the Euro-American emphasis on hierarchy and 'dominant/subordinate' social roles" (511). At times the authors critique the religious and political ideologies that mainstream society has tried to force on them through acculturation and assimilation. Often these acts of criticism are subversive in that the authors show how indigenous peoples have made certain aspects of the dominant culture and colonization work to their advantage. These Native literary texts treat subversive acts as acts of resistance for survival, in which women play a major role:

> Contrary to those images of meekness, docility, and subordination to males with which we women typically have been portrayed by the dominant culture's books and movies, anthropology, and political ideologues of both rightist and leftist persuasions, it is women who have formed the very core of indigenous resistance to genocide and colonization since the first moment of conflict between Indians and invaders. (Jaimes and Halsey 311)

Therefore, one of the major preoccupations of new historicism, "subversion and containment," as defined by Culler, does not apply in the same way to Native literary texts, which have always been concerned with resistance.

The ideology of gender complementarity must be understood within the larger social, political, and religious structure of the tribe. In the same way that one cannot disconnect the Native American literary work from the author's/tribe's historical and cultural contexts, neither can one separate gender complementarity from the communal life of the tribe. To do so would be antithetical to the holistic philosophy of the tribe. This book focuses on gender complementarity in order to discuss the political ramifications for women; in reality this one area does not exist in a vacuum. This part of tribal life, as any part, is interconnected in important ways. The concept of gender complementarity is only one part of Native American women's identity. They also know who they are by their membership in the tribe, which fosters a communal worldview, as opposed to an individualistic one; tribal language, origin myths, and legends; connection to the land; tribal traditions, ceremonies, and rituals; to name but a few of the other considerations that contribute to a people's sense of who they are. Rather than an overview of important historical events and cultural information that affect Native Americans today, specific issues that authors highlight in their texts are addressed accordingly.

The four authors—Zitkala-Ša, Leslie Marmon Silko, Louise Erdrich, and Sherman Alexie—were chosen for this book because their combined work spans almost a hundred-year timeline, illustrating that the traditional tribal concept of gender complementarity has survived into the twenty-first century. Additionally, although the focus of the book is on the political ramifications of gender complementarity for women, the four authors are not only females. To illustrate that gender complementarity is understood by both men and women, a male author, Sherman Alexie, is included. Also, the tribal affiliations of the authors represent both patriarchal and matriarchal structures, which demonstrate that regardless of the political structure of the tribe, gender complementarity still exists as an inherent part of both those structures.

Chapter 2 gives a brief overview of the introduction of Native American literature into the academic literary canon, the critical works that focus on the place of Native women in their communities, Native women authors, and Native female characters in the literature. Examining what Native women have to say about their experiences addresses why they do not see white feminist theory as applicable to their lives, or, therefore, to their literature.

Chapter 3 discusses rhetorical sovereignty in selected works of Zitkala-Ša, a well-known figure in Pan-Indianism in the 1920s. Leaving her Yankton Reservation at a young age for an off-reservation boarding school education, she mastered rhetorical strategies in the English language, which she would use for the rest of her life to promote political causes for the welfare of American Indians. A successful educator, accomplished musician, published fiction writer, and political activist, Zitkala-Ša focused on the premise of American freedom and equality for all, which included American Indians. Within the context of gender complementarity, this chapter looks at how she employs the themes of freedom and equality in her first award-winning speech, later autobiographical essays, personal correspondence, and, in particular, her contribution to *Oklahoma's Poor Rich Indians: An Orgy of Graft and Exploitation of the Five Civilized Tribes—Legalized Robbery?* (1924). The power that Zitkala-Ša experienced in public forums grew out of a combination of her sense of gender complementarity and her mastery of the English language, which allowed her to write a literature of resistance.

Chapter 4 deals with one of the most-often anthologized short stories in American Indian literature, Leslie Marmon Silko's "Lullaby," published in 1974. Silko prefers promoting a political agenda through her stories rather than any other format, and in "Lullaby," she privileges the political power of Navajo women. Writing outside her own Laguna Pueblo tradition in "Lullaby," Silko draws on her cultural and linguistic knowledge of the Navajo (Diné). "Lullaby" presents the challenge to the reader of having to know not only Silko's tribal heritage but also that of the Navajo in order to understand better the power of the female protagonist, Ayah. Although the story is often read as ending on a tragic note, understanding the Navajo worldview, gender complementarity, and the political implications of the role of the

Navajo female allows for an alternative resolution that also implies continuity, survival, and hope in the face of sometimes overwhelming obstacles.

Chapter 5 focuses on the intellectual sovereignty and strength of female characters in selected works of Louise Erdrich. Throughout her writing—nonfiction memoirs, children's books, and the North Dakota cycle of novels—Erdrich portrays strong female characters, both Ojibwe women and non-Native women, who live their lives as single women, married women, and women passing as men. The political ramifications of gender complementarity for the Ojibwe characters grow out of their intellectual sovereignty, having indigenous knowledge that helps them perform male- and female-gendered tasks to survive. This indigenous knowledge is particularly evident in Ojibwe midwifery, which helps pregnant women in the delivery of their babies, and in comparison to the Western medical establishment's approach to laboring mothers, Erdrich definitely privileges the former. Erdrich's construction of a non-Native female character, Agnes Dewitt, who passes as a Catholic priest, offers more information on how she views the role of strong, powerful women, even those who subvert a patriarchal religious organization. In a context of gender complementarity, Erdrich creates women who are autonomous creatures, living the lives they choose.

Chapter 6 looks at contemporary female warriors in selected works of Sherman Alexie. As a writer who depicts both contemporary Spokane Reservation and urban Indians in short stories and novels, Alexie goes beyond portraying merely strong female characters as transmitters of culture and indigenous knowledge and represents women of both heterosexual and homosexual orientations as married women, college students, and political activists. He clearly establishes a context of gender complementarity in which women are autonomous figures, who win battles with mythic status, words, education, and, at times, physical intimidation. He also focuses on how survival humor can save marriages and help women learn to cope with the anticipated death of a spouse. Alexie sees contemporary women as politically empowered, and his worldview expresses the concept of gender complementarity.

Chapter 7 offers some concluding remarks on the political ramifications of gender complementarity for women in the literature of the authors covered, looking specifically at how Zitkala-Ša, Silko, Erdrich, and Alexie construct female characters who embody and practice the acts of sovereignty, power, strength, and contemporary female warrior status. Despite external factors that either historically misrepresented Native women as "princess" or "squaw" or eroded traditional tribal structures that empowered Native women, these authors imbue female literary characters with the realities of American Indian women's lives, thus revising previously erroneous portrayals.

Finally, with regard to the nomenclature for Native Americans, throughout this book the name of the specific tribe is used whenever possible. In other instances, the inclusive terms *Native Americans* and *American Indians* are used when referring to the indigenous peoples of North America, although many writers use other terms, such as *Indians, First Nations People,* and *Natives.* To clarify the sometimes-confusing issue of what the preferred or correct term is when referring to Indians, Inés Hernandez (Nimipu) has the following to say:

> Native people know that the term "Indian" is a misnomer, but we have made it our own, just as we have made "American Indian" and more recently "Native American" our own, even though in our original languages, each of our peoples had (and have) their own name for themselves and for this part of the earth that is now known as "America." We refer to each other by tribe or nation that we are from—that is one of the first questions we ask each other, "Who are your people?" and "Where are you from?" [...] The labels "Native American" or "American Indian" are in the end simplistic generalizations, generic terms, that at best acknowledge the fact that indeed indigenous peoples in this hemisphere did and do have something in common. (8–9)

Although Native Americans use and prefer specific tribal identifications, they realize that other generic terms have, in fact, become common usage. In conducting a survey about what indigenous peoples want to be called, Michael Yellow Bird (Sahnish/Hidatsa) begins with the knowledge that *American Indian* and *Native American* are the most common labels used to identify indigenous peoples in the United States, but on the basis of his research he finds, "neither term has been without controversy, and no clear consensus exists on which label is most preferable" (1). The majority of the respondents in Yellow Bird's study prefer specific tribal identity, but after that, they prefer to use *American Indian,* and many indicated that they use several terms interchangeably, mostly *Indian, American Indian, Native American, Native,* and *Indigenous Peoples* (7–8). The tribe with which someone self-identifies is used in this book, regardless of whether the person is an enrolled member or whether others have challenged that affiliation. Thus, with the understanding that certain labels are not always the most accurate, various terminologies are used throughout this work.

CHAPTER 2

"The Old Lady Trill, the Victory Yell"
Why Feminist Theory Does Not Apply to Native American Literature

In Louise Erdrich's (Ojibwe) *Bingo Palace,* Lulu Lamartine "dances the old-lady traditional" as federal marshals arrest her for stealing government property and escort her to a waiting vehicle. They believe that she has helped her son, Gerry Nanapush, escape from the authorities. In celebration of confusing the agents, Lulu lets go "the old lady trill, the victory yell" (*Bingo Palace* 264–65). This act symbolizes Lulu's ability to wield power over the U.S. government officials who are looking for her son. Moreover, "the old lady trill" represents continuity and survival of cultural customs, the women's role after the men have returned triumphant from battle. Her son has eluded his captors, and Lulu celebrates with "the victory yell," demonstrating gender complementarity. Lulu has done her job well, acknowledges it with her voice, and entices the community to join in with her. Lulu is a strong woman but not in the usual white feminist sense; she is a strong woman in the Ojibwe sense, in a context of gender complementarity. A brief overview of the evolution of the critical works that focus on the place of Native women in their communities, Native women authors, and Native female characters in the literature will provide a clearer context in which to understand why white feminist theory is not applicable to their lives, and, therefore, limited in its approach to their literature.

Native American literature entered the academic literary canon in the late 1960s and the 1970s in conjunction with the social movements of feminism,

African-American civil rights, Red Power, and protests by students on major urban campuses across the United States, who demanded a multicultural curriculum that was more relevant to their lives. Michael Dorris (Modoc) notes, however, that Native American literatures have always been a part of Native life: "During the past several thousand years, Native American people have produced literatures rich in diversity and imagery, ancient in tradition, and universal in significance" ("Native" 232). Dorris goes on to explain that there is not a singular Native American literature but many because of the diversity of cultural and linguistic groups in the pre-1942 western hemisphere: "More than three hundred cultures, each differentiated to a greater or lesser degree by language, custom, history, and life way, were resident north of the Rio Grande in 1492" (233). Joseph Bruchac (Abenaki) lists the extensive and complex oral traditions of Native North America, "epic poems, religious liturgy, personal and communal songs, tribal and personal histories, legends and myths," and notes their "great importance to the North American Native writers of the last hundred years, the period in which written literature by Natives has achieved its greatest audience" (xl).

The first wave of noted Native American authors who entered the canon were Leslie Marmon Silko (Laguna Pueblo), Vine Deloria, Jr. (Standing Rock Sioux), James Welch (Blackfeet/Gros Ventre), Simon J. Ortiz (Acoma Pueblo), and N. Scott Momaday (Kiowa), who won the 1969 Pulitzer Prize in fiction for *House Made of Dawn* (1968). Bruchac notes that 1969 was a turning point for Native American literature,

> a year which saw both a new birth of Native activism with the takeover of Alcatraz Island by the "Indians of All Tribes," and [...] the first major literary award ever given to a work written by an American Indian. Not only did Momaday's book gain attention from the European-American critics, it also served as an inspiration to a whole new generation of Native writers just embarking on their own careers [...]. (xl)

With the seemingly sudden influx of Native writings, some critics often refer to this period as the Native American Renaissance, but as Dorris and Bruchac state, Native American literatures have always existed. This choice of questionable terminology illustrates an example of the existing tension between Native and non-Native scholars and their views of Native American literatures.

Rayna Green's (Cherokee) "Essay Review: Native American Women" (1980) looks at works written on Native American women across various disciplines, but there is a lack of literary critical works cited. Mentioned, of course, are some of the standard autobiographies, such as *Life among the Piutes: Their Wrongs and Claims* (1883, 1994), by Sarah Winnemucca Hopkins; *American Indian Stories* (1921, 1985), by Zitkala-Ša; and *Me and*

Mine: The Life Story of Helen Sekaquaptewa (Hopi) (1969, 1993), as told to Louise Udall. Green, however, notes that the "real experience of Indian women's lives" does not appear until the 1970s, when the work of Indian women poets is published: "Corn Mother and Changing Woman—the symbolic referents of Indian female life—join the powwow princesses, grandmothers, and female doctors, lawyers, and Indian chiefs of the real Indian female world to create an often harsh, unromanticized, truthful version of Native American women's lives" (Green 263). As a bibliographic guide to some major works by Native American women poets and writers as well as examples of their writing, Green recommends *The Third Woman: Minority Women Writers of the United States* (1979), edited by Dexter Fisher.

Bruchac supports what Green observes about the lack of early literary writing by Native American women:

> That the voices of North American women went almost unheard until the start of the 20th century may be surprising to anyone who knows the vital, central places which women held and continue to hold in most, if not all, indigenous nations on the continent. It may also be surprising when one considers that some of the most acclaimed contemporary Native writers, Laguna novelist Leslie Silko, Creek poet Joy Harjo, Chippewa novelist Louise Erdrich, for example, are women and that, numerically, there appear to be more native women in print in the 1990's than there are Native men! (Bruchac xlii–xliii)

Bruchac goes on to discuss the difficulty that Native women would have had early in the century in publishing their own works in the male-oriented and male-dominated European-American institution of publishing. He cites John Mohawk's (Seneca) belief that "European-Americans saw the world in such different terms, in terms of hierarchies, male force and control, that they were blind to the fact that Native cultures were, in fact, community and woman-oriented and non-abusive in nature" (xliii). If European-American women had difficulty publishing their work, then the Native women would have had an almost impossible task. Therefore, people such as Zitkala-Ša who published autobiographical essays might be described as one of the Native "women who opened the doors for their sisters to follow through" (xliii).

Important critical works on Native women begin to appear in the 1980s and 1990s. In *American Indian Women: Telling Their Lives* (1984, 1989), literary critics Gretchen M. Bataille and Kathleen Mullen Sands focus on Indian women's autobiographies and demonstrate the diversity and centrality of women in American Indian cultures. The book includes a comprehensive annotated bibliography of works by and about American Indian women. In *The Sacred Hoop: Recovering the Feminine in American Indian Traditions* (1986, 1992), noted scholar Paula Gunn Allen (Laguna Pueblo/Sioux) writes a pioneering work in American Indian and feminist scholarship, a collection of essays that explore a matrifocal feminine spirituality in the context of Native American traditions. She challenges old stereotypes of American Indians and proposes new images of Native woman-centered social systems. In *"Yellow Woman"/Leslie Marmon Silko* (1993), Melody Graulich edits and introduces a collection of critical essays on the traditional mythological Laguna figure of Yellow Woman, whom Silko has rendered in several retellings. In addition to a chronology of Silko's life, the text of the story itself, and a bibiliography, the essays look at storytelling, cultural inheritances, memory, continuity, identity, interconnectedness, ritual, and tradition. Although these texts are about Native women, there is not a narrow focus on gender complementarity in the discussions.

Two important books by Native authors in Native American literary criticism include chapters on Silko and Erdrich, but the focus is not necessarily on woman-centered issues. In *Other Destinies: Understanding the American Indian Novel* (1992, 1994), Louis Owens (Choctaw/Cherokee) offers a critical analysis of novels written by Native authors, including Silko and Erdrich, between 1854 and today. Owens, however, focuses on marginalization and cultural survival, not on literary constructions of strong women: "The Very Essence of Our Lives": Leslie Silko's Webs of Identity," and "Erdrich and Dorris's Mixedbloods and Multiple Narratives." In *Narrative Chance: Postmodern Discourse on Native American Indian Literatures* (1989, 1993), Gerald Vizenor (Ojibwe) edits a collection of critical essays on Native authors, including Silko and Erdrich: "The Dialogic of Silko's *Storyteller*," by Arnold Krupat; "Tayo, Death, and Desire: A Lacanian Reading of *Ceremony*," by Gretchen Ronnow; and "Opening the Text: *Love Medicine* and the Return of the Native American Woman," by Robert Silberman. Silberman discusses how the beginning of Erdrich's novel speaks to the tradition established in previous Native novels in which the male protagonist returns home to the reservation, but Erdrich replaces the male protagonist with a female, June Kashpaw, who returns home:

> The beginning of *Love Medicine* therefore signals a recasting of the tradition represented by the other works even as it partly continues to work within the older conventions and share many of the same concerns: the consequences of an individual's return or attempted return to the reservation, the significance of home and family, the politics of language and the relations between speaking and writing. (103)

Although Silberman notes Erdrich's introduction of the Native woman in an established convention, he does not comment on the power of June Kashpaw in relation to the other characters in the novel.

A collection of essays from the seminar "The Construction of Gender and the Experience of Women in American Indian Societies," held in January

1996 at the Newberry Library, D'Arcy McNickle Center for the History of the American Indian, are grouped into five sections: course outlines, bibliographies, and methodologies for teaching about various aspects of American Indian gender; historical and ethnohistoric essays on gender in American Indian communities; gender-related subjects in American Indian biography and autobiography; gender and the work of one American Indian poet; and evaluations of the first gender seminar by Peter Iverson, the McNickle Center's acting director in 1994–95. Clearly, this collection is of importance in the discussion of Native women and gender, but the focus is not entirely on literature but on several disciplines that converge in American Indian studies. Most notable in this collection is the absence of European-American feminism to discuss Native women and gender.

When discussing Native women, Native scholars do not engage in the same critical discussion as Western feminists do. For example, poet, author, and American Indian studies educator Elizabeth Cook-Lynn (Crow Creek Sioux) notes that until recently Native American women probably did not think about how "societal and professional status was achieved or denied on the basis of gender" (*Why I Can't Read* 99). She goes on to describe how Native women see themselves:

> Sex difference [...] was a "given" in tribal life and, often, the roles and status of the two sexes in the community seemed not to be a matter of conflict or ambiguity. Indeed, it may still seem so for many of us who recognize that more central to tribal thinking are the matters of individual choice and preference, personal dignity, privacy, industry, competence, political issues, treaty rights, litigation, and sovereignty—all significant considerations in rather egalitarian cultures developing tribalistically. (99)

Cook-Lynn describes a tribal system based on relationships of gender complementarity in which people are not so concerned with issues of power between the genders because they already have equal importance and a worldview that privileges a communal perspective as well as individual rights. Other Native critics, such as Kathryn Shanley (Assiniboine) and Devon Mihesuah (Oklahoma Choctaw), also see gender in tribal contexts. For example, Mihesuah writes: "White feminists tend to focus on gender oppression and to overlook racial issues, thus alienating many Indian females. Traditional Indian women have been more concerned about tribal or community survival than either gender oppression or individual advancement in economics, academia, or other facets of society" ("Commonality" 40). Although current white feminism has worked to include women of color, the nature of Indian women presents challenges that are difficult to accommodate. "There was and is no such thing as a monolithic, essential Indian woman," explains Mihesuah. In her *Indigenous American Women: Decolonization, Empowerment, Activism* (2003), Mihesuah "explores how modern American Indigenous women have empowered themselves tribally, nationally, or academically. Additionally, she examines the overlooked role that Native women played in the Red Power Movement as well as some key differences between Native women 'feminists' and 'activists' (University of Nebraska Press Online).

Poet, scholar, and educator Laura Tohe (Navajo) points out that although there is no word for feminism in the Diné language, the women have always been strong and powerful leaders (104), and this fact explains why viewing Native American literature through the lens of feminist criticism often presents an incomplete view, at best, of the female characters:

> In undergraduate school I came across the term "feminism" in a women's studies class. I thought if that term applied to women, it must also apply to Indian women. When Indian women joined the feminist dialogue in the 1970s, we found that equality for women was generally directed toward white women's issues. The issues that were relevant to our tribal communities were not part of white feminist dialogue. Most Indian families were struggling just to survive. How could Indian women discourse in the feminist dialogue of the 1970s or participate in the symbolic act of burning their bras? Some probably owned only one bra and would not even consider burning it. (109)

For Indian women, as Tohe notes, "white" feminism does not apply to issues that are of vital importance to the survival of American Indians. Issues pertaining to the whole tribal community—such as sovereignty and land entitlement—take precedence. Further, issues of economics, health care, and education that affect the day-to-day lives of all Indians are more important than the concerns of white feminism. Lorelei DeCora Means (Minneconjou Lakota), an American Indian Movement (AIM) member and one of the founders of Women of All Red Nations (WARN), explains: "'We are *American Indian* women, in that order. We are oppressed, first and foremost, as American Indians, as peoples colonized by the United States of America, *not* as women. As Indians, we can never forget that. Our survival, the survival of every one of us—man, woman and child—*as Indians* depends on it'" (Jaimes and Halsey 314). Working for equality between men and women, a "white" feminist issue, is not the most pressing matter in Indian communities.

Often Indian women see "white" feminism as just another act of colonialism, as Janet McCloud (Tulalip) states:

> Many Anglo women try, I expect in all sincerity, to tell us that our most pressing problem is male supremacy. To this, I have to say, with all due respect, *bullshit*. Our problems are what they've been for the past several hundred years: white supremacism and colonialism. And that's a supremacism and a colonialism of which white feminists are still very much a part. (Jaimes and Halsey 332)

The oppression that white feminists experience is not the oppression that most concerns Indian women. In fact, rather than male supremacy, the concept of gender complementarity more accurately describes the traditional relationship between Native men and women and helps in understanding the political ramifications for women in the literature.

Exploring the political ramifications of gender complementarity for women in Native American literature arises from an often-erroneous view of female characters by critics who use feminist criticism. For the purposes of this discussion, *feminist criticism* will be defined as a "deconstruction of the opposition man/woman and the oppositions associated with it in the history of Western culture" (Culler 128). Granted, this characterization oversimplifies a complex category that surely deserves more elaboration; however, the merits of feminist criticism are not the main focus of this book. That this definition embeds itself within the context of Western ideology illustrates a key concept that conflicts with Native American worldviews. A patriarchal culture denotes a hierarchy with women in subordinate position to men, a relationship of unequal power. Critiquing Native American literature with the application of feminist criticism, which originates in a different environment, assumes that all things are equal, and that, of course, is not always the case with regard to race, tribe, culture, and gender. Even postcolonial feminist criticism still sees Native women as "Other," as objects not subjects, without tribal distinctions or tribal identities. In critiquing imperialism, postcolonial critic Gayatri Chakravorty Spivak grounds her discussion in a context of East–West relations without consideration of Indigenous issues, particularly in the western hemisphere (7–8). Despite postcolonial feminism's attempts to be more inclusive of marginalized and oppressed women, the theory and practice fail by not recognizing and including tribal specificity.

For example, in *Feminist Readings of Native American Literature: Coming to Voice*, Kathleen M. Donovan writes, "The relevance of even the term 'feminisms' to Native American communities is debatable among women" (7). Donovan asserts that although Native women might have problems with the significance of feminism when applied to their culture, what matters most is the issue of voice and who has the authority to speak for Native women (7). She goes on to note that women of color find ways to resist, and that political action is embedded in culture and gender. Despite these valid observations in the introduction and the contexts in which Donovan examines Native literature—"feminist literary and cultural theories, and the related fields of ethnography, ethnopoetics, eco-feminism, and post-colonialism"—the chapters that follow continue a pattern of displacing Native voices (10). Donovan inconsistently acknowledges specific tribal cultures and histories of the author/work in question. The resulting work perpetuates a pattern of speaking for Native women in literature with a filter of Western theories, thereby negating her original objective of communicating "across cultural, class, sexual, national, and gendered borders" (8). A more productive approach, viewing tribal histories and cultures, the voices of women within the contexts of gender complementarity, and Native theories, helps minimize the consequence of appropriation.

In *The Sacred Hoop: Recovering the Feminine in American Indian Traditions,* Gunn Allen writes, "Traditional tribal lifestyles are more often gynocratic than not, and they are never patriarchal" (2). The ability of women to bear children was highly valued. Involved in military, political, social, and spiritual leadership roles, women were regarded as equals to men rather than inferiors. Responsible for socioeconomic decisions, women in many indigenous societies owned all or most of the property. In their essay "American Indian Women: At the Center of Indigenous Resistance in Contemporary North America," scholar M. Annette Jaimes (Juaneño/Yaqui) and educational activist Theresa Halsey (Standing Rock Sioux) note, "Although Gunn Allen's conclusion is undoubtedly overstated and misleading, this is not to say that Native American women were not politically powerful" (316). Traditional tribal views of women persist in today's Native literatures as politically powerful female characters. Therefore, feminist criticism that does not account for differing tribal paradigms will not produce an accurate reading of Native American literature. Furthermore, "the opposition man/woman and the oppositions associated with it" must be considered differently than the patriarchal view when the cultural paradigms shift. When the male–female construction represents tribal gender complementarity, a situation in which there is balance, critics spend less energy discussing how women are denied equal status and power and instead look at how women's contributions are valued.

Bataille writes that although many historians have generally ignored Native American women, and literature has stereotyped Indian women as "squaws" and "princesses," researchers continue to confirm the importance of their roles in both traditional and contemporary cultures (xi). For example, in *Women and Power in Native North America,* the anthropologists Laura F. Klein and Lillian A. Ackerman have compiled a collection of essays that examines Native women in different culture areas, including the Inuit, Tlingit, Chipewyan, Plateau, Seneca, Blackfoot, Pomo, Southern Paiute, Navajo, San Juan Pueblo, Muskogee, and Cherokee. The chapters "challenge the stereotypes of gender relations and replace them with a much more complex reality that includes real respect and usually power for Native women within their societies" (vii). Looking at women's roles within their societies, the essays discuss their power, authority, and prestige in the areas of politics, economics, domestic life, and religion. The collection demonstrates that the important issue associated with power is autonomy—how individuals are autonomous in living their lives, making their own decisions. The editors conclude that Native women have (and had) more power than previous observers have claimed, and they summarize four themes in the ethnography of Native North America that contribute to the understanding of gender complementarity:

> First is a cultural notion of the self that stresses individual autonomy and relative freedom independent of one's gender. Second is a relative lack of social domination and submission in defining interpersonal relations, including relations between men and women, [...]. Third is a cultural elaboration and valuation of feminine principles in mythology and belief. Fourth is relative availability of positions of power to women as well as men. (246)

Unfortunately, these observations about gender complementarity, autonomy, and power have not always crossed over into other academic disciplines, particularly literary criticism of Native American literature.

Another collection of essays, *The Hidden Half: Studies of Plains Indian Women,* edited by anthropologists Patricia Albers and Beatrice Medicine (Standing Rock Sioux), focuses on the role and status of Plains Indian women in the historical period and in the modern reservation era. Similarly to *Women and Power in Native North America,* these essays indicate that the role, status, and identity of Plains Indian women, contrary to "their secondary place in popular myth and stereotypes," are not universal but varied and changing over time; they "cannot be explained in terms of some consistent and reductionist set of criteria" (Albers and Medicine 2, 14). Gender complementarity, however, was the norm, as Albers observes:

> In early Sioux households, the ideal relationship between men and women was based on principles of complementarity. Under these principles, the members of each sex were expected to be proficient in their respective work activities and self-sufficient as well. Work autonomy and prior claims on the products of one's labor, however, did not mitigate against voluntary sharing between the sexes. For just as each sex was accorded a certain degree of independence from the other, men and women were expected to be generous and willingly share the products of their respective labors. (189)

Albers describes gender complementarity as it existed in historical Sioux culture, but this ethos of gender complementarity, autonomy, and the value of men and women's work still can be seen in the contemporary Native American literary constructions of female characters. Gender complementarity has not disappeared.

Rebecca Tsosie (Pascua Yaqui) observes, "The modern conflict between genders, for many Indian groups, has largely resulted from patterns learned from white colonial authorities whose policies destroyed traditional egalitarian systems among Indian people" (520). Zitkala-Ša, Silko, Erdrich, and Alexie counter this colonial legacy with female characters in their writing who exhibit sovereignty, power, strength, and the autonomy of contemporary female warriors. "Like my mother and other Indian women who grew up in a matrilineal culture," writes Tohe, "when we cross into the Western world, we see how that world values women differently" (107). In Native communities, however, gender complementarity continues to exist, as Tohe notes: "Though I write about the women from my family and tribal community, I see many of the same qualities in the women I have met from other tribes. We didn't need to fight for our place in our societies because it surrounded us constantly" (110).

Likewise, the female characters in the works examined in this book do not have to fight for their place in their societies because it surrounds them constantly, just as Lulu Lamartine so efficaciously proves as she lets loose "the old lady trill, the victory yell." These Native female characters do not have to worry about whether they have power; they know they are powerful. Lulu *knows* that her community will recognize her authority and follow her lead. She does not need white feminist theory to explain why she is powerful; it does not apply. Lulu is powerful in a tribal context of gender complementarity.

CHAPTER 3

"We Must Be Masters of Our Circumstances"
Rhetorical Sovereignty as Political Resistance in the Life and Works of Zitkala-Ša

Zitkala-Ša (Lakota for "Red Bird") was born Gertrude Simmons on February 22, 1876, the child of a Yankton-Nakota mother from the Yankton Sioux Reservation, South Dakota, and a white father.[1] Her birth occurred during the period historians refer to as the Sioux War for the Black Hills, or Sitting Bull and Crazy Horse's War of 1876–77, which includes the well-known Battle of Little Bighorn (Greasy Grass) on June 25, 1876. The people generally referred to as the "Sioux" prefer to call themselves Lakota, Nakota, or Dakota, and they speak three eponymous dialects of the Siouan language. The Yankton originally used Nakota, but many adopted the Dakota dialect in the mid-1800s when they split from the Dakota and moved from a region east of the Mississippi in what is currently Minnesota to the prairies in the region that is now southeast South Dakota (Strom). During her childhood Zitkala-Ša would have learned her mother's dialect Nakota, perhaps would have become familiar with the Dakota dialect from her exposure to the Yankton groups, and would have understood Lakota well enough to choose a pen name in that dialect (Picotte xi). Her facility with language would prove to be one of her greatest strengths throughout her life.

The Yankton Sioux held the distinction of choosing to be at peace with the whites and not to persist in fighting with them. Vine Deloria, Jr. (Standing Rock Sioux), writes: "In the winter of 1916–17, a devoted Episcopal church-woman, Miss Sarah Emilia Olden, came from the eastern United States to write a book, *The People of Tipi Sapa*, on my grandfather, Philip Joseph Deloria, who was one of the most prominent Native clergy in that denomination" (*Singing* 3). Olden recounts that although other Sioux bands did not agree to remain peaceful, the "Yankton Dakotas seem to have been honestly pacific toward the whites and to have used whatever influence they had with other tribes to bring about a friendly attitude. It is doubtful, however, whether their attitude was either recognized or appreciated" (206). Deloria supports Olden's account of the Yankton's pursuing peaceful relations with the whites because he heard the stories passed down through his family from his grandfather, Tipi Sapa:

> Tipi Sapa was particularly proud of his association with peace efforts before he became a Christian, since it confirmed for him the idea that his life's mission was one of bringing peace and harmony to the Sioux people. During the prolonged period when the Yanktons were negotiating for compensation for the Pipestone Quarry in Minnesota, the old chiefs, led by Struck-by-the-Ree, told their lawyers that the Yanktons were custodians of the quarry on behalf of the whole Sioux Nation. They said that one reason why they sent out bundles of tobacco and pleaded with the other Sioux tribes to make peace was that they had obligations to try and make peace when the whole nation was at war with another nation. (*Singing* 210)

Although the Yankton Reservation did not participate in the Sioux conflicts with the whites and did what they could to promote peaceful relations, undoubtedly Zitkala-Ša's people still would have felt the effects of an enraged American nation's learning of the defeat of its golden-haired hero, Lt. Col. George Armstrong Custer.

Despite America's animosity toward Native peoples, however, in the early years of the twentieth century Zitkala-Ša was one of the few American Indian women who successfully moved as a public figure between her own Native culture and the dominant white culture. According to scholar Alison Bernstein, "Bonnin was easily the most valuable Indian woman reformer of the 1920s and early 1930s, having long been active in Indian reform organizations" (13). How she was able to accomplish as much as she did in the way of publishing literature and working for America Indian reform has received relatively little critical attention. Rather, both literary critics and historians tend to report biographical facts about her life; seldom do they offer critical analysis of why she could do what she did. "The Indian woman," as Bernstein notes, "remains a shadowy figure even in the best scholarship" (13).

This chapter examines how Zitkala-Ša, within the contexts of gender complementarity and knowledge of rhetorical strategies, uses her writing talents to work for the rights of all American Indians, creating a literature of resistance. To begin with, this discussion looks at some of her early writings—speeches, short stories, and autobiographical essays, then it situates her in the historical framework of the political activities of the General Federation of Women's Clubs (GFWC). The language that she uses in her personal writing will be compared to her fiction and nonfiction publications, particularly her contribution to *Oklahoma's Poor Rich Indians: An Orgy of Graft and Exploitation of the Five Civilized Tribes—Legalized Robbery?* (1924), which she coauthored with Charles H. Fabens and Matthew K. Sniffen. This document describes the results of an "investigation into the probate settlements of Indian land in Oklahoma after apportionment and oil strikes. The abuses outlined are incredible; the individual cases reviewed are pathetic" (Stout 77). Zitkala-Ša consciously chooses very specific rhetorical strategies that she knows will elicit a strong response from the American public regarding the exploitation of Oklahoma Indians' material wealth. As Mary Stout observes, "It is evident in her report, *Oklahoma's Poor Rich Indians*, and other writings, that she has discovered how to skillfully use the language to arouse the emotions in others" (74). A native Nakota speaker, Zitkala-Ša expertly manipulates her second language, English, to influence the American people, thereby empowering herself in a public way not usually enjoyed by marginalized minority women of her era. According to Hazel W. Hertzberg, she was "the most important figure in reform Pan-Indianism during the twenties" (303).

Zitkala-Ša's Yankton Nakota mother was Ellen Simmons (Taté Iyóhiwin, which means "Every Wind"), and her father was a white man who deserted the family before she was born.[2] Ellen named her daughter after her second husband, Simmons, rather than her birth father. Zitkala-Ša spent her first eight years on the Yankton Reservation in South Dakota and then began her assimilationist education at White's Manual Labor Institute, a Quaker missionary school for Indians in Wabash, Indiana, where she first learned to speak and to write English. After three years at White's, she returned to the reservation (1887–89), attended the Santee School (1889–90), and once again stayed with her mother (1890–91). She went back to White's, where she earned her diploma (1891–95); went on to study at Earlham College in Richmond, Indiana (1895–97); and while there she won prizes in oratory at the age of twenty. She taught at the Carlisle Indian Industrial School in Carlisle, Pennsylvania (1897–99), and after that, she attended the New England Conservatory of Music to study the violin (1899–1901). She also appeared as a soloist with the Carlisle Indian Band. Three of her autobiographical essays were published in the *Atlantic Monthly* in 1900, and her short stories appeared in *Harper's Monthly* in 1901. Later these articles, along with some additions, were collected and published as *American Indian Stories* (1921). In addition to this collection, she earlier had published *Old Indian Legends* (1901), a collection of Dakota Iktomi (trickster) tales.

By the age of twenty-four, Zitkala-Ša had traveled, become educated, taught school, performed music and oratory, and published her literature. Dexter Fisher notes that Zitkala-Ša had become very aware of her white audience: "She had already become the darling of a small literary coterie in Boston whose members were enthusiastic about the autobiographical sketches and short stories" (Foreword vii). In 1901 Zitkala-Ša was engaged to Dr. Carlos Montezuma (Yavapai), but she broke off the engagement and returned to the Standing Rock Reservation, South Dakota, where she worked as an issue clerk (1901–2). There on May 10, 1902, she married Raymond T. Bonnin, a Yankton Sioux; both were employed by the Indian Service. They moved to the Uintah and Ouray Reservation in Utah, where they worked for fourteen years (1903–16), and where their son, Raymond O. Bonnin (1903), was born. In 1913, Zitkala-Ša and Professor William Hanson of Brigham Young University composed and transcribed traditional Native melodies for *The Sun Dance Opera*. While in Utah, Zitkala-Ša became a correspondent for the Society of the American Indian (SAI), and after she was elected secretary of SAI (1916), she and Raymond moved to Washington, D.C. (1917–38). In her association with the SAI, she worked ceaselessly for Indian reform. When the organization disbanded in 1920, Zitkala-Ša went on to work with the GFWC (1920–23) and convinced them to develop the Indian Welfare Committee in 1921: "One concrete result of the collective efforts of Zitkala-Ša and the Federation was an investigation into government treatment of certain Oklahoma tribes, which led to the formation of the Meriam Commission and the subsequent appointment by President Hoover in 1928 of members of the Indian Rights Association to the top two positions in the Bureau of Indian Affairs" (Fisher, Foreword xv–xvi). In 1926, Zitkala-Ša formed a new Pan-Indian organization, the National Council of American Indians (NCAI), and presided over the group until her death in 1938. Her husband, Raymond, the secretary-treasurer of the NCAI, died in 1942. Zitkala-Ša's many accomplishments as an orator, teacher, musician, essayist, short story writer, editor, and political activist are examples of how her education successfully acculturated and assimilated her so that she could mediate between the dominant white mainstream society and her own tribal culture.

Zitkala-Ša's gender did not present any obstacles for her in accomplishing her work. In other words, she never shied away from the very public work she chose for fear that because she was a woman people would not listen to her or take her seriously. The image of the American Indian woman denied access to political forums was not part of Zitkala-Ša's consciousness even though the Indian woman did not hold the same fascination for the American imagination as the Indian man did. "The side of Plains Indian life most often seen by the American public," notes American Indian studies scholar Patricia C. Albers, "is the male half" (Albers and Medicine 2). Albers goes on to say, "Indian women are not portrayed autonomously, as having skills, conversations, and participating in areas of life that exist in partial independence of those of men" (2–3). Regardless of how the American public viewed the lives of Indian women, Zitkala-Ša knew that the roles of each gender were important to the welfare and health of the tribal community, neither subordinated to the other but rather both complementing each other. Deloria's discussion of the gendered division of labor among the Dakota Sioux reflects this same point of view: "The men and the women acted the parts in life that they considered to be allotted to them. The bearing of burdens seemed to be shared by both sexes to an almost equal degree" (*Singing* 95).

Zitkala-Ša frequently mentions work in her various publications and its importance whether performed by women or men. In her childhood, her mother is the main female role model, and although the father figure is absent, there are still many male figures in the tribe to act as male role models. Zitkala-Ša describes in her autobiographical essay, "Impressions of an Indian Childhood," how as a young girl of seven years she learns about the traditional work done by females in the tribe. She observes and models her behavior on her mother's example, including performing jobs such as drawing water from the Missouri River for household use (*American* 7), preparing meals and offering hospitality to guests (12, 27–28), learning the art of beadwork (19–20), and caring for the sick and elderly (31). Although the main focus is on what the females do, Zitkala-Ša portrays the males' work as that of warriors (12, 31) and storytellers (13, 15–16, 27). Because there is no "tendency to *rank* 'duties' into hierarchical layers of 'status,' thereby ascribing notions of 'inferiority' to women's domestic duties, and 'superiority' to men's roles in politics and warfare," there is a sense of responsibility and pride in doing one's part to help others (Tsosie 510). Zitkala-Ša, for example, reassures her mother of her help when she says, "Mother, when I am tall as my cousin Waraca-Ziwin, you shall not have to come for water. I will do it for you," and again when she serves an old grandfather a piece of bread and a cup of cold coffee, she "offered them to him with the air of bestowing generous hospitality" (*American* 9, 28). Zitkala-Ša learns at a young age that others will value the contributions she makes to the tribe, and the tasks do not reflect her lack of status.

For Zitkala-Ša, the gendered division of labor does not indicate a reduction in power for women. Legal scholar Rebecca Tsosie (Pascua Yaqui) writes, "Although clearly many Indian societies did ascribe to a degree of task differentiation according to gender, the variable of 'importance' attached to these tasks may be a purely European invention" (510). The power of women is not based on the work they do but on the way others perceive them. Paula Gunn Allen (Laguna Pueblo/Sioux) affirms this idea when she writes about how traditional roles for women have changed since colonization and westernization:

> While women still play the traditional role of housekeeper, childbearer, and nurturer, they no longer enjoy the unquestioned positions of power, respect, and decision making on local and international levels that were not so long ago their accustomed functions. Only in some tribes do they still enjoy the medicine or shamanistic power they earlier possessed. No longer, except in backwoods pockets of resistance, do they speak with the power and authority of inviolable law.
>
> [...] Patriarchy requires that powerful women be discredited so that its own system will seem to be the only one that reasonable or intelligent people can subscribe to. (*Sacred* 202–3)

Regardless of how the dominant culture might view Native women, Zitkala-Ša's sense of power and autonomy does not stem from the gendered division of labor. She does not see herself or her work as unimportant. If anybody views her as powerless merely because she is a woman, that perception arises outside her tribal community. Relationships among the Sioux, argues Patricia Albers, allow "all people a degree of autonomy and the right to exert influence through their own work and example" (217).

The attitude of helping others continues into Zitkala-Ša's adulthood, appearing in an article she writes for *The American Indian Magazine*, "A Year's Experience in Community Service Work among the Ute Tribe of Indians." She details how the wives of Indian employees agree that by "donating their services to prepare and serve a simple, wholesome lunch to these 'Monday Indians,' a mutual benefit would be gained to all concerned" (308). She adds: "The soup, pies and coffee were prepared by the Indian women under my supervision. [...] The Indian men hauled the wood and cut it up for us. They were good enough to carry buckets of water for us, too" (308). Even within a different tribe from her own and a change in geographical location, women and men still cooperate, complementing each other's work, and she notices it and values it.

In Zitkala-Ša's "Address" at the 1919 Annual Convention of the Society of American Indians, she makes a Pan-Indian appeal, requesting that the Indian men take the Indian women to the next meeting (153). She speaks about the important role of the women in transmitting the culture to the next generation and notes the importance of work for everyone in a way that illustrates gender complementarity:

> We have had to change from the old style of hunting, have had to leave the old trails. We have got to learn the new trails—we can do it. We have the power, we can think. We can be fair. Work is honorable as long as men and women are honest. There is no work that is degrading. It is all honorable. I do not need to

repeat that, because Indians know it. Our forefathers knew it was no disgrace to go on the hunt to bring the meat home for the family. It was no disgrace for the mother to prepare the meal. Work is honorable. We must have a work and each day do it to the best of our ability. (154)

Again, Zitkala-Ša does not differentiate work done by women and done by men in terms of its worth; all of it has equal value and importance because everyone's work contributes to the welfare of the whole community. She has moved from the work she learns as a young female child on the Yankton Reservation, to the work she does in the community for the Utes, and finally to the political arena, where she encourages both women and men to participate in the political process of working for change and improvements in the quality of life among American Indians. Zitkala-Ša does not doubt the ability of Indian women to think as competently as men. Perhaps her vision of women's work has changed from that which her mother performed in the domestic role to that which she now performs in the public role. Both roles contribute to the welfare of the tribal community, the former as the traditional caretaker of the people and the latter as the public guardian of the laws that affect the people. Even in traditional Plains Indian cultures, there were roles available to women in which they could assert their power outside the traditional avenues.

In discussing the "warrior role for women" in Plains Indian societies, anthropologist Beatrice Medicine (Standing Rock Sioux) argues, "it was one of several culturally accepted positions which accorded women power and prestige in areas typically identified as 'masculine'" (268). In her lifetime Zitkala-Ša, of course, did not participate in any kind of warfare in the usual sense of the term, but she would have known about this role for women. In her short story "A Warrior's Daughter," originally published in a 1902 issue of *Everybody's Magazine*, Zitkala-Ša portrays the heroine, Tusee, as a fearless woman who single-handedly risks her own life to enter an enemy camp to rescue her captive lover. Ruth Spack, a specialist in English for speakers of other languages and Native American studies scholar, notes that in this story Zitkala-Ša privileges the Sioux women's status and inverts the well-known story of Pocahontas's rescue of John Smith (164). Tusee saves a Native man, not a white man. She makes a plea to the Great Spirit for protection and success: "'Great Spirit, speed me to my lover's rescue! Give me swift cunning for a weapon this night! All-powerful Spirit, grant me my warrior-father's heart, strong to slay a foe and mighty to save a friend!'" (*American* 146). Displaying bravery and ingenuity, Tusee speaks in the enemy's "own tongue" (149) to entice the foe away from the camp. When he asks Tusee, "'Pray tell me, are you a woman or an evil spirit to lure me away?'" (150), Tusee adopts aggressive male warrior behaviors: "Turning on heels firmly planted in the earth, the woman gives a wild spring forward, like a panther for its prey. In a husky voice she hissed between her teeth, 'I am a Dakota woman!' From her unerring long knife the enemy falls heavily at her feet. The Great Spirit heard Tusee's prayer on the hilltop. He gave her a warrior's strong heart to lessen the foe by one" (150–51). The Great Spirit facilitates Tusee's coup by helping her first to use her young female charms to tempt the proud victor and ultimately to use her warrior skills to destroy him.

In order to approach her lover, who "in his tight-binding rawhide ropes hangs in hopeless despair" (151), unnoticed, Tusee adopts the disguise of an "old bent woman":

> With a stroke upward and downward she severs the cruel cords with her sharp blade. Dropping her blanket from her shoulders, so that it hangs from her girdled waist like a skirt, she shakes the large bundle into a light shawl for her lover. Quickly she spreads it over his bare back.
> "Come!" she whispers, and turns to go; but the young man, numb and helpless, staggers nigh to falling.
> The sight of his weakness makes her strong. A mighty power thrills her body. Stooping beneath his outstretched arms grasping at the air for support, Tusee lifts him upon her broad shoulders. With half-running, triumphant steps she carries him away into the open night. (152–53)

Tusee's schemes consist of the identities of a young sexual woman, a harmless old woman, and a strong warrior woman. To achieve her goals, she must draw on all her available resources, both feminine and masculine behaviors. Within her own personality the female and male complement each other. Zitkala-Ša creates a heroine who performs superhuman feats in the face of overwhelming odds, not unlike what she herself accomplishes in her own lifetime.

Medicine views these sex role reversals as "normative statuses which permitted individuals to strive for self-actualization, excellence, and social recognition in areas outside their customary sex role assignments. In this light, changing sex role identity becomes an achieved act which individuals pursue as a means for the healthy expression of alternative behaviors" (269). Therefore, in addition to Zitkala-Ša's views about the equal value of men and women's work, she would not necessarily have seen her role of political fighting with words as a departure from the traditionally accepted work for women. She was still serving Indian peoples and thinking of the welfare of the whole community.

Ironically, English, the language that proponents of assimilationist education believed would move American Indians into mainstream society, becomes a tool for Zitkala-Ša to defend tribal rights. In his essay "Rhetorical Sovereignty: What Do American Indians Want from Writing?" Scott Richard

Lyons (Ojibwe/Mdewakanton Dakota) defines *rhetorical sovereignty* as "the inherent right and ability of *peoples* to determine their own communicative needs and desires in this pursuit, to decide for themselves the goals, modes, styles, and languages of public discourse" (449–50). Zitkala-Ša uses rhetorical strategies in the oppressor's language as political resistance to the injustices suffered by American Indians. She practices rhetorical sovereignty when she subverts the English language to her own advantage. Muscogee Creek poet Joy Harjo explains how this strategy works for those writing in the oppressor's language: "In our tribal cultures the power of language to heal, to regenerate, and to create is understood. These colonizers' languages, which often usurped our own tribal languages or diminished them, now hand back emblems of our cultures, our own designs: beadwork, quills if you will. We've transformed these enemy languages" (21–22).[3]

Zitkala-Ša, indeed, transforms the enemy's language as she offers resistance in her oratory, autobiographical essays, and political writing. As she writes in the preface to *Old Indian Legends,* she hopes that people will learn to respect American Indians and their worldviews: "If it be true that much lies 'in the eye of the beholder,' then in the American aborigine as in any other race, sincerity of belief, though it were based upon mere optical illusion, demands a little respect. After all he seems at heart much like other peoples" (vi). Zitkala-Ša's writing strives to educate people about American Indians, to rectify the crimes perpetrated against them, and to promote their welfare. Her understanding of rhetorical strategies, both her own Yankton oral traditions and the Western literary traditions that she learned in school, provided her with the necessary tools to move comfortably and successfully as a writer among different rhetorical contexts and genres.

In 1901, Zitkala-Ša publishes *Old Indian Legends,* a collection of Dakota stories. One tale in particular, "The Toad and the Boy," offers an analogy of how Zitkala-Ša remains firmly connected to her heritage despite her assimilationist education. The narrator relates how a young mother leaves her sleeping baby boy in the tepee so that she can gather willow sticks for the fire, and while she is gone, a toad steals the baby to raise as her own child. When the mother returns and discovers her child missing, everyone in the camp searches for him but to no avail. Consequently, the distressed parents return yearly to the same location to search for their lost child. On the tenth anniversary of the child's abduction, the little boy hiding in the tall grasses sees his weeping mother, and he begins to cry. He runs home to his toad mother, demanding, "'Tell me what voice it was I heard which pleased my ears, but made my eyes grow wet!'" and "'Tell me why my little brothers and sisters are all unlike me'" (124). Anticipating that she might soon lose her stolen human son, the toad mother orders one of her own children to stay with him wherever he goes. One day an Indian hunter sees the boy, and having heard of the baby stolen long ago, he realizes who the child must be. The hunter runs to tell the people, and soon the heretofore-unhappy parents reunite with their long lost son, reestablishing tribal and family connections.

In much the same way that the young boy does not feel that he fits in with his toad family, Zitkala-Ša experiences discomfort in both white society and her own Nakota family. Her white education makes her feel out of place when she returns to the Yankton Reservation after her first three-year period of schooling at White's Manual Labor Institute. At the same time, her Indian identity creates problems for her in a white racist society. The staff of the boarding school failed if they did not enable Zitkala-Ša to help her people when she returned to her reservation. In effect, she is caught within a relationship of negative reciprocity: She is not able to feel comfortable giving to or receiving from her community. However, as the young boy in the story intuits a connection to his birth mother, Zitkala-Ša never forgets her heritage or relinquishes her relationship to it. On the contrary, she spends the major part of her life reaffirming the Indian identity that the boarding school tried to erase. As Agnes M. Picotte (Lakota Sioux) states in the foreword to *Old Indian Legends,* "her attachment to her roots in the primary Nakota culture gave her strength and endurance" (xii). Undeniably, those qualities of strength and endurance support Zitkala-Ša as she lives a life of resistance in her words and deeds in response to the wrongs imposed on American Indians by the dominant society.

In January 1896, Zitkala-Ša enters her first oratorical contest just five months into her first year at Earlham College and only five years after the December 29, 1890, Massacre at Wounded Knee. At the time, according to historian Francis Paul Prucha, press coverage offered two opposing analyses of the battle: "Some papers saw the battle as a victorious triumph of the soldiers over treacherous Indians. Others condemned the action as a brutal revenge for Custer's defeat (the soldiers were of the same regiment), in which women and children were wantonly butchered" (729). Following in the wake of this political climate and public opinion regarding American Indians, Zitkala-Ša speaks passionately for Indian rights.

Zitkala-Ša demonstrates at a young age her ability in using rhetorical strategies as she privileges the American Indian position and perspective. Her speech, "Side by Side," recounts the history of America, life before the invasion of the Europeans and life for the American Indians since that time. Biographer Doreen Rappaport notes how Zitkala-Ša reminds the audience of the "gentle, generous culture of her people and how badly the *wasí un* [white man] had treated them" (61). She seems to play on the romantic notions of the noble savage in the pristine Eden of the "New World," using the phrase "forest children," made popular by William Apess (Pequot) in *A Son of the Forest* (1829), and later by S. Alice Callahan (Muscogee) in *Wynema: A Child of the Forest* (1891). Zitkala-Ša portrays the early American Indians as having innate natural simplicity and virtue uncorrupted by European civilization:

> The reverent and poetic natures of these forest children feel the benign influence of the Great Spirit; they hear his voice in the wind; see his frown in the storm cloud; his smile in the sunbeam. Thus in reverential awe the Red man lived. His was the life that is the common lot of human kind. Bravely did he struggle with famine and disease. He felt his pulses hasten in the joyous freedom of the hunt. Quick to string his bow for vengeance; ready to bury the hatchet or smoke the pipe of peace; never was he first to break a treaty or known to betray a friend with whom he had eaten salt. (Simmons 177–78)

In this excerpt, Zitkala-Ša emphasizes that the Indians integrate spirituality holistically in their lives to the extent of the natural world around them. Although they practice respect for their environment, they do not hesitate to exact revenge for wrongs committed against them but also are quick to reconcile. She claims that they are honorable, never breaking a promise, and thereby implies that the whites are guilty of violating agreements with the Indians. After all, how could noble savages conceive of dishonesty and intentional deceit? According to Zitkala-Ša's description of American Indians, they could not possibly be corrupt.

Justifying the Indians who fought to defend their territories, Zitkala-Ša appeals to the audience's sense of patriotism:

> He loved his family and would defend them. He loved the fair land of which he was rightful owner. He loved the inheritance of his fathers, their traditions, their graves; held them a priceless legacy to be sacredly kept. He loved his native land. Do you wonder still that in his breast he should brood revenge, when ruthlessly driven from the temples where he worshipped? Do you wonder still that he skulked in forest gloom to avenge the desolation of his home? Is patriotism a virtue only in Saxon hearts? (178)

She notes the reasons that the Indians would naturally want to protect themselves and their families, and respectfully honor their elders and traditions. She uses sentimental and religious language of the period—"driven from the temples where he worshipped"—to elicit sympathy from a Christian audience who, although perhaps not appreciating a different way of understanding the world, might relate to the importance that the Indians place on their spirituality and "church." She moves the focus back to a question of "patriotism," an idea that she introduces at the beginning of her speech with a description of America as a "starry emblem of liberty" (177).

Arguing for equality among Indians and whites, Zitkala-Ša appeals to the audience's patriotic ideals, upon which America is founded:

> America entered upon her career of freedom and prosperity with the declaration that "all men are born free and equal." Her prosperity has advanced in proportion as she has preserved to her citizens this birthright of freedom and equality. Aside from the claims of a common humanity, can you as consistent Americans deny equal opportunities to an American people in their struggle to rise from ignorance and degradation? (179)

At this point in her speech, as Rappaport correctly observes, Zitkala-Ša "conclude[s] by regurgitating the lessons of boarding school that had been drummed into her: If Indians were to rise from their ignorance, they had to adopt the 'white man's ways'" (Rappaport 61):

> We come from mountain fastnesses, from cheerless plains, from far-off low-wooded streams, seeking the "White Man's Ways." Seeking your skill in industry and in art, seeking labor and honest independence, seeking the treasures of knowledge and wisdom, seeking to comprehend the spirit of your laws and the genius of your noble institutions, seeking by a new birthright to unite with yours our claim to a common country, seeking the Sovereign's crown that we may stand side by side with you in ascribing royal honor to our nation's flag. America, I love thee. "Thy people shall be my people and thy God my God." (Simmons 179)

Ending her speech with an Old Testament reference from Ruth 1.16, Zitkala-Ša personifies white Christian America as a worthy mother-in-law, not the birth mother of American Indians but a chosen surrogate. Although she privileges the white people's institutions, reinscribing the rhetoric that argues for white superiority, she still acknowledges an equal claim to the land and an equal standing of Indians and whites. Thus, she uses to her advantage the rhetoric of American equality and freedom for all to support her position for the Indian. Because she is persuasive in her rhetorical strategies, the Earlham judges award her first place.

The victory gives Zitkala-Ša her first concrete evidence that she, a Yankton woman whom all the American public does not see as an equal, can speak out for American Indians in a public forum and make a difference. This political triumph, using the rhetoric upon which America was founded, sets her on a path of political work that she will follow for the rest of her life.

One month later, in February 1896, Zitkala-Ša goes on to represent Earlham in a competition of college orators at Indianapolis and wins second place (Rappaport 64). In a later autobiographical essay, "The School Days of an Indian Girl," published in the February 1900 issue of *Atlantic Monthly*, she recalls the prejudice she encounters during the contest from the other student bodies: "There, before that vast ocean of eyes, some college rowdies threw out a large white flag, with a drawing of a most forlorn Indian girl on it. Under this they had printed in bold black letters words that ridiculed the college which was represented by a 'squaw.' Such worse than barbarian rudeness embittered me" (*American* 79). Perhaps the humiliation and embarrassment that she experiences during the competition fuel the resistance growing inside her. As Harold Bloom points out in *Native American Women Writers*, Zitkala-Ša's speech "touched on what would be the abiding themes of her other writings: the tension and difficulty of being part Native American, the inequities of the United States government's policies towards the Dakotas and other Native Americans, and the loss of the traditional way of life" (118). Even though critics tend to take notice of Zitkala-Ša's mixed-blood heritage, she never discusses this personal issue: "Any tensions from her mixed-blood heritage are not acknowledged in her remembrances" (Hafen, Introduction xv). She does address the racial intolerance of her peers, however, when she highlights the emotional damage that discrimination causes, and as literary critic Margo Lukens rightly asserts, by characterizing the slur—"squaw"—as "worse than barbarian rudeness," Zitkala-Ša "puts the 'savage' shoe on the white foot that she believes it truly fits" (334). By strategically inverting the civilized–savage polarity, Zitkala-Ša demonstrates who the truly civilized person is in this scenario—the Indian.

Looking at Zitkala-Ša's life in the context of how women were perceived in the dominant mainstream culture, that is, as individuals who did not have a lot of power, underscores how her education and political activism prepared her to write her report on the Oklahoma Indians. First, Zitkala-Ša attended off-reservation boarding schools that operated under policies common to the goals of the United States government with regard to American Indians: to acculturate and to assimilate the Indians as efficiently as possible, to convert them to Christianity, and to educate them in the ways of the whites. In "Motivations of Indian Children at Missionary and U.S. Government Schools," historian Michael Coleman writes, "These schools, it was believed, would 'civilize' and Christianize tribal children and thus accelerate the assimilation of all Indians into white society" (30). Zitkala-Ša attended these boarding schools during a period when the schools employed the governmental and maternalistic attitude of "We know what is best for you." She would later go on to exercise a similar kind of ideology in working for Indian reform. She sincerely believed that she could help American Indians because she knew what was best for them: "[S]he would fight for Sioux freedom and self-determination through educational reform" (Johnson and Wilson 27).

Also, the boarding schools would have indoctrinated Zitkala-Ša with the Victorian model for women known as the cult of true womanhood—"queen of the hearth" or "angel of the house." In "Educating Indian Girls at

Nonreservation Boarding Schools, 1878–1920," historian Robert Trennert states that the U.S. government tried to educate Indian girls so that they in turn could help their husbands assimilate (24). The prevailing image of women during this period was that they were responsible for the moral stature of their families. Rather than focus on changing Indian men, the government followed the current trend and opted for directing its energy toward educating the Indian women in the art of becoming "proper middle-class housewives" (230). In this way, the government transferred the definition of white womanhood to Indian women. This model was one more source from which Zitkala-Ša would have learned about white expectations for women.

Expectations of women who subscribed to the Victorian model contrast to those of Yankton women. In general, although the white women controlled the private domestic realm and through their example modeled the moral behavior that they expected their spouses to follow, they still were subjugated to the rule of their husbands, who held the economic, political, religious, and social power in public. Thus, women and men did not have equal power, and their work was not valued in the same way. The Yankton women, on the other hand, held traditional domestic roles as "housekeeper, childbearer, and nurturer"; however, the women's roles were complementary, not of lesser value than those of men (Allen, *Sacred* 202). Still grounded in her own worldview of gender complementarity, Zitkala-Ša is able to exploit the white expectations of how she should behave through her ability to mediate between the two cultures. She has the persona of a female who wants to model the appropriate moral behavior for American Indians, abstinence from alcohol and drugs. This stance fits the Victorian model for women. However, she also exhibits the behaviors of a strong Yankton woman who lobbies for the welfare of all Native peoples. Using the rhetoric of the dominant culture, Zitkala-Ša maintains political power, characteristically for a Yankton woman.

Zitkala-Ša's understanding of how to deal with a white audience helped her gain the support of the General Federation of Women's Clubs (GFWC). Founded in 1890, the GFWC drew together two hundred clubs, and by 1920 it had a membership of 1 million. Historian Sara M. Evans details the agenda of the GFWC as ranging from "self-development and literary activities [...] to] a variety of benevolent activities in behalf of women and children" (150). Not only did Zitkala-Ša understand the cult of domesticity because of her boarding school experience, but also she understood the role of Christianity in white society. Another key factor that would have helped her build a following among the GFWC members was her political lobbying for a ban on the use of peyote among the Native American Church members.

On the basis of her personal observations of peyote use among the Utes, Zitkala-Ša concluded that peyote was detrimental to the health and well-being of American Indians. Along with Paul Jones, a bishop of Utah, Henry B. Lloyd, a government physician, and Albert H. Kneale, a government officer in charge, Zitkala-Ša wrote in a sworn statement of April 28, 1916, the following evaluation of peyote's effects on the people:

> "The effect of the 'peyote' appears to be like that of an opiate. The users are stimulated to dreams and hullucinations [sic] in regard to themselves and others, and between times become sullen and uncommunicative. While under the influence, moral restraints are forgotten.
>
> "In connection with its use in sickness, several deaths have been reported as due to its influence. The continued use of 'peyote' on the health and character of the Indians appears to be so serious that we believe immediate steps should be taken by the government to prevent its sale and distribution to them, and we should therefore ask you to bring this statement to the attention of the proper authorities to secure that action." (*Sherman* 2)

Zitkala-Ša worked for restrictive legislation to include peyote in a ban on alcohol on reservations. In an interview with *The Washington Times*, she says, "I am now engaged in testifying before the Senate Committee on Indian Affairs in regard to the baneful effects of the use of peyote among the tribes. A hundred and fifty thousand dollars are to be appropriated to prevent the use of alcohol among the tribes, and it is our wish that the peyote be included in the legislation" (Bonnin, "*Indian Woman*"). Naturally, this rhetoric would appeal to the GFWC, especially to groups like the Women's Christian Temperance Union (WCTU).

Zitkala-Ša argued that peyote was like alcohol, a leading cause of the disintegration of the family unit because men under its influence did not work to support their families and were abusive to wives and children. If white women believed her rhetoric, then the WCTU would lobby their congressmen for political action in order to protect American Indian women and children. During hearings before the House Subcommittee of the Committee on Indian Affairs in February and March 1918, Congressman Bill Hayden offered evidence that, among others, groups like the Anti-Saloon League of America, the National Women's Christian Temperance Union, and the National Congress of Mothers and Parent-Teachers Associations opposed the use of peyote and supported its prohibition (Hertzberg 259, 264).

One more reason that the GFWC would have been drawn to Zitkala-Ša's causes would have been her very presence. Zitkala-Ša represented the "vanishing American Indian," and she played up that role by dressing in the appropriate costume whenever she gave a speech. In "The First Amendment, Anglo-Conformity and American Indian Religious Freedom," William Willard (Cherokee) asserts that Zitkala-Ša "found her best audience to be women's clubs whose attention was first caught by her elaborate buckskin dress and jewelry" (31). In other words, she played into the cultural image, the visual rhetoric, of what whites thought an Indian should look like. Willard notes that in 1918 when Zitkala-Ša testified before the House Subcommittee of the Committee on Indian Affairs, James Mooney, an ethnologist employed by the Bureau of American Ethnology, countered her charges and undermined her authority by critiquing her Indian garb: "'The dress is a woman's dress from some southern tribe, as shown by the long fringes; the belt is a Navajo Man's belt; the fan is a peyote man's fan, carried only by men, usually in the peyote ceremony'" (Willard, "First" 33). Mooney's attack on the authenticity of Zitkala-Ša's Indian identity and clothing bears closer scrutiny. He had been studying peyote as early as 1891 and had always been a promoter of its use among the Indians (Hertzberg 265, 262). He had such a personal investment in the continued use of peyote that he was instrumental in the legitimatizing of the Native American Church, "which was incorporated in the State of Oklahoma on October 10, 1918" (272). Hence, his opinions concerning the weight of Zitkala-Ša's testimony should be regarded with some skepticism.

In addition, Zitkala-Ša's critics do not seem to ask why she would wear clothing from a tribe other than her own Yankton tribe. She could have acquired this dress while living among the Utes, or her choice could fit more closely what her white audience expected to see on a "real" Indian. Working for a Pan-Indian organization, Zitkala-Ša used whatever means she needed, in clothing or words, to capture and persuade her white audience. Regardless of the tactics she chose, they worked. In "Zitkala-Ša: A Woman Who Would Be Heard," Willard writes: "Her beaded and fringed costume may have served to catch their attention but her descriptions of the reality of the corruption and brutality of the Bureau of Indian Affairs system kept their attention and moved them to political action on a national scale through a new GFWC committee" (13). Finally, in "The Transformation of Tradition," Dexter Fisher argues, "The influence of the white reading audience upon the early Indian writers cannot be exaggerated because within the American imagination, Indians have always been regarded as 'exotic,' 'primitive,' or 'romantic'" (209). Certainly, the GFWC also perceived Zitkala-Ša as the "exotic" Other.

The relationship between Zitkala-Ša and the GFWC can be described loosely in terms of gender complementarity. First, her Yankton worldview includes this concept. As her work complements the work of males in a tribal context, the GFWC's work allows the women a way to enter the social and political work of men in the dominant society. There is not an equal sharing of power as there is in the tribal context, but at least the GFWC provides an entrance for the women into these male-dominated public areas. Further, Zitkala-Ša's work and the GFWC's work complement each other.

Zitkala-Ša profits by her association with the GFWC, its power and access to public forums. Simultaneously, the GFWC benefits from Zitkala-Ša's public persona, attracting attention to its causes. Thus, Zitkala-Ša and the GFWC have a mutually advantageous relationship.

Although Zitkala-Ša sincerely believed that use of peyote would prevent American Indians from fully participating in their own self-determination, there seemed to be a contradiction of sorts in her position. If she truly supported self-determination for American Indian tribes, how could she criticize their choice of religion, which included peyote, and how could she request government interference? Both attitudes challenged her concept of self-determination and legal tribal sovereignties. P. Jane Hafen (Taos Pueblo) notes how the issue of peyote was argued both for and against by the first Pan-Indian group, the Society of American Indians, founded in 1911:

> In an additional irony, though, the Society of American Indians was simultaneously most united and most divided by the issue of peyote use. Opposition to peyote even brought bitter adversaries such as Colonel Richard H. Pratt, Carlisle founder, and his former employee, Zitkala-Ša, into unanimity. Pan-Indianism has had one of its most successful manifestations in the peyote culture of the Native American Church. As an accommodating strategy, this organization is a product of cultural mediation, blending traditional practices with Christianity and developing new rituals. ("Pan-Indianism" 9)

In its adaptation, the Native American Church exhibits a familiar problem of traditional versus progressive attitudes. There were others, such as Zitkala-Ša, who did not endorse the new religious practices because they did not see how American Indians could fully participate in their future if they were under the influence of peyote.

In opposition to Zitkala-Ša's antipeyote stance and proposed ban was another former Carlisle student, Cleaver Warden (Arapaho). He attended the Senate hearings to defend the use of peyote after reading in the newspapers about Zitkala-Ša's testimony: "'That Indian lady is not right but is instigated by wrong advice,' Warden commented. 'We only ask a fair and impartial trial by reasonable white people, not half breeds who do not know a lot of their ancestors or kindred. A true Indian is one who helps for a race and not that secretary of the Society of American Indians. Our intentions are good but obstructed by such persons'" (Hertzberg 269). Proponents of peyote, such as Warden, saw the controversy as a direct affront to their ability to self-determine what was best for them. People on both sides of the issue felt strongly about their positions. As Hafen points out, peyote was an issue that "most united and most divided." Despite Zitkala-Ša's long fight to ban peyote from the reservations, legislation was never passed. With the founding and continued growth of the Native American Church, after 1923, the subject of peyote disappeared from the Indian Rights Association *Annual Reports* (Hertzberg 275).

The outcome of the struggle to ban peyote did not prevent Zitkala-Ša from continuing to work for Indian reform. She chose not to give up, and evidence of this determination in her personality is apparent from a very early point in her career. She displayed it as a young woman in her personal correspondence with Carlos Montezuma. In one letter to him, dated February 20, 1901, Zitkala-Ša expresses her convictions about self-determination and tribal sovereignty, the ideas that American Indians as members of sovereign nations should have the right to decide their own future without interference from the United States government: "If we would claim our full heritage we must be masters of our circumstances" (Montezuma).[4] And in a letter dated March 5, 1901, she states, "I won't be another's mouthpiece. I will say just what I think. I fear no man. Sometimes I think I'd not fear God" (Montezuma). And she offers additional insights regarding her thoughts on groups and gender in a letter dated May 2, 1901. She and Montezuma have been writing about establishing a Pan-Indian organization. In response to Montezuma's suggestion that she could form a separate group for women, she becomes rather indignant:

> Your idea of an organization seems a plausible project. Why do you think the men are able alone to do it—and in a queer after thought suggest the Indian women should have theirs too? For spite, I feel like putting my hand forward and simply wiping the Indian men's Committee into no where!!! No—I should not really do such a thing. Only I do not understand *why* your organization does not include Indian women. Am I not an Indian woman as capable to think in serious matters and as thoroughly interested in the race as any one or two of you men put together? Why do you dare to leave us out? Why? Sometimes as I ponder the preponderous [sic] actions of men which are so tremendously out of proportion with the small results I laugh. (Montezuma)

Educated and firmly established in mainstream ideologies, Montezuma seems to have expectations of Zitkala-Ša that imply he sees no problem with separate spheres for men and women. Once again, Zitkala-Ša reveals her orientation within a context of gender complementarity. The assertive tone and style of her forceful personality can be seen in her direct, no-nonsense language. Her diction is clear and free of frivolous, flowery words. This commentary on her ability to think as well as any other person, male or female, perhaps explains why she appointed herself as president of the National Council of American Indians. She has no doubts about what she is capable of accomplishing. She displays a sense of liberation that Medicine claims Indian women have always had (Bataille and Sands viii): "[T]here was considerable variation in the roles of women," and "it is clear that they had other options which included assertiveness and independence" (Medicine 267, 276).

Zitkala-Ša writes to Montezuma in a letter dated May 7, 1901, about her feelings regarding marriage: "I swear I am not yours! I do not belong to anybody. Do not wish to be! First I like roaming about too well to settle down anywhere. Second, I know absolutely nothing about house-keeping. I would be restless and a burden" (Montezuma). Again she communicates her position on marriage in a very strong, clear style. Also, her remarks concerning housekeeping are interesting in light of the fact that most boarding schools focused on teaching the Indian girls domestic chores so that they could become middle-class housewives. In "The School Days of an Indian Girl," Zitkala-Ša describes how she was sent to the kitchen to mash turnips: "I bent in a hot rage over the turnips. I worked my vengeance upon them" (*American* 59–60). She had to do chores in the kitchen while she was at boarding school. Either she deliberately lied to Montezuma because she did not want to become a housewife, or she wanted to escape the necessity to perform daily domestic chores. That she was more interested in her political activism is more likely, as later she writes about performing those very same domestic chores that she complains about to Montezuma. In another letter to him, dated January 23, 1902, Zitkala-Ša writes about not taking responsibility for a deceased friend's orphaned two-year-old child: "That would mean my giving up my writing, and that is out of the question" (Montezuma). As a young woman, Zitkala-Ša has an independent spirit that she never loses as a mature adult. She has a clear vision of how she sees herself spending her life: writing, working, and striving for Indian reform.

Zitkala-Ša's individualistic approach to her life seems strange because she is from a worldview that values the tribal and communal perspective. Within the communal worldview, however, is space for respect for the individual's ability to make the choices that affect her life. In addition, the influence of her assimilationist education may have increased her sense of the ethos of American individualism. Thus, even though she spoke and worked in an individualistic manner, she claimed that all her work was for the benefit of all American Indians. Addressing the GFWC national council convention at Salt Lake City on the subject of the creation of a national Committee on Indian Welfare, she expresses her deep appreciation:

> "The Great Spirit knows my heart is full! Words are so deep in my heart I cannot utter them without tears. As an educated woman I have tried as interpreter to make America, which is so generous to all other races of the world, understand the longing of her own people, the first Americans, to become citizens of this great republic. Children of the Great Spirit they are, the same as you, and as worthy as any other race of recognition." ("Indian Welfare" 9)

Zitkala-Ša genuinely cared about American Indians and their future. She spent her life working to improve conditions for them in education, citizenship, employment, land claims, and self-determination.

Zitkala-Ša's concern over the policies regarding treatment of American Indians is found in her autobiographical essays. She shapes the narratives around the criticism of her boarding school experience, the resistance that she exercises as a young girl, and her continuing struggle throughout her adult life both to raise the consciousness of the white reading public and to improve the lives of American Indians. In her first autobiographical essay "Impressions of an Indian Childhood," published in the January 1900 issue of *Atlantic Monthly,* Zitkala-Ša's initial desire to go east corresponds to the first time she resists her mother: "This was the first time I had ever been so unwilling to give up my own desire that I refused to hearken to my mother's voice" (*American* 43). However, this scene is not the first time that Zitkala-Ša displays a distinct streak of defiance in her nature. When she learns that her mother fears the whites may still take more land away from the Sioux, she voices a strong opposition to them: "Stamping my foot on the earth, I cried aloud, 'I hate this paleface that makes my mother cry!'" (9). In this passage, Zitkala-Ša accomplishes more than recalling her act of childhood defiance. In a child's outburst within the confines of one sentence, she couches her criticism of how by 1892 the United States government acquires over 30 million acres of Indian lands through treaties, allotment processes, purchases, and outright thefts (Nabokov 369). In agreeing to allow Zitkala-Ša to travel east to attend school, her mother rationalizes that the government has an obligation to the Indians: "The palefaces, who owe us a large debt for stolen lands, have begun to pay a tardy justice in offering some education to our children" (*American* 44). Therefore, Zitkala-Ša not only crafts her own story for those with, as she describes, "an ignorant curiosity" about the life of the American Indian but also embeds in that narrative a harsh critique of how the federal government manages the Indians' land resources (98).

Although Zitkala-Ša's mother consents to her daughter's request to go with the missionaries, she realizes that her daughter will pay a high price and says, "I know my daughter must suffer keenly in this experiment" (44). With the advantage of hindsight, Zitkala-Ša renders this account in the all-knowing mother's language that signifies foresight of the pain ahead and uncertainty as to the outcome of her daughter's education. In her third autobiographical essay, "An Indian Teacher among Indians," published in the March 1900 issue of *Atlantic Monthly,* Zitkala-Ša recognizes how the white system of education in its goal to civilize the Indians instead contributes to their cultural genocide. Her brother, who was also educated in the eastern school, loses his job as a government clerk because he complains to

Washington of injustices on the reservation. After learning about his firing, she questions the value of white education for Indians if they do not benefit from it. Resigning her position as teacher, she concludes, "[F]ew there are who have paused to question whether real life or long-lasting death lies beneath this semblance of civilization" (*American* 99). Again, Zitkala-Ša challenges the government's policy of assimilation through education by questioning the value of that education, asking whether anyone has considered the long-range effects on those whom it supposedly helps.

Turning to political activism, Zitkala-Ša hopes to make a more valuable contribution to the welfare of American Indians by working for Indian reform. Among her many activities, she works as a research agent for the Indian Welfare Committee of the GFWC. Along with Charles H. Fabens, representative of the American Indian Defense Association, and Matthew K. Sniffen, secretary of the Indian Rights Association, Zitkala-Ša coauthors the pamphlet *Oklahoma's Poor Rich Indians: An Orgy of Graft and Exploitation of the Five Civilized Tribes—Legalized Robbery*, published February 5, 1924. The three authors investigate the probate settlements of Indian land in Oklahoma after apportionment and oil strikes. Herbert Welsh, the president of the Indian Rights Association, opens the pamphlet with "In Explanation," which describes their work:

> These experienced investigators spent five weeks in Eastern Oklahoma during the months of November and December, 1923, making a first-hand study of the conditions [...] and gathering information from all available sources. Their report discloses a situation that is almost unbelievable in a civilized country, and makes it clear that a radical and immediate change of the system in vogue is necessary if the members of the Five Civilized Tribes are to be saved from pauperization and virtual extermination. (Bonnin, Fabens, and Sniffen 3)

Welsh refers to the Indian probate conditions in Oklahoma that allow a corrupt system to exploit and steal from the Indians. Judges, attorneys, guardians, and businesspeople all conspire to steal thousands of dollars from unsuspecting Indians, and some go so far as to commit kidnapping, rape, and murder.

Although Zitkala-Ša worked alongside Fabens and Sniffen throughout their research, inquiries, and writing, the report attributes only one specific portion to her. In "Regardless of Sex or Age," the voice changes completely in tone and style from the rest of the writing, which is formal, factual, and legalistic. This part of the report, then, which might easily be characterized as female in style and subject matter, complements the rest of the report, which might be characterized as more traditionally male in style and subject matter. As always, Zitkala-Ša would have seen her involvement in this project from her own concept of gender complementarity and work. Fabens and

Sniffen needed Zitkala-Ša to interview the Native women. The interviewees most likely would have felt more comfortable talking to another woman as opposed to a man and also would have trusted another Native far more than a white man, considering what they had been through. In other words, Zitkala-Ša would not have seen herself as less than an equal participant or her work as less important than that of the male coauthors. Fabens and Sniffen, however, socialized in a European-American perspective that privileges patriarchy, feminize her contribution, thereby creating a hierarchy that implies their superior male position of authority.

Zitkala-Ša's writing in this document also changes in tone and style from her writing in her personal letters to Montezuma. The male coauthors write: "There are some phases of our investigation that can be presented best by a feminine mind, and we leave it to Mrs. Bonnin to describe the following three cases" (Bonnin, Fabens, and Sniffen 23). Even this decision is a political rhetorical strategy in presenting the material they discovered in Oklahoma. They want to show the public and Congress examples of the outrageous crimes being committed against Indian women and children, and a woman's discussing these acts in emotional language, which is more often associated with females, creates pathos and carries even more persuasive power. Finally, Zitkala-Ša's involvement offers an additional example of gender complementarity. In working with Fabens and Sniffen, she gives the necessary female perspective to a project that requires a woman with whom other Indian women and children will speak.

Because of the subject matter in the *Oklahoma's Poor Rich Indians*, Zitkala-Ša carefully selects her words to create the exact effect on the reader that she wants to have. The three cases are about Millie Neharkey, an eighteen-year-old Indian women; Ledcie Stechi, a seven-year-old Choctaw minor; and Martha Axe Roberts, a Shawnee widow of an Osage. In "Tender Violence: Literary Eavesdropping, Domestic Fiction, and Educational Reform," Laura Wexler writes that the "expansive, imperial project of sentimentalism [...] was intended as a tool for the control of others" (158). Normally, the "others" would have been the "races who were compelled to play not the leading roles but the human scenery before which the melodrama of middle-class redemption could be enacted" (158). In this case, the American Indians play the leading roles, but the scenario is not fiction. Nevertheless, Zitkala-Ša uses the language of sentimentalism to portray the events in such a way as to invoke the same kind of response from the white readers. Wexler notes, "The typical objects of sentimental compassion are the prisoner, the madman, the child, the very old, the animal, and the slave" (160). The three cases that Zitkala-Ša writes about are all females of different ages, and in different senses of the words, they are all prisoners and slaves to their guardians, who control their money. She would know how to tap easily into the language of sentimentalism because as Wexler points out, she attended White's Manual Institute, where sentimental culture was enforced (173).

The first case, of Millie Neharkey, reveals the rhetorical strategies that Zitkala-Ša employs throughout her contribution to the report. Abductors kidnap Millie Neharkey, feed her alcohol, sexually assault her, force her to sign over her deed, and forge her checks. The newspaper account included in the report gives the typical journalistic reporting: just the facts. Then Zitkala-Ša gives her account of interviewing Millie. Now the language changes to the emotional, melodramatic, and sentimental. For example, the newspaper account talks about the kidnappers' sexually assaulting Millie: "[O]ne of them, according to the evidence, made an unlawful assault upon her" (Bonnin, Fabens, and Sniffen 26). Zitkala-Ša reports the events in a much more dramatic style: "Mutely I put my arms around her, whose great wealth had made her a victim of an unscrupulous, lawless party, and whose little body was mutilated by a drunken fiend who assaulted her night after night" (26). Whereas the newspaper account relates only one assault—"an unlawful assault"—in a simple sentence, Zitkala-Ša claims that after a "private conference" with the child, she learns that Millie was repeatedly assaulted. Zitkala-Ša uses the language of the "seduction" narrative that Mary E. Odem claims expresses "female reformers' deep anger about women's sexual vulnerability in a male-dominated society. They shifted the blame for moral wrongdoing from the young woman to her male seducer, whom they described in various accounts as 'fiend,' 'devil,' 'wild beast,' and 'moral monstrosity'" (18). In addition to the language of sentimentalism, Zitkala-Ša intensifies the emotional impact of her writing by using the language of the seduction narrative.

In the sentence cited, Zitkala-Ša describes Millie as "little" and a "victim" (Bonnin, Fabens, and Sniffen 26). Even though the young woman has just turned eighteen years old, Zitkala-Ša continually calls attention to her diminutive size, thereby increasing her vulnerability. In addition to the preceding sentence, the following words appear in Zitkala-Ša's commentary on Millie: "smallness of stature," "child's voice," "timidity," "girl," "immature," "sixth grade," and "little Millie." Zitkala-Ša repeats these images to remind the reader that Millie is young, small, and helpless. Zitkala-Ša calls to mind the seduction narrative, with which the white middle class is very familiar; however, whites apply the narrative to young white women who leave home and go to the dangerous big city. In this case, kidnappers seize Millie from where she lives. To ensure that Americans will feel outrage at this injustice, Zitkala-Ša appeals to their patriotism and upstanding reputations as American citizens: "This is an appeal for *action, immediate action,* by the honest and fair-minded Americans of this 20th century. We believe they are in an overwhelming majority over the criminal class, and the power is in their hands to redeem not only the helpless Indians, but a sister state of the Union from the petty thieves that infest her" (26). Zitkala-Ša plays to the image of Americans as powerful and capable of solving all problems as good humanitarians, much as she does in her speech "Side by Side" at the oratorical contest. Unfortunately, the image of the powerful American hero and the helpless Indian victim does nothing to equalize the power relationships between the races, but the comparison accurately reflects the then-existing conditions in Oklahoma.

In the second case, seven-year-old Ledcie Stechi "lived with her old grandmother in a small shack" (26). Zitkala-Ša has chosen an example that has not just one sentimental character, the small sick child, but two, the second an old frail grandmother. If the first case scenario did not enrage the reader, then the second one should pull at the heartstrings. The small, undernourished child does not get enough money from her guardian to eat or clothe herself. At one point, when the child is ill, she is placed in an Indian school and begins to regain her health. Her guardian, however, demands that she be returned to him. The grandmother is never reunited with the child, and one month later Ledcie dies. There is suspicion that she has been poisoned so that the guardian can claim her land:

> Greed for the girl's lands and rich oil property actuated the grafters and made them like beasts surrounding their prey, insensible to the grief and anguish of the white-haired grandmother. Feebly, hopelessly, she wailed over the little dead body—its baby mouth turned black, little fingernails turned black, and even the little breast all turned black! In vain she asked for an examination of the body, believing Ledcie had been poisoned. "No use. Bury the body," commanded the legal guardian. (28)

Once again, Zitkala-Ša uses the language of the "seduction" narrative to describe the perpetrators in the case of Ledcie Stechi. The villains are "like beasts surrounding their prey." To conclude the second case, Zitkala-Ša adheres to the same format she uses in the first case, patriotic rhetoric to move people's consciences: The grandmother "will go the way of her grandchild, as sheep for slaughter by ravenous wolves in men's forms, unless the good people of America intervene immediately by remedial Congressional action. Such action is the duty of all loyal Americans for the protection of America's wards" (28). Zitkala-Ša knows how to tell the reader the same thing repeatedly: Do something and do it now before any more people die.

In the final case, Zitkala-Ša interviews Martha Axe Roberts, a Shawnee widow with two small children. This is a case of a woman who has been declared mentally incompetent and not capable of handling her own finances. And she does not receive enough money from her guardian to meet expenses for her family and herself. She wants to live with her parents in another county, but her guardian will not allow it. After a lengthy in-person interview, Zitkala-Ša concludes that "Martha is not crazy but perfectly sane, and her love for her parents, which draws her to them, is wholly admirable. She is a victim of exploitation" (32). And one last time, Zitkala-Ša ends her account with a patriotic message: "The human cry of this Shawnee woman is a call to America for defence and protection" (32).

These three examples, in which Zitkala-Ša uses sentimental language and a "seduction narrative," show how well she can manipulate the language to achieve the desired effect of moving the reader to action. Because she was educated at a school that enforced the sentimental culture, she was very familiar with the discourse. And because the GFWC supported her, she was in tune with the discourse that would not only appeal to their sensibilities of domesticity and the protection of women and children but would also speak to their outrage at the sexual victimization of these females. The findings published in *Oklahoma's Poor Rich Indians* "[alert] the nation to the scandals and [bolster] the resolve of responsible citizens of Oklahoma to end the evils in their state" (Prucha 907).

Scott Lyons describes those Natives who have won victories with writing as "Native people who learned how to fight battles in both court and the culture-at-large, who knew how to read and write the legal system, interrogate and challenge cultural semiotics, generate public opinion, form publics, and create solidarity with others" (466). Zitkala-Ša certainly falls within that description, as a person who exercises rhetorical sovereignty as a form of political resistance in her oratory, autobiographical essays, and political writing. Zitkala-Ša was able to mediate and accommodate between two cultures, American Indian culture and white dominant mainstream culture, because she had a command of the English language and knew how and when to use it to her best advantage. Her talent with language accounted for her success as much as her ability to play to the public's cultural image of the Indian. The wonderful irony about how well Zitkala-Ša uses the English language is that she manipulates the language of the oppressor to further the rights of Indians. Thus, in a subtle way she creates resistance and liberation literature with sentimentalism. Her core beliefs, however, are situated within the context of gender complementarity. She sees her writing and work as necessary with that of men to make for a complete whole. As she writes in her letter to Dr. Carlos Montezuma, "Why do you think the men are able alone to do it [. . .]?" Plainly, Zitkala-Ša demonstrates that a Yankton woman like her successfully applies rhetorical sovereignty as political resistance in her life and works.

CHAPTER 4

"The Men in the Bar Feared Her"
The Power of Ayah in Leslie Marmon Silko's "Lullaby"

Leslie Marmon Silko, of Laguna Pueblo, Mexican, and Anglo-American descent, was born on March 5, 1948, in Albuquerque, New Mexico, and grew up in Old Laguna. Her white great-grandfather, Robert G. Marmon, settled in Laguna in 1872. His brother, Walter Marmon, had gone there from Ohio in 1869 to survey the pueblo boundary and later become a government schoolteacher at Laguna in 1871. Both brothers served terms as pueblo governors during the 1870s, experiencing political power and leaving a legacy that would influence their great-granddaughter years later. Robert G. Marmon's second wife was Maria Anaya, a Laguna, who was Silko's great-grandmother, whom she called "Grandma A'mooh." Her aunt Susie Reyes Marmon, also Laguna, was the wife of her grandfather's brother. Both women played an important role in the transfer of traditional Laguna cultural knowledge to Silko when she was a child (Clements and Roemer 277).

Using her cultural knowledge of the Laguna people in her writing, Leslie Marmon Silko has established herself as one of the most important contemporary American Indian writers. Alan R. Velie canonizes her, along with N. Scott Momaday (Kiowa), James Welch (Blackfeet/Gros Ventre), and Gerald Vizenor (Chippewa), in his examination of *Four American Indian Literary Masters* (1982). "During the early 1970s—the emergent years of what Kenneth Lincoln has called the 'Native American Renaissance'—Leslie Marmon Silko was perhaps the movement's preeminent writer of short fiction," write William M. Clements and Kenneth M. Roemer (277). Although her importance in American Indian literature cannot be overstated, this group of writers received attention and high praise from the academy, in part, because of Momaday's high-profile 1969 Pulitzer Prize. Just as the term *Native American Renaissance* is misleading, causing people to think that Native literatures were stagnant before this period, so is the assumption that there were no other Native women authors. In fact, Native women were writing before Silko, during the same period, and soon after, just as Native American literatures have always continued to evolve.

Although Silko's writing reflects her Laguna background, she also has written about indigenous peoples outside her own tribe, in particular the young Yupik female protagonist in the short story "Storyteller" (*Storyteller* 1981), the Navajo medicine man Betonie in the novel *Ceremony* (1977), and a cast of characters from Mexico and South America in the novel *Almanac of the Dead* (1991). In the short story "Lullaby," which is "among the most often reprinted stories in American Indian literature," Silko draws on Navajo (Diné) characters (Graulich 19). First published in 1974 in both *Chicago Review* and *Yardbird Reader*, "Lullaby" was later selected by Martha Foley as one of twenty works for *The Best American Short Stories of 1975*. Silko then included it in *Storyteller* (1981), a collection of short stories, poems, autobiographical anecdotes, and photographs. Silko's writing outside her own Laguna Pueblo tradition in "Lullaby" presents the challenge to the reader to be aware of not only Silko's tribal heritage but also that of the Navajo.

In "Lullaby," Ayah searches for her husband, Chato, as she walks in the falling snow to Azzie's Bar, where he has gone to buy wine. During her walk, she reminisces about her life, remembering, among other things, scenes from her childhood, the loss of her son in the war, the removal of her two young children from her home, and Chato's firing from his cattle rancher's job. Silko juxtaposes the past and the present to show both how Ayah maintains her sense of tribal identity in the face of change, disillusionment, and loss, and by extension how problems still exist today not just for the Navajo but for many American Indians. The story ends on a dual note, one that implies death, but more importantly one that signifies continuity, survival, and hope.

About this particular story, Silko states her political agenda: "I feel it is more effective to write a story like 'Lullaby' than to rant and rave. I think it is more effective in reaching people" (Seyersted, *Two Interviews* 24). According to Silko, understanding context provides more accessibility to a story. "Depending on how familiar you are with the context," she says, "you'll get more or less" (Fisher 22). Most biographical writings about Silko and critical pieces about her fiction include the influence of her Laguna Pueblo heritage. Along with that influence, this chapter also examines how the history and culture of the Navajo impact "Lullaby" and why she feels at ease writing about a Native culture other than her own. As Silko's Laguna Pueblo heritage and Navajo culture and history combine to shape "Lullaby," taking into account the story's Navajo historical and cultural contexts illuminates more fully the political ramifications of gender complementarity for the female protagonist, Ayah. Regarding her own position on feminism and political activism, Silko adds, "Artists can't work with a chip on their shoulders, and that's what has happened to a lot of feminists. Politics can ruin anything. It will ruin a picnic. Politics in the most crass sense—rally around the banner kind. I'm political, but I'm political in my stories" (Fisher 21–22). Hence, for Silko, her stories supersede both feminism and political activism. To discern her stand on American Indian issues, and in particular on women and power, understanding the cultural and historical contexts of her story is necessary.

In Laura Tohe's (Navajo) essay "There Is No Word for Feminism in My Language," she writes about the cultural role of Navajo women in general as important members of the family and tribe:

> As long as I can remember, the Diné (or Navajo, as we are also referred to) women in my life have always shown courage, determination, strength, persistence, and endurance in their own special way. My female relatives lived their lives within the Diné matrilineal culture that valued, honored, and respected them. These women passed on to their daughters not only their strength, but the expectation to assume responsibility for the family, and therefore were expected to act as leaders for the family and the tribe. Despite five hundred years of Western patriarchal intrusion, this practice continues. (103)

Tohe's description of Navajo women suggests that Ayah should be viewed in the context of her own family: her grandmother, mother, husband, and children. Also, the way in which Tohe characterizes the Navajo women certainly applies to Ayah, the "courage, determination, strength, persistence, and endurance" that she shows "in [her] own special way," in view of the hardships that she has endured.

Silko's own mixed ancestry—Laguna Pueblo, Mexican, and white—perhaps explains, in part, why she feels entitled to write about other cultures with which she has had contact, such as the Navajo. Discussing the all-embracing nature of her people in the essay "Fences against Freedom," Silko writes, "The cosmology of the Pueblo people is all-inclusive [...]. The oldtime people believed that we must keep learning as much as we can all of our lives" (*Yellow Woman* 103). Discussing Silko's background, Melody Graulich remarks that "she grew up in a family that practiced and celebrated the traditional ways of Pueblo life but also borrowed freely from Anglo and Mexican cultures, a family that valued learning" (7). Viewing the practice of "borrowing freely" from other cultures as a way of learning does not seem to present Silko with any concerns about the question of appropriation in her writing, an important issue in American Indian literary studies.

On the contrary, in her essay "The Border Patrol State," Silko seems to see the issue of cultural boundaries, at least with regard to indigenous peoples, in much the same way that she does physical boundaries that affect those same groups:

> It is no use; borders haven't worked, and they won't work, not now, as the indigenous people of the Americas assert their kinship and solidarity with one another. A mass migration is already underway; its roots are not simply economic. The Uto-Aztecan languages are spoken as far north as Taos Pueblo near the Colorado border, all the way south to Mexico City. Before the arrival of the Europeans, the indigenous communities throughout this region not only conducted commerce; the people shared cosmologies, and oral narratives about the Maize Mother, the Twin Brothers, and their grandmother, Spider Woman, as well as Quetzalcoatl, the benevolent snake. The great human migration within the Americas cannot be stopped; human beings are natural forces of the earth, just as rivers and winds are natural forces. (*Yellow Woman* 122–23)

Actually, the Uto-Aztecan languages are spoken as far northwest as Idaho and Oregon and as far south as Central America ("American Indian Languages"). Although each American Indian tribe has its own unique culture, Silko chooses to focus more on commonalities among Southwest tribes, including worldviews and origin stories. Her mixed ancestry might account for this relaxed attitude about tribal specificity in her writing and her habit of straying from a strict Laguna Pueblo context. More importantly, her view of storytelling coincides with the Navajo. In "Language and Literature from a Pueblo Indian Perspective," Silko quotes the old people as saying, "'If you can remember the stories, you will be all right. Just remember the stories'" (*Yellow Woman* 58). Ray Yazzie (Navajo) states his view on the value of tribal stories similarly: "A long time ago people used to say that if you remembered the stories that were passed down, they would make you strong. Even just a little portion of the stories—that part would keep you and your children strong so you could face whatever is in the future" (Evers ix). For Silko, the shared view of the oral tradition of storytelling seems to overshadow any problems writing about the Navajo culture. The story itself is more important than any other consideration.

In *Leslie Marmon Silko*, Per Seyersted discusses the Laguna Pueblo culture and notes the mediating position in which Silko lived: "The family lived in one of the Marmon houses, which were situated below the village, close to the river. [...] This in-between position was also seen in such facts as that the family was included in clan activities, but not to the same extent as full bloods, and that the young Leslie helped out at ceremonial dances, but did not dance herself" (13). As a result of this mediating position, Silko displays sensitivity to the issues that mixed-blood peoples face when interacting not only with the dominant mainstream culture but with their own as well. In an autobiographical entry for *The Man to Send Rain Clouds: Contemporary Stories by American Indians,* Silko comments on her identity: "I am of mixed-breed ancestry, but what I know is Laguna. This place I am from is everything I am as a writer and human being" (Rosen 176). Her description of the Pueblo cosmology as an all-inclusive one that continues to learn from other peoples and her own admission of her mixed ancestry make clear her position that she feels comfortable writing about not only the Laguna Pueblo but also any indigenous culture with which she has contact, particularly the Southwest Pueblos and Navajo tribes.

Silko admits that in the past she was not as aware of her connection to the Navajo: "I guess I underestimated my involvement or my sense of some kind of relationship with Navajo people and Navajo culture" (Fitzgerald and Hudak 33). As a writer, Silko has a sense of an autonomous self, one grounded in the concept of gender complementarity, that allows her to move freely among the cultures of the Laguna Pueblo, the Navajo, and the dominant mainstream. She does not see any drawbacks to her mixed heritage. On the contrary, she sees the advantages to having access to several cultures, and as a result, she becomes more powerful in her writing, drawing on a variety of resources. In effect, Silko's political statement in her stories is that people can cross cultural boundaries if they have intimate knowledge of the people and the land. Thus, Silko's stories, including those about the Navajo, have played their part, as Ray Yazzie says, in making her strong.

Perhaps the sixteenth-century history that the Puebloan peoples share with the Navajo partially accounts for Silko's seeing more of the similarities than of the distinctions: "[T]he Navajos became readily distinguishable from other Athabaskans only after these bands were joined by Puebloan peoples fleeing Spanish persecution" (Bailey and Bailey 12). According to the findings of fact decided on February 28, 1967, before the Indian Claims Commission, the "Navajo in New Mexico were first found on the San Juan River in the sixteenth century. It was their custom to move frequently," and in the 1700s they were settled, among other places, "on the northern edge of the Cebolleta Mountains" and as "neighbors of the Laguna on the north" (Horr 188). In "Lullaby," Silko introduces the geographical setting of Cebolleta in the first paragraph as she locates the protagonist, Ayah, in the landscape: "She was sitting on the edge of Cebolleta Creek, where in the springtime the thin cows would graze on grass already chewed flat to the ground" (*Storyteller* 43).[1] Silko uses a setting that has a history of Navajo and Laguna habitation, a history that she heard while growing up through oral accounts.

The Indian Claims Commission also notes, "The first reference to the Navajo in the Laguna area dates from the middle of the eighteenth century, when the Navajo permitted themselves to be settled at Encinal, under Fray Juan Sanz de Lezaun, and at Cebolleta, under Fray Manuel Vemejo" (Horr 188). After the Navajo grew tired of the settled way of life and the Christian faith, they ejected the friars and moved westward. The few who remained over the next 125 years bothered the Lagunas and Acoma, sometimes at the prompting of the Spanish authorities who requested their help: "Throughout the Spanish period small bands of Navajos continued to move in and out of the area, sometimes cultivating small plots in the Cebolleta, Cubero Pedro Padilla Canada, on the Rio, and in the Canon [sic] of Juan Tafoya in the Agua Salada, northeast of Cebolleta" (189). The documents filed before the Indian Claims Commission argue that the Laguna always lived in these areas regardless of whether the Navajo came or went.

In the opinion of the commission, the records indicate that "from the middle of the 18th century until 1864 when they were taken to Bosque Redondo the Navajo moved in and out" of lands occupied by the Laguna:

> Sometimes small groups would be raising crops at various places and be on friendly terms with the pueblos. At other times the Navajos would raid the pueblos causing them to move their herds closer to the home villages for protection. During the intermittent periods of peace the pueblos would again reoccupy the outlying areas as they had before. From time to time during this period military forces of the Spanish, Mexican and American governments would attempt to stop the raiding by carrying out campaigns against the Navajos and making peace treaties with them, and encouraged them to live a more settled existence. However, raids continued until the Navajos were taken to Bosque Redondo in 1864. The raids, at least in part, were a retaliation by the Navajos for members of their tribe who were taken and sold as slaves by both Indians and whites. (230–31)

Silko writes about all these aspects of Navajo–Laguna Pueblo relations: friendly interactions with various Navajo, Navajo raiding of Laguna sheep, and a reference to a Navajo woman who was stolen by slave hunters as a child and later worked for her Great-Grandmother Helen. One expert witness, anthropologist Dr. Florence H. Ellis, who testified on behalf of both the Acoma and Lagunas, based her conclusions supporting Laguna claims on archaeological, historical, and ethnological materials. Commenting on the Navajo presence in the area, Dr. Ellis notes that the few Navajos in the Laguna territory before Bosque Redondo (1864–68) "were by all accounts friendly to the Lagunas" (232–33). She goes on to note that Navajos "moved down into the main Canoncito [sic] area in the late 1800's and early 1900's" (236). In "Lullaby," Silko refers to Cañoncito, where Ayah takes her children to the clinic. The secondary source of documented history gathered and compiled by the "experts" confirms the primary oral history that Silko learned while growing up at Laguna Pueblo.

Beyond the historical relationship among the Pueblos and Navajo, Silko asserts that her role as a storyteller involves seeing the connections among people: "It's that whole deeper experience of seeing life and seeing what everyone's doing as being interrelated, sets of stories and story-telling—that's the part of my growing up that's really important to me as a writer" (Fitzgerald and Hudak 25). Expounding on this same point about connections, Silko continues:

> The only thing that means anything is to really feel how it is you fit into this larger scheme, and then once you understand that, you don't feel alone or isolated... you continue on. So for me the stories and that whole process are just a kind of reaffirming where everything stands in relation to everything else, and at the same time you get figured into that yourself. (32)

According to Silko's philosophy of storytelling, writing about other American Indian tribes provides another means of discovering more about an individual's place in this world and how that position fits into the larger scheme. In *Laguna Woman*, a collection of her poems, Silko acknowledges in the biographical information that her writing is an effort to define who she is: "I suppose at the core of my writing is the attempt to identify what it is to be a half-breed or mixed blooded person; what it is is [*sic*] grow up neither white nor fully traditional Indian" (35). Silko's project when writing about another culture entails a search for her own sense of self. In other words, if Silko writes a story about a Navajo woman, in essence she still wants to explore issues that will contribute to a fuller understanding of her own personhood and perhaps gender. In that sense, she does appropriate other cultures to further her own understanding of what "it is to be a [...] mixed blooded person" (35).

Possibly this strategy of writing about other American Indian cultures suggests Silko's theme of adaptation:

> Silko shows how Laguna tradition can and must adapt to the twentieth century. While Laguna culture remains distinct and viable, it does so through flexibility and an ability to incorporate and shape outside influences. Just as Laguna society had incorporated the Marmon family, so the rituals, customs, patterns of storytelling, and other aspects of culture have survived by adapting to and exploiting the modern world. (Clements and Roemer 278)

Conceivably, Silko sees the use of other cultures in her writing as a form of adaptation, a means of drawing on the world around her in a positive manner. In a brief summary of the history of Laguna Pueblo, Kathleen M. Sands concludes that the inevitable result is change:

> According to Laguna stories, the people, migrating south from the Mesa Verde area, settled near the lake at Laguna in the late 1300s and founded Old Laguna around 1400 where groups from other pueblos (Hopi, Zuni, Jemez) joined them, creating a multi-cultural society. Following a move to the present site of Laguna in the early 1500s, the Spanish entered the area but did not force surrender until 1692. Other groups fleeing drought and Spanish reprisals after the Pueblo uprisings in the late 1600s, joined the pueblo along with a few Navajos who married into the tribe. Thus a tradition of incorporation of ritual and story from other tribes was established from the beginnings of Laguna society and became an ongoing practice. Change, accommodation, and growth are inherent to the tribe [...]. (4)

Clearly, Silko envisions her use of ritual and story from the Navajo as a continuation of Laguna Pueblo tradition. As a storyteller from Laguna Pueblo, she merely incorporates what she sees around her, in this case the Navajo culture; manipulates it to her advantage; and issues a new rendering that contributes to the growth of her own tribe. In demonstrating her power of knowledge and language to utilize cultures in ways that she wants, Silko herself becomes a powerful negotiator. By writing about the change, adaptation, and continuity of the Navajo, Silko in essence claims the same kind of progress and development in light of similar problems for the Laguna Pueblo.

Yet Silko does not condone this practice of "incorporation of ritual and story from other tribes" by just anyone. On the contrary, she abhors appropriation of American Indian materials in the work of European-American writers. In "An Old-Time Indian Attack Conducted in Two Parts," she critiques the imperialist assumption of "Euro-American cultural superiority [that] allows writers to master the essence of Native American worldviews so expeditiously that they can write from an Indian point of view" (Clements and Roemer 281). For Silko, American Indians' including materials from different tribes in their writing is neither problematic nor equivalent to European Americans' including materials from American Indian cultures in their writing. She bases her position on the imperialist assumptions of European Americans, something of which she does not find herself guilty; therefore, she must reason that American Indians have enough in common culturally to remove any possibility of the idea of appropriation, at least in a pejorative sense. In fact, while teaching Navajo students Oliver La Farge's 1927 novel *Laughing Boy,* about a Navajo man, she stresses how the class concluded, "as an expression of anything Navajo, especially with relations to Navajo emotions and behavior, the novel was a failure" ("Old Time Indian Attack" 77). Silko rejects the possibility of a white writer's successfully portraying American Indian characters; yet she personally feels competent to explore the "Navajo emotions and behavior" of the characters in "Lullaby." By refusing "to forget how generous, how expansive, how inclusive the way of the old people [Laguna Pueblo elders] was, of seeing the world and of seeing human beings," she delves into the Navajo world to tell her story (Arnold 11).

Silko's knowledge of Navajo culture has several different sources. As a child, Silko heard family-related stories involving Navajos, which she fashions into new stories for her collection in *Storyteller*. In one, Silko's Grandma A'mooh recounts how when she was a child, she heard the story of the hungry Navajos who stole a herd of Laguna sheep. A'mooh's uncles and grandfather were among those who caught the Navajos and told them the next time they were hungry they should ask for something to eat and the Laguna people would feed them. Silko contends that today Laguna homes always welcome Navajo people during Feast time (210). In addition to the historical account of sheep raiding, this story's theme focuses on the tribal characteristic of sharing, an important concept in a communal culture.

In another story from *Storyteller*, Silko's Great-Grandpa Stagner hired Juana, an adult Navajo woman who as a child was kidnapped by slave hunters. Juana went to live with Silko's Great-Grandmother Helen to help raise her children. As a child, Silko along with her Grandma Lillie would place flowers on Juana's grave (88–89). Although Silko does not explain why Juana might be well suited to help in the raising of children, the Navajo concept of mothering might explain her propensity for this kind of work. This idea will be dealt with in greater detail later in this chapter.

In a third story from the collection, Silko writes about the Navajos who visited every year at Laguna Feast time: "Navajos used to jam the hillsides with their wagons and horses. [...] My father made all of us kids come outside and watch the last wagon come" (202). In one anecdote, Silko relates how her grandfather became good friends with one Navajo man:

> Grandpa Hank had a friend like that, an old man from Alamo. Every year they were so glad to see each other, and the Navajo man would bring Grandpa something in the gunny sack he carried—sometimes little apricots the old man grew or a mutton shoulder. [...] I remember the last time the old Navajo man came looking for my Grandpa. [...] we told him, "Henry passed away last winter." The old Navajo man cried, and then he left. He never came back anymore after that. (187)

Growing up in proximity to the Navajos along with hearing stories about the relationships among them and the Laguna people are just two of the ways in which Silko learned about her neighbors. The stories reveal details of intimate friendships, employer-employee relationships, historical events involving sheep raiding and kidnapping, traditional tribal ceremonies, family customs, and other information about the Laguna and Navajo lifestyles. Evidently, these family stories of personal experiences with the Navajo carry enough importance in Silko's life that she feels compelled to share them in her own storytelling, and she shows a deep abiding respect for the role these Navajo people have played in her family's history. Having this much personal information about the Navajo at her disposal would certainly explain Silko's comfort with writing the short story "Lullaby."

Silko undoubtedly met more Navajos when she attended the University of New Mexico, where she earned a B.A. in English in 1969 and afterward completed three semesters of law school. Later, Silko taught for approximately two years at the Navajo Community College in Tsaile, Arizona. In an interview, Silko responds to a question about the character Betonie in *Ceremony* by speaking about one particular Navajo friend with whom she had long conversations:

> Betonie is partly based on things that I began to perceive from the two years I spent in Navajo country and from one Navajo man who was a friend of mine. What he told me in our long discussions was that he was constantly probing the Navajo beliefs he had grown up with. [. . .] He has this tremendous mind, and he's constantly examining and reexamining basic assumptions and presumptions. Not just in Navajo culture, but . . . he went to St. John's College in Santa Fe, and he studied Greek. He has an incisive mind. From talking with him, I began to appreciate the kind of conservatism I'd been taught to connect with Navajo culture, Navajo thought. (Fitzgerald and Hudak 33)

Silko seems to have spent a substantial amount of time in the company of enough other Navajo people to assume that she acquired a degree of familiarity with Navajo culture. After leaving the Navajo reservation, Silko moved to Ketchikan, Alaska, in 1973, and while living there, she wrote "Lullaby" (30).

Apart from the personal contact that Silko has had with Navajo people, she has incorporated both the Navajo landscape and Navajo characters in her own creative work. One of the most obvious references to the actual geographical location of Navajo reservations near Laguna Pueblo occurs in the reworking of a Laguna traditional tribal abduction story, "Yellow Woman." Silko positions Silva, the narrator's lover, so he can see the Navajo reservation: "'From here I can see the world.' He stepped out on the edge. 'The Navajo reservation begins over there.' He pointed to the east. 'The Pueblo boundaries are over here.' He looked below us to the south" (*Storyteller* 57–58). Silko also suggests that Silva might be Navajo: "Even beside the horses he looked tall, and I asked him again if he wasn't Navajo" (60). Finally, when the narrator returns home, she decides to tell her family that "some Navajo had kidnapped [her]" (62). A. LaVonne Ruoff points out this "allusion to the old Navajo practice of raiding Pueblo settlements for food and women" ("Ritual" 13). The consequences of both the historical events and the physical proximity of the Navajo to the Pueblo people lend themselves to the narrative structure of Silko's "Yellow Woman." The short story "Lullaby," about a Navajo family, is not an anomaly in Silko's writing. She has established a pattern of writing about Navajo characters based on both her personal history and the larger history of the two tribes.

Silko refers to the Navajo in several other places in *Storyteller*. In the poem "Storytelling," Silko inverts the usually gendered paradigm of the abductor-abducted relationship, and three Navajo men become the kidnapped victims of four Laguna women: "'We couldn't escape them,' he told police later./ 'We tried, but there were four of them and/only three of us'" (96). Later in the same poem, the speaker accuses a Navajo of threatening her life:

> It was
> that Navajo
> from Alamo,
> you know,
> the tall
> good-looking
> one.
>
> He told me
> he'd kill me
> if I didn't
> go with him (97–98)

The historical influences of kidnapping as well as the mythical influence of Yellow Woman's leaving the pueblo and engaging in sexual relationships permeate the poem. Not understanding Silko's larger personal and historical contexts for using the Navajo in so much of her work might lead to a misinterpretation of what at times on the surface appears to be a negative although humorous portrayal of them, and this reading, of course, would not be correct. In fact, the women's abducting the men is a perfect example of gender complementarity, in which the women are as strong, powerful, and capable of playing the role of kidnappers, as well as acting as the sexual aggressors. As for the woman who claims that the Navajo man threatened her, she uses language to defend herself, to blame him, when she most likely went willingly.

Also, two of the Lee H. Marmon photographs in *Storyteller* deal with Navajo subjects. For one landscape photograph, Silko provides a note that explains a Navajo legend: "The Navajos say the black peaks in this valley are drops of blood that fell from a dying monster which the Twin Brothers fought and fatally wounded" (n. 14, 271). The second photograph, from the early 1950s, pictures Navajo wagons at the Laguna Fiesta (n. 14, 271). Her knowledge of the Navajo has been gained from the oral stories she heard growing up and from the photographs that her father took. She saw for herself many of the objects and events in the photographs and had the pictures to remind her of those images. In story and picture, Silko weaves the Navajo people, culture, and history throughout her work as if they form a natural part of her own intellectual landscape.

Another aspect of Silko's affinity for integrating the Navajo in her work arises from the similarities between the Navajo and Laguna Pueblo in terms of matriarchies or matrilineal societies. In an interview, Silko explains the role of Laguna Pueblo women:

> In a matrilineal society, in a matriarchy, and especially in this particular matriarchy, the women, as I've already said, control the houses, the lineage of the children, and a lot of the decisions about marriages and so forth. In a sense, the women have called the shots pretty much in the world of relationships and the everyday world. While the Pueblo women were kind of running the show, buying and selling sheep, and *of course the Navajos are the same way too,* the women making many of the business decisions, the Pueblo men would be taking care of ceremonial matters or maybe out hunting. (emphasis added, Barnes 96–97)

Silko describes the Laguna Pueblo as a matrilineal, matriarchal, and matrilocal society, and she asserts that the "Navajo are the same way." In reality, the Navajo "tribe is matrilineal and matrilocal (preferred) with apparent high status for women" (Shepardson 159). On the basis of these similarities, that Silko would feel open to using Navajo characters in "Lullaby," as well as in her other works, is understandable. Again, she focuses on commonalities rather than any differences among the tribes, and specifically she considers issues of women's power and gender complementarity in matrifocal societies.

The abundance of evidence for Silko's use of Navajo material in her writing is necessary to defend against any critique of her choice to write about another culture than her own Laguna Pueblo tribe. Noted scholar Elizabeth Cook-Lynn (Crow Creek Sioux) speaks to the current problem of appropriation as she perceives it in American Indian literary studies:

> A great deal of the work done in the mixed-blood literary movement is personal, invented, appropriated, and irrelevant to First Nation status in the United States. If that work becomes too far removed from what is really going on in Indian enclaves, there will be no way to engage in responsible intellectual strategies in an era when structures of external cultural power are more oppressive than ever. (130)

The appropriation of cultures other than the author's leads to the fear of misrepresentation of that culture. American Indians resent cultural outsiders' defining who they are. The evidence for Silko's knowledge of the Navajo and her sincerity in portraying them within their own cultural and historical contexts cannot be denied. Cook-Lynn's concern, however, also speaks to whether the writing will address the issues most important to the future survival of American Indians:

> Does this art give thoughtful consideration to the defense of our lands, resources, languages, children? Is anyone doing the intellectual work in and about Indian communities that will help us understand our future? While it is true that any indigenous story tells of death and blood, it also tells of indigenous rebirth and hope, not as Americans nor as some new ersatz race but as the indigenes of this continent. (134)

In telling Ayah's story in "Lullaby," Silko addresses those very issues of resources, language, and children. In writing images that reflect the past and present of the Navajo, she tells about death, but by taking into account Navajo mythology, she also offers continuity and survival for them.

Silko portrays the Navajo woman Ayah as a character who shares common experiences with other American Indian women. She has lived through a variety of historical and cultural changes and still retains an intact connection to her Navajo identity. Some historical information and general principles about Navajo culture offer a better understanding of Ayah and what a Navajo woman's life entails. One major historical event is the Navajo War of 1863–64. Under the military leadership of Gen. James H. Carleton and the command of Col. Kit Carson, federal and volunteer troops captured and killed Navajos, burned their hogans, destroyed their crops, and seized their herds (Bailey and Bailey 9). In August 1863, surviving groups of Navajo prisoners began the Long Walk to Bosque Redondo, where almost eighty-five hundred Navajos were eventually imprisoned (10). The Treaty of 1868 allowed the Navajo to return to their sacred homeland after they had suffered for four years. Clyde Kluckhohn and Dorothea Leighton describe the lasting negative impact the effects of the war and subsequent imprisonment have had on the Navajo: "Fort Sumner [Bosque Redondo] was a major calamity to The People; its full effects upon their imagination can hardly be conveyed to white readers. ... One can no more understand Navaho attitudes ... without knowing of Fort Sumner than he can comprehend Southern attitudes without knowing of the Civil War" (qtd. in Bailey and Bailey 10–11). The plot structure of Ayah's remembering injustices suffered in her past and *walking* to find her husband recalls the Long Walk that her ancestors endured. That the Navajo returned, survived, and flourished also indicates a potentially positive reading of the end of "Lullaby." On the basis of her tribal history, Ayah could have negative feelings about the whites even before she experiences personal injuries by them.

A second important historical event that would color Ayah's perceptions of whites would be the U.S. government's 1930s stock reduction programs. The government and the Navajo saw the problems of erosion and the resulting damage to the grazing lands from completely different perspectives: "Indian Service officials saw the problem as overgrazing [. . .] and stock reduction as the only solution" (Bailey and Bailey 185). Ruth Roessel (Navajo) and Broderick H. Johnson, on the other hand, note that the Navajos "perceived a different set of factors which produced the erosion—namely, the reduction of stock 'caused the rain clouds to diminish,' which kept the grass from growing, and this in turn resulted in the erosion" (qtd. in Bailey and Bailey 185–86). Destroying thousands of animals to which the Navajos had complex and profound cultural and economic attachments did not make any sense to them. This key event of enforced herd reductions could color the way that Ayah perceives Anglo-Americans.

Language creates origins, and Silko knows that Ayah's worldview begins with a Navajo origin myth. As do the Laguna Pueblo, the Navajo have an emergence myth. They believe that they have emerged through several worlds to the present one. Peter Iverson offers a brief summary of the emergence myth, which includes stories of the Four Worlds, First Man and First Woman, and the animals. He goes on to describe how the world as the Navajos know it continued to be shaped:

> The stories tell of the first hogan being constructed, the first sweat bath being taken, the four seasons being established, day and night being created, the stars being placed in the sky, and the sun and the moon coming into existence. The Glittering World encompasses both beauty and difficulty. In one episode after another, listeners hear the consequences of improper behavior, and learn about the difficulties that may ensue through carelessness or thoughtlessness. (9–11)

The Navajo find not only their relationship to this world and the land in their origin myth but also their identity. The central idea in Navajo religious thinking, *hozho,* "translates as balance or harmony, and they strive to maintain this harmony" (Tobert and Pitt 34):

> [I]t is not something that occurs only in ritual song and prayer; it is referred to frequently in everyday speech. A Navajo uses this concept to express his happiness, his health, the beauty of his land, and the harmony of his relations with others. It is used in reminding people to be careful and deliberate, and when he says good-bye to someone leaving, he will say [. . .] ("may you walk or go about according to *hozho*"). (Witherspoon, *Language* 18)

Traditional Navajo elders Chauncy Neboyia and Dorothy Neboyia summarize the Navajo philosophy in the following way: "The earth is our mother; she sustains us. Those who give birth nurse their young. It is the same with the earth. Living and working well will bring a good life and a good reputation" (*Seasons*). Navajo worldview encompasses life in a holistic way; the people, environment, work, and spirituality are interconnected at all times, and this worldview is omnipresent in "Lullaby." Therefore, an understanding of Navajo cultural and historical contexts opens up the reading of "Lullaby" in a necessary way that no other approach offers.

The Navajo practice three general kinds of ritual to maintain, ensure, or restore *hozho:* Blessingway rites, Holyway rites, and Evilway rites (Witherspoon, *Language* 34–35). The opening paragraph of "Lullaby" contains a wealth of information that hints at Navajo culture, including a reference to ceremony:

> The sun had gone down but the snow in the wind gave off its own light. It came in thick tufts like new wool—washed before the weaver spins it. Ayah reached out for it like her own babies had, and she smiled when she remembered how she had laughed at them. She was an old woman now, and her life had become memories. She sat down with her back against the wide cottonwood tree, feeling the rough bark on her back bones; she faced east and listened to the wind and snow sing a high-pitched Yeibechei song. (*Storyteller* 43)

Teams of masked dancers perform the Yeibechei songs during the last two evenings of the Nightway ceremony, a healing ritual. They are "widely known as the most dramatic of Navajo songs" and "have been described as being 'piercingly powerful,' having 'hypnotic power,' and 'displaying almost acrobatic feats of bounding back and forth between octaves.' [...] All these differences are intentional for it is the voices of the gods that are heard [...] and they should not sound like ordinary singing" (McAllester and Mitchell 609). Clearly, Silko references the Yeibechei song to allude to the healing and ritual nature of the story that follows, an attempt to restore *hozho*— "everything that is good, harmonious, orderly, happy, and beautiful"—the opposite of *hocho:* "the evil, the disorderly, and the ugly" (Witherspoon, *Language* 34). In light of the negative events in Ayah's life, she would need to concentrate on a healing ceremony to restore *hozho*.

In addition to the introduction of the protagonist, the ceremonial nature of the story, and the seasonal aspect in the opening paragraph, there are other conventional elements of the short story: the setting, style, and indication of plot. Unsurprisingly, a detailed description of the natural environment coincides with the worldview of *hozho*, one of harmony and balance with surroundings: "snow," "wind," "new wool," "cottonwood tree," "bark," "east," "arroyo," "Cebolleta Creek," "grass," "trickle of water," "skinny cows," "winding paths," and "manure." Elaine Jahner calls this Silko's "signature opening move, the use of nature descriptions to refer to psychological and cosmic temporality" (503). Silko presents a seasonal panorama that illustrates the close connection between the landscape and Ayah, the importance of water in an arid Southwest geographical location, and a glimpse of the gendered economic enterprises of the Navajo. Even the direction "east," that of the rising sun, balances the implied direction of west in the opening line, "The sun had gone down." This reference to day and night represents the American Indian view of space as spherical and time as cyclical, concepts in opposition to the models of linear space and sequential time of many non-Indians. The "east" also resonates with the Navajo cultural practice of constructing the door to face the east in the hogan, the Navajo house, which has now come to mean the traditional eight-sided log house with a domed, earth-covered roof. A close reading of the introductory paragraph reveals a setting that supports the Navajo worldview.

The gendered economic enterprises alluded to in the first paragraph are weaving for women and herding for men. The traditional roles of the Navajo women center around the maintenance of the home, the care of the children, and the spinning, carding, dyeing, and weaving of the wool. Later, when Ayah wants to block out memories of Jimmie's death, she comforts herself with thoughts of her mother and grandmother's working with the wool:

> She did not want to think about Jimmie. So she thought about the weaving and the way her mother had done it. On the tall wooden loom set into the sand under a tamarack tree for shade. She could see it clearly. She had been only a little girl when her grandma gave her the wooden combs to pull the twigs and burrs from the raw, freshly washed wool. And while she combed the wool, her grandma sat beside her, spinning a silvery strand of yarn around the smooth cedar spindle. (*Storyteller* 43)

Silko provides insights into how the process of weaving has been a major force in shaping Ayah's life. As a traditional activity, it binds her to her mother and grandmother, emotionally and culturally. The memories sustain her and provide solace during times of great emotional pain and grief. Therefore, the weaving becomes therapeutic beyond the actual act.

Not only do the Navajo blankets serve a utilitarian function for the family, but they also most likely would serve an economic purpose:

> With the unemployment percentage for Navajo adults exceeding 60 percent (in 1973) and with many of the limited jobs being seasonal and uncertain, such as fighting forest fires, working on the railroads, and farm labor, the role of women in weaving to provide a reliable source of food and clothing is of extreme importance to the existence of Navajo family life. The Navajo have always been matrilineal with women holding a position of prestige in Navajo culture, and weaving helps assure the continuation of this position for women. (Roessel 595)

Thus, in addition to memories that keep her connected to her people, weaving in Ayah's life represents an economic means of survival for the women and their families in her tribe. Tohe points out, "Diné women have always worked to help support the family, even before the reservation system was established. Later, when the white man established trading posts on the reservation, the women wove and sold blankets in exchange for food and supplies" (104). Unlike the women, however, Navajo men did not always fare so well.

Tohe adds, "While the male roles diminished as protectors and providers for the family, the women's roles persisted and, in many instances, the women adapted more easily" (104). In "Lullaby," through all the setbacks that Chato and Ayah experience, Ayah fares better than Chato. For Navajo men, herding sheep and cattle, gathering and cutting firewood, and helping the elders complement the roles of women. Ayah knows that Chato misses the wage labor he used to do: "She knew he did not like walking behind old ewes when for so many years he rode big quarter horses and worked with cattle" (*Storyteller* 50). The plot revolves around Ayah's memories of her past, specific things that have changed, seen in the metaphorical snowfall: "[S]he could watch the wide fluffy snow fill in her tracks, steadily, until the direction she had come from was gone" (43). Though the "direction" seems to have vanished, as Charlene Taylor Evans notes, "The reader can experience the fluidity of time; the past is omnipresent" (176).

Silko, however, does not necessarily lament the changes that have occurred, because in juxtaposing images of the past and present, she again demonstrates adaptation and continuity, lessening the nostalgic effects. Indeed, she intends a political statement about some of these changes, but one needs to keep the idea of *hozho,* or balance, in mind in the following examples of the past and present: her mother's woven blankets and Jimmie's army blanket, high buckskin leggings wrapped over elkhide moccasins and black overshoes with metal buckles, the traditional hogan and the boxcar shack, a traditional medicine man and the children's clinic at Cañoncito, and traditional Navajo names and English names. Yes, contemporary versions have replaced traditional items and customs, but one aspect of the story preserves and privileges the traditional way of life. Ironically, the English language of "Lullaby" will keep the traditional Navajo way of life alive for future generations to read about, so the past lives on despite change. This sentiment can be found in Silko's dedication in *Storyteller:* "This book is dedicated to the storytellers as far back as memory goes and to the telling which continues and through which they all live and we with them" (title page).

Other elements in the opening paragraph of "Lullaby" allude to Changing Woman. The story's season is winter, and Ayah is "an old woman" (43). An important principal female deity, Changing Woman was raised by First Man and First Woman. She symbolizes nature and the mystery of birth; cyclic, she never dies but grows old in the winter and is forever young again in the spring. Anthropologist Mary Shepardson discusses the implications of Changing Woman for Navajo women:

> Puberty rites are celebrated for girls, not for boys. A great goddess in Navajo mythology is Changing Woman, who created the Navajo and the four original clans. She was the first to be honored with Kinaaldá, the girl's puberty rite. She was the mother of the hero twins, who rid the world of monsters. She symbolizes, through changes from youth to age and return to youth, the four seasons of the year. She is the Earth Mother. All these factors mean high status for Navajo women. (160)

Silko mentions two other seasons in the opening paragraph, "springtime" and "summer." Setting the story during winter, noting the cyclic nature of the seasons that will follow, and placing Ayah in old age generate a wealth of contextual background for anyone who understands the influential role of Changing Woman in Navajo culture. Her presence is felt during the later telling of the birth of Ayah's son, Jimmie, and in the implied death of Chato at the end of the story. Knowledge, however, that Changing Woman connotes a cyclic return—a rebirth—softens the focus on the otherwise tragic ending, and a positive note of continuity and survival appears.

Additionally, knowledge of the high status that Changing Woman provides Navajo women precludes Ayah's being seen as a powerless figure, buffeted about by events perpetrated by the dominant culture. Laura Tohe writes with great respect about Changing Woman and confirms the findings of anthropologist Shepardson:

> Changing Woman, sometimes known as White Shell Woman, is the principal mythological deity in the Diné culture. She gave to the Diné the first clans and the guidelines of how the Diné should live their lives. She birthed the Twin Heroes who destroyed the monsters that were ravaging the people. She underwent the first Kinaaldá ceremony, the puberty ceremony for young women. Through her, the matriarchal system of the Diné was established. (Tohe 104)

Although in the story Ayah does not interact with members of her community other than her kinship-based residence group, within that environment she would have a degree of standing and integrity that outsiders might not recognize, and Changing Woman is, in part, to be credited with that status.

The positive valence of Ayah's role as a mother appears in the opening paragraph as she recalls laughing at her babies' reaching for snowflakes, warm memories in contrast to the cold snow that surrounds her, another example of balance. Ayah is in a culture that values women for their ability to bear children, a natural physiological function and part of the life cycle. Tohe claims that the Navajo woman "is groomed for motherhood, which carries a different connotation in Diné culture than in Western culture" (105). Ayah's affectionate memories of her children indicate that she obviously takes great satisfaction in her role as a mother. Although the premature loss of children most certainly always causes sadness, the knowledge that motherhood carries such power in Navajo culture seems to add even more poignancy in view of Ayah's loss.

Silko offers an additional indication of the importance of the role of motherhood in Navajo culture by describing Ayah's memories of the birth of her son, Jimmie:

> She felt peaceful remembering. She didn't feel cold anymore. Jimmie's blanket seemed warmer than it had ever been. And she could remember the morning he was born. She could remember whispering to her mother, who was sleeping on the other side of the hogan, to tell her it was time now. She did not want to wake the others. The second time she called to her, her mother stood up and pulled on her shoes; she knew. They walked to the old stone hogan together, Ayah walking a step behind her mother. She waited alone, learning the rhythms of the pains while her mother went to call the old woman to help them. The morning was already warm even before dawn, and Ayah smelled the bee flowers blooming and the young willow growing at the springs. She could remember that so clearly, but his birth merged into the births of the other children and to her it became all the same birth. They named him for the summer morning and in English they called him Jimmie. (*Storyteller* 44)

This passage presents the customs associated with giving birth: the use of a separate hogan for labor and delivery, the assistance of a midwife, and the presence of the mother. Also, elements of the natural landscape intimately entwine with Ayah's physical sensations of painful contractions: the time of day, the warm temperature of the summer morning, the fragrant smell of the flowers, and the willow situated near the water. The landscape creates balance and harmony with the work and pain associated with giving birth, an example of the Navajo worldview, *hozho*. These details of the surrounding environment ingrain themselves in Ayah's memories of her physical sensations, and in keeping with circular time, Jimmie's birth becomes much like the births of all her children, equally important and memorable. Finally, the double naming, both in Navajo and in English, comments on the Navajo people's mediation between both cultures through language, a major theme in "Lullaby."

To balance the memory of Jimmie's birth, Ayah also remembers receiving the news of his death. Her recollections suggest the period of the story, her feelings regarding Jimmie's service to the U.S. armed forces, and Navajo customs surrounding death:

> It wasn't like Jimmie died. He just never came back, and one day a dark blue sedan with white writing on its doors pulled up in front of the box-car shack where the rancher let the Indians live. A man in a khaki uniform trimmed in gold gave them a yellow piece of paper and told them that Jimmie was dead. He said the Army would try to get the body back and then it would be shipped to them; but it wasn't likely because the helicopter had burned after it crashed. (44)

With the serviceman's news of Jimmie's death, the narrative reveals that Jimmie has served in the army and dies in a helicopter crash. In Lawana Trout's introductory contextual notes to "Lullaby," she explains briefly the role of the Navajos in World War II:

> Navajos served in the U.S. armed forces in disproportionately large numbers during World War II The Marine Corps recruited a special "Code Talker" unit deployed in the Pacific theater. Navajo "code talkers" created codes in their own language so that no Japanese hearing their messages radioed in the open could understand them. Consequently, Silko's Navajo family is typical in losing a son overseas. (389–90)

Concluding that Jimmie serves during World War II (1941–45) seems logical in view of the well-known role of the Navajo "code talkers." Silko, however, does not specify in which war Jimmie serves, and his dying in a helicopter crash complicates the period of the story. World War II saw limited use of helicopters, and the Korean War (1950–53) used them for medevac missions, cargo delivery, and vertical deployment. Not until the Vietnam War did the U.S. forces use helicopters as offensive weapons ("Evolution"). Silko does not offer any details about Jimmie's mission, but the Vietnam War has the distinction of being known as the "Helicopter War" ("Vietnam"). Thus, Jimmie's death by helicopter crash strongly suggests that he dies sometime during the Vietnam era, from the 1960s to the early 1970s. More important, however, is the ambiguity that Silko creates by not specifying the period. The resulting anachronistic quality more appropriately fits the American Indian sense of time and removes the story from any one specific time. Silko would want all Navajo war veterans honored and memorialized.

In fact, part of Ayah's anger upon hearing the news of her son's death might be attributed to her scorn for the white society's treatment of Navajo veterans when they returned home from World War II. While enlisted, many American Indians for the first time experienced respect from whites. Then, when they were discharged, they received the same kind of shabby treatment they had before entering the service:

> American society had never before conferred such respect upon Indian people, and native servicemen and women came to like the resulting feelings of self-worth and national worth. When the war ended, however, and the uniforms came off, Indians found that America's respect had vanished as well. Indian people, even the most "assimilated," would seemingly always be second-class citizens, kept in their places by both the subtle snub and the sign reading "No Dogs or Indians Allowed." After the liberating experience of wartime, America's return to prewar discrimination proved doubly humiliating for many Indians and raised the level of frustration in Indian country to new heights. (Deloria, "The Twentieth" 427)

Not only did returning war veterans face poor treatment from American citizens but they also had to worry about finding employment. For the

Navajos, World War II followed on the heels of the stock reduction programs, from which some herds never recovered: "Returning Navajos discovered that their herds and farms could not support their families even at bare subsistence, and that opportunities for wage labor were minimal" (Bailey and Bailey 220). Silko heard veterans talk about their war experiences and sympathized with the employment problems they faced: "When I was really small, I listened to World War II and Korean War veterans. They had drinking problems and lacked regular jobs, but they had good souls and spirits" (Boos 243). Thus, to understand Ayah's anger at hearing the news of Jimmie's death, the history of veterans' returning home to the Navajo reservation from previous wars must be considered.[2]

Knowing how the Navajo think of the dead clarifies why Chato tells the army official to keep Jimmie's body and not return it (*Storyteller* 45). Traditionally, the Navajo guard against any unnecessary or unwise contact with the dead:

> The anxieties and extraordinary precautions concerning death, burial, and the visits of ghosts were greatly relaxed when it was an infant or a very old person who died. An infant could not have developed animosities, it was thought, and an aged person who had lived out his life fully was considered beyond rancor. It was the person who dies with his promise and hopes unfulfilled who was to be feared. (Opler 378)

An example of lack of anxiety about the death and burial of infants occurs when Ayah gives an account of her own babies who died and how she buried them:

> There had been babies that died soon after they were born, and one that died before he could walk. She had carried them herself, up to the boulders and great pieces of the cliff that long ago crashed down from Long Mesa; she laid them in crevices of sandstone and buried them in fine brown sand with round quartz pebbles that washed down the hills in the rain. She had endured it because they had been with her. (*Storyteller* 47)

On one level Ayah has no problem dealing with the death and burial of her young babies, and once again, Silko grounds even death and burial in a descriptive context of the natural environment. Jimmie died, however, before he had had an opportunity to live a full life. His death is one that must be feared and handled with precautions "in order to prevent unnatural illness and premature death" (Witherspoon, "Language and Reality" 571). Hence, Chato and Ayah do not care whether the army recovers his body. They do not want to deal with it.

The implied death of Chato at the end of "Lullaby" presents a more complex situation. Has Chato lived long enough to release any bitterness, so death would not create any anxiety for anyone left behind? In light of his unemployment, the resulting alcoholism, and the loss of children, he probably has not. Yet, Silko's reference to the Yeibechei song at the beginning of the story—the implied healing nature of this telling—and the lullaby at the end of the story should help to counterbalance any hostility that Chato still feels. Moreover, "[f]or the Navajo death from old age is considered to be both natural and highly desirable," and "[t]he goal of Navajo life in this world is to live to maturity in the condition described as *hózhó*, to die of old age, the end result of which incorporates one in the universal beauty, harmony, and happiness [...]" (Witherspoon, *Language* 19, 25). Therefore, rather than a tragic ending to the story that plays into the myth of the vanishing American Indian, the possibility of Chato's death signifies sadness not because death in itself is a negative event but because his death might be a premature death due to alcoholism. Silko seems to attribute Chato's drinking, which did not begin until after loss of his job, to "the dislocations of acculturation and social change" (Kunitz and Levy 5).[3] The rate of alcohol-related deaths is ten times greater for American Indians than for the non-Indian population (Forbes 40). Chato's alcoholism, its causes and effects in his life, is the tragedy, one that does not incorporate his death "in the universal beauty, harmony, and happiness."

That Ayah does not become alcoholic might be attributed to Silko's keeping her more connected to the traditional aspects of Navajo women. Although Ayah accompanies Chato, she does not leave the reservation to find wage labor as he does. Unlike Chato, Ayah manages to maintain a degree of standing afforded Navajo women. Shepardson lists the following considerations as indicators of the gender status of Navajo women: clan affiliation, kinship-based residence group, social rights to divorce and custody of children, puberty rites, and inheritance rights. The Navajo women are "born into" their mother's clan and "born for" their father's clan. This kinship structure provides the "network of relations of responsibility and expectation of helpfulness" (Shepardson 160). In "Lullaby," Silko illustrates that the mother's clan is of chief importance by focusing on the female protagonist and her family line: her children, her mother, and her grandmother. As Ayah thinks of Jimmie's death, she reveals the importance of his role in the family:

> And she mourned him as the years passed, when a horse fell with Chato and broke his leg, and the white rancher told them he wouldn't pay Chato until he could work again. She mourned Jimmie because he would have worked for his father then; he would have saddled the big bay horse and ridden the fence lines each day, with wire cutters and heavy gloves, fixing the breaks in the barbed wire and putting the stray cattle back inside again. (*Storyteller* 45)

That Jimmie would have worked for his injured father indicates more than just a good-natured son willing to help his family. In truth, the child's role in the family involves a kind of solidarity: *k'é* is characterized by love and unsystematic sharing, whereas nonkinship solidarity is characterized by reciprocity or systematic exchange (Witherspoon, *Language* 84–85). The latter describes the husband-wife bond; the former describes the mother-child bond. Gary Witherspoon notes: "The mother-child bond involves what might be called cognatic or kinship solidarity. The giving of life and the sharing of sustenance is considered to be the most powerful, the most intense, and the most enduring of these two bonds, and is considered to be the ideal pattern or code for all social interaction" (85). Understanding this kind of family dynamic in which the mother-child bond takes precedence over all other relationships sheds light on Ayah's expectation of helpfulness from Jimmie. The intense degree of regard in the mother-child relationship also contributes to an understanding of her deep and lengthy mourning of his death.

Although Silko privileges Ayah's perspective in "Lullaby," this point of view should not be interpreted as diminishing the husband's role, for two reasons. First, telling Ayah's story from the third-person limited point of view draws attention to the fact that she does not speak English; she cannot tell her story from the first-person point of view unless the reader speaks Navajo. Silko resists the oppressor's language, English, by not writing the story in the first person; in one sense, she makes the telling from the third person perspective a political act to privilege Ayah's native tongue. Second, Silko does not diminish the husband's role because the primary bond of nonkinship solidarity in Navajo culture is found in the husband-wife relationship. Hence, this relationship does not carry the same import as the mother-child relationship. Witherspoon explains Navajo custom provides for easy divorce if the husband or wife feels the union does not satisfy the needs of either party: "[W]hen a husband is irresponsible or immoral, a wife usually sends him away. If a wife is barren, a husband usually goes elsewhere. In other words, if either sees the relationship as without merit to himself or herself, it will likely be dissolved. The relationship is supposed to be advantageous to both parties through mutual obligations" ("Navajo Social" 525). Given that "a woman could divorce her spouse simply by leaving his personal possessions outside the door," Ayah could have dissolved her relationship with Chato at any time (Tohe 108). Obviously, Ayah has fulfilled her duties in that she has given birth to numerous children, even though those children have either died or been removed from her home. Chato, on the other hand, has behaved irresponsibly in Ayah's eyes. She blames him for the papers she signs in English, enabling the white doctors and Bureau of Indian Affairs (BIA) policeman to take away her young children, Danny and Ella. Thus, again the story critiques the English language and how poorly it has served American Indian peoples.

At first, Ayah takes pride in having learned how to write her name, an act that the dominant culture values: "Chato had taught her to sign her name. It was something she was proud of" (*Storyteller* 45). Later, Ayah resents Chato for teaching her anything of the English language, causing the loss of her children: "She hated Chato, not because he let the policeman and doctors put the screaming children in the government car, but because he had taught her to sign her name. Because it was like the old ones always told her about learning their language or any of their ways: it endangered you" (47). By criticizing literacy, Silko privileges the oral tradition. She esteems the elders' advice, favors the Navajo language, and calls attention to a history of treaties among the U.S. government and American Indian tribes, legal agreements in which tribal members often unknowingly signed away land and other rights.

Similarly to tactics often used by the U.S. government officials, the authorities must know that Ayah does not understand the repercussions of signing the papers:

> She was at the shack alone that day they came. It was back in the days before they hired Navajo women to go with them as interpreters. She recognized one of the doctors. She had seen him at the children's clinic at Cañoncito about a month ago. They were wearing khaki uniforms and they waved papers at her and a black ball-point pen, trying to make her understand their English words. She was frightened by the way they looked at the children, like the lizard watches the fly. (45)

Alone and afraid, Ayah has no defenses against the intruders. The officials do not consider Ayah's lack of knowledge of the English language; nor do they offer to find someone who can translate for them. This episode marks another reason that Ayah regrets Jimmie's death: "If Jimmie had been there he could have read those papers and explained to her what they said. Ayah would have known then, never to sign them" (46). Silko associates not speaking English with Ayah's traditional ways, which have a positive valence; she then associates speaking English as a second language with Chato and Jimmie, an unemployed alcoholic and the other a dead serviceman, respectively, which have negative valences. Although Jimmie's knowledge of English might have helped Ayah, Silko seems to reconcile the ambivalent attitude toward the adoption of English by using it to tell stories that resist the United States' history of oppression and marginalization of Native peoples.

The doctors and BIA policeman claim that they have to remove Ayah's children from her home because of the threat of tuberculosis: "[I]t was the old woman who died in the winter, spitting blood; it was her old grandma who had given the children this disease" (46). American Indians experience a rate of tuberculosis that is 7.4 times greater than that in the non-Indian population (Forbes 40). In addition to the officials' refusing to honor Ayah's request for a tribal medicine man to treat her children, they offer no consideration of her feelings in the way they remove her young ones. In fact, the Indian Child Welfare Act of 1978 was a response to authorities' removing American Indian children from their tribal homes without any regard for the breakup of families and the damaging results to the children: "The law requires state courts, adoption agencies and anyone else placing Indian children to first notify the child's tribe or tribes. In most cases it gives tribal courts jurisdiction over the child's placement and requires those courts to give priority to members of the family, members of the tribe and other Indians who want to adopt the child" (Smith 403). Granted, nobody adopts Ayah's children, and supposedly she has signed papers giving permission for them to go to Colorado. Nevertheless, the children suffer a great loss—their language—as Ayah can see when they return to visit. During the first visit, "Danny had been shy and hid behind the thin white woman who brought them. And the baby had not known her until Ayah took her into her arms [. . .]" (*Storyteller* 49). By the end of that first visit, the children were "jabbering excitedly" in Navajo (49). They have not completely lost their language yet, but Ayah realizes as she watches them leave that they soon will lose their culture: "Ayah watched the government car disappear down the road and she knew they were already being weaned from these lava hills and from this sky" (49). Ayah clearly understands the image of the land's nourishing the people with their identity and the children's losing their cultural identity through the loss of their language and displacement from their home. By the last visit, Ayah knows that she has lost them for good:

> Ella stared at her [. . .]. Ayah did not try to pick her up; she smiled at her instead and spoke cheerfully to Danny. When he tried to answer her, he could not seem to remember and he spoke English words with the Navajo. But he gave her a scrap of paper that he had found somewhere and carried in his pocket; it was folded in half, and he shyly looked up at her and said it was a bird. She asked Chato if they were home for good this time. He spoke to the white woman and she shook her head. "How much longer?" he asked, and she said she didn't know; but Chato saw how she stared at the boxcar shack. Ayah turned away then. She did not say good-bye. (49)

Silko alludes to more than just removing American Indian children from their tribal homes because of illness. She exposes how well-meaning federal authorities can destroy culture and obliterate family structures, all in the name of acculturation and assimilation.

Silko calls attention to another practice that involves removing American Indian children from their tribal homelands—off-reservation boarding schools. The historical reason for parents' resistance to sending children to distant schools arises from the Treaty of 1868: "The compulsory school attendance provision of the peace treaty of 1868 further alienated Navajo parents who tried to protect their children from meddlesome Indian agents bent on sending children off the reservation to far away schools" (Emerson 659). Edith Blicksilver does not even credit the removal of Ayah's children to medical reasons but attributes their removal to the off-reservation boarding school. She writes: "Ayah recalls [...] the snatching of her remaining two small children by Anglo educators. After their time in the white man's school they return only briefly and feel uncomfortable in what now seems to them her alien and culturally backward world" (150). Perhaps because the children speak English when they return for a visit home, Blicksilver attributes their removal to the influence of the off-reservation boarding school rather than to the doctors. Regardless, the language issue speaks to the effects of the U.S. government's assimilationist education policies.

To attain the government's goals, that the children learn English and assimilate into the dominant culture, they must attend school. About the history of off-reservation boarding schools, Silko writes:

> When the United States government began to forcibly remove Pueblo children to distant boarding schools in the 1890s, the Pueblo people faced a great crisis. Like the slaughter of the buffalo, the removal of Native American children to boarding schools was a calculated act of cultural genocide. How would the children hear and see, how would the children learn and remember what Pueblo people, what Native Americans for thousands of years had known and remembered together? (Foreword 7)

Silko rightly questions the impact of the off-reservation boarding school experience on the future generations of American Indians. "Lullaby" clearly shows what happens to the children who lose their language, identity, and connection to the land. They become detribalized, strangers to their heritage.

After Danny and Ella are gone, Ayah can leave Chato if she wants; yet she stays with him. Having lost her children, Ayah in one sense replaces them with Chato; he becomes like a child for whom she must care. Granted, her change of heart toward him does not occur immediately, but she does assume the role of caretaker for her sick husband:

> She slept alone on the hill until the middle of November when the first snows came. Then she made a bed for herself where the children had slept. She did not lie down beside Chato again until many years later, when he was sick and shivering and only her body could keep him warm. The illness came after the white rancher told Chato he was too old to work for him anymore, and Chato and his old woman should be out of the shack by the next afternoon because the rancher had hired new people to work there. That had satisfied her. To see how the white man repaid Chato's years of loyalty and work. All of Chato's fine-sounding English talk didn't change things. (*Storyteller* 47)

Ayah's anger prevents her from sleeping with her husband, but perhaps she has another reason for rejecting him. Maybe she cannot bear the possibility of becoming pregnant again only to lose another child. Although she feels vindicated in her contempt for the English language when it does not assure Chato that he will remain employed, she does not turn her back on him when he becomes ill. She nurses him in much the same way that she would a sick child. Once Ayah's children no longer constitute part of her everyday life, she merely transfers her mothering to Chato, not only tending him during his illness but also watching over him as he repeats a cycle of spending government welfare checks on alcohol and passing out at Azzie's Bar (*Storyteller* 48). Ayah continues to care for Chato when nobody else will, looking for him when he becomes intoxicated: "She walked north down the road, searching for the old man. She did this because she had the blanket, and there would be no other place for him except with her and the blanket in the old adobe barn near the arroyo" (49). Regardless of how Ayah has felt toward Chato or treated him in the past, she will not allow him to pass out and suffer exposure to the cold; she will protect him. Ayah displays *k'e*, which "includes love, compassion, kindness, cooperativeness, friendliness, and peacefulness"; it is "[t]he ideal mode of all social relations" (Witherspoon, *Language* 194).

Ayah's caring for Chato should not be confused with loving him as a husband. The narrator says that Ayah thinks of Chato as a stranger: "[F]or forty years she had smiled at him and cooked his food, but he remained a stranger" (*Storyteller* 48). For that reason, Ayah's wifely duties might be compared to the treatment that she might give a dependent child. Witherspoon notes how this kind of relationship can exist between individuals other than mother and child:

> The solidarity of mother and child symbolized in patterns of giving life and sharing items which sustain life, is projected in Navajo culture as the ideal relationship between and among all people. All one's kinsmen are simply differentiated kinds of mothers; and, since everyone is treated and addressed as a kinsman, all people are bound together by the bond of *k'e*. [...] the *k'e* that exists between mother and child provides the foundational concepts and forms for all relationships in Navajo social life. (*Navajo Kinship* 125–26)

Consequently, Ayah chooses to remain with Chato and to worry about him despite her anger and resentment. In her Navajo worldview, Ayah would consider sustaining of Chato's life more important than her own feelings of bitterness and disappointment.

Returning to Shepardson's list of indicators of the gender status of Navajo women, the social rights to custody of children, inheritance rights, and kinship-based residence group also must be considered. Already mentioned, the matrilineal nature of the social structure of the Navajo accounts for the women's social rights to custody of the children and inheritance rights. The last indicator of kinship-based residence group speaks to Ayah's right to use land for settling, cultivating, and grazing livestock: "Preferably, the groom on marriage comes to live in the bride's residence group. Women share in the work of grazing, agriculture, and crafts, all of which makes [*sic*] a substantial contribution to the subsistence economy and is [*sic*] valued. They own their own stock and control the disposal of their own handicraft products" (Shepardson 160). Silko acknowledges Ayah's kinship-based residence group when she describes Ayah's desire to return home: "If the money and the wine were gone, she would be relieved because then they could go home again; back to the old hogan with a dirt roof and rock walls where she herself had been born. And the next day the old man could go back to the few sheep they still had, to follow along behind them, guiding them, into dry sandy arroyos where sparse grass grew" (*Storyteller* 49). Ayah still lives in the hogan where she was born, an indication that she has inherited the home. She also owns the few sheep that they still tend and has rights to use the "dry sandy arroyos" for grazing. The small number of sheep might be an allusion to Ayah's family's never really having recovered from the enforced herd reductions of the 1930s. Nevertheless, even though Chato no longer has his job or housing provided by the cattle rancher, Ayah owns a home and livestock, both of which add to their meager economic resources.

Ayah's lack of sympathy for Chato's plight is no surprise in view of her low opinion of the whites and what she has suffered because of them. Conversely, Chato's effort to assimilate into the dominant mainstream society by speaking English and working as a wage laborer does not represent an anomaly. If Ayah's children no longer make up part of her resident extended family, then there are no other members to help with the support of the basic social unit. If herding on the reservation could no longer supply even basic subsistence needs for Ayah and Chato, then naturally he would have to look elsewhere for employment.

Despite events that might portray Ayah as a victim, someone marginalized by the dominant mainstream society, she, in fact, transcends loss and disappointment in her life to emerge as a powerful figure. Viewing Ayah in the context of gender complementarity helps explain the resulting image of a strong woman. Considering the role, status, and autonomy of Ayah in the narrative sheds light on how this character survives. She has displayed autonomy in terms of how she functions in the marriage, choosing when she will sleep with Chato: she has control over her own body. She has retained ownership of her hogan and livestock. She has kept her tribal identity alive with her connections to the land and memories of family. Having a structure of balanced reciprocity between women and men contributes to Ayah's sense that she can capably do anything. Silko has voiced this same philosophy about the ability of women: "I never thought that women weren't as strong as men, as able as men or as valid as men. I was pretty old before I really started running into mainstream culture's attitudes about women. And because I never internalized the oppressor's attitude, I never behaved in a passive, helpless way. Instead of being crushed by sexism, I was sort of amused or enraged, but never cowed" (Perry 319). In much the same way, Silko does not allow Ayah to feel "cowed" by the dominant culture's male authority. On the contrary, when Ayah realizes that the authorities want to take her children, she does not hesitate to protect them:

> She moved suddenly and grabbed Ella into her arms; the child squirmed, trying to get back to her toys. Ayah ran with the baby toward Danny; she screamed for him to run and then she grabbed him around his chest and carried him too. She ran south into the foothills of juniper trees and black lava rock. Behind her she heard the doctors running, but they had been taken by surprise, and as the hills became steeper and the cholla cactus were thicker, they stopped. (*Storyteller* 45–46)

Ayah responds to danger as a brave female warrior, never thinking for a moment that she does not have the strength, courage, or conviction to succeed in escaping those who want to abduct her children. Knowledge of the landscape also aids Ayah in her getaway. She knows the terrain and is accustomed to traveling it, but the authorities do not know how to maneuver among the steep hills and cholla cactus. They are at a disadvantage and soon cannot continue the chase. Although her act of resistance might seem only to delay the inevitable, that Ayah should even attempt the flight signals a woman who feels empowered to change the course of events.

In terms of Ayah's strength, the most telling moment of the story occurs during her search for Chato in Azzie's Bar when she faces the discrimination of the bar owner. Knowing that the bar owner does not want her on his property does not prevent her from entering. She does not fear him:

> The bar owner didn't like Indians in there, especially Navajos, but he let Chato come in because he could talk Spanish like he was one of them. [. . .] She held herself straight and walked across the room slowly, searching the room with every step. [. . .] She felt calm.
>
> In past years they would have told her to get out. But her hair was white now and her face was wrinkled. They looked at her like she was a spider crawling slowly across the room. They were afraid; she could feel the fear. [. . .]
>
> She felt satisfied that the men in the bar feared her. Maybe it was her face and the way she held her mouth with teeth clenched tight, like there was nothing anyone could do to her now. (48–49)

What would make men fear an old woman? As a Navajo woman, Ayah knows who she is, where she is from, and where she belongs. The comparison of Ayah to the "spider" alludes to one of the Navajo Holy People, Spider Woman, who taught the Navajo how to weave (Shepardson 171). Comparing Ayah to the spider implies that she has the power to weave her own story.

Linda L. Danielson agrees and sees the connection between Ayah and Spider Woman as one in which Ayah has control over her life, certainly a powerful image:

> Web imagery reinforces the structural statement in the story "Lullaby" as the old Navajo woman, Ayah, spins a narrative of the end of her and her husband's lives. One could see her as a victim. Her children have been taken by white people who "know best." Her husband's loyalty to an employer has been rewarded by callous dismissal and eviction. The husband, Chato, is evidently drinking himself into discouraged oblivion. But the structural context of the spider web, combined with the story's imagery, associates Ayah with Spider Woman, and thus with control over the making of her life. (335)

That Ayah walks proudly, determined not to let anyone prevent her mission of finding her husband, exemplifies taking control of the situation. Such an act of overt confrontation by an old Navajo woman makes a strong political statement. Nobody in the mainstream culture can intimidate her or prevent her from carrying out her intentions. As Ayah has control of her life at other times and in other places, at this particular moment in the world of Azzie's Bar, a place where she is not wanted, Ayah is a powerful woman who controls the making of her life.

That Silko uses the image of the spider is not surprising because for the Laguna Pueblo, Spider Woman is another name for Thought Woman, who brought everything in the universe into creation by thinking it. Silko begins her novel *Ceremony* with this creation myth: "Thought-Woman, the spider, / named things and / as she named them / they appeared" (1). Thus, the significance: the "spider" allusion for both author and Ayah connotes one of great power, one of creation in language and/or weaving. By association the allusion gives Ayah an aura of power that the men in the bar can sense and fear. As noted earlier, Silko believes that the Indians of the Southwest "shared cosmologies, and oral narratives about [...] their grandmother, Spider Woman" (*Yellow Woman* 123). Including what the spider signifies to Silko in reading "Lullaby," however, is an inappropriate strategy because it combines deities from different tribes who mean different things to different people. Conflating the Laguna Pueblo and Navajo meanings of the spider is a mistake that should be avoided.

Ayah's sense of survival humor also displays her strength. How does a person successfully cope with loss of children, unemployment, poverty, alcoholism, illness, and death? In keeping with her worldview of *hozho,* a sense of balance and harmony, Ayah must have laughter in her life. "The more desperate the problem," writes Vine Deloria, Jr., "the more humor is directed to describe it" (*Custer* 147). Chato's drunken, disheveled appearance—he "smelled strong of woodsmoke and urine"—and his delusional ramblings, signs of mental deterioration due to alcohol, certainly indicate a man with a desperate problem, and Silko directs humor to it: "[H]e walked on determined, limping on the leg that had been crushed many years before. [...] The rags made his feet look like little animals up to their ears in snow. She laughed at his feet; the snow muffled the sound of her laugh" (*Storyteller* 50). That Ayah can find humor in and laugh at the sad physical state of her husband might amaze someone who does not understand survival humor. Deloria explains, however, that laughter in these circumstances is necessary: "When a people can laugh at themselves and laugh at others and hold all aspects of life together without letting anybody drive them to extremes, then it seems to me that that people can survive" (*Custer* 167). Ayah laughs; Chato drinks. The one holds her life together, and the other chooses the extreme path of alcohol. Ayah survives through humor and maintains *hozho.* Silko agrees, "in order to have perfect balance or harmony you have to have humor" (Perry 336). Through humor, Ayah finds her strength.

The concluding lullaby that Ayah sings at the end of the story offers one more example of her strength. She understands that Chato might freeze to death: "She recognized the freezing. It came gradually, sinking snowflake by snowflake until the crust was heavy and deep. It had the strength of the stars in Orion, and its journey was endless. Ayah knew that with the wine he would sleep. He would not feel it" (*Storyteller* 51). Alcohol would make Chato feel warm, giving him a false sense of security and preventing him from recognizing the dangerously cold temperatures. Perhaps Ayah acts benevolently, knowing that Chato's death will be painless. Ayah has no evil intentions, however, even though she understands the possibility that Chato might die. As already explained, this reading does not fit with Ayah's cultural worldview of sustaining life.

Contrary to one of the alternative readings that Elaine Jahner posits, Ayah does not methodically plot "to murder her sick husband by getting him drunk and then watching and singing while he freezes in the cold" (505). The only evidence of Ayah's planning their stop occurs during the snowstorm when she suggests, "Let's rest awhile" (*Storyteller* 50). "The Storm passed swiftly," and while waiting, Chato falls asleep (51). In fact, in Tohe's description of the strength of Navajo women, she relates a similar situation in which she knows her own mother would not let any harm come to her and her siblings in a snowstorm: "I grew up knowing that my mother, who divorced my father several years before, would drive us through the thirty miles of muddy reservation road to get groceries. I never doubted that she would get us through the dizzying snowstorm that fell on the deserted dirt road alone with my brothers and me in the back seat" (109). Navajo women know how to take care of their families in severe circumstances. More than likely, Ayah has reached the end of her story, accomplished the healing that she set out to do, let go of her resentments, and merely sees that perhaps the time is right if Chato should peacefully pass away in his sleep. Rather than see his freezing to death as due to alcohol, she might feel that to look death in the face and to accept it at this point in her life simply acknowledge that she has reached the Navajo goal of living to old age. Death is the natural and inevitable next step, but the actual dying is only implied and not the most important part of the ending.

Silko's views on death shed more light on the ending of "Lullaby." Discussing animals dying in a hunt, she claims that European Americans have an unnatural fear of death, and she sees death more as a sacred part of the life cycle:

> It's sort of puritanical abhorrence of blood and a tremendous fear of death that western European people have; Americans especially. That's why everyone is out jogging and not eating salt because he's so scared of death; those are like amulets to keep death away. So on the literal level, it's not something nasty or awful or horrible or something to avert one's eyes from: look at it. It's actually almost like a sacred or ritualistic kind of thing, that giving up of the life. Of course, I also mean for it to transcend that and for people to be able to see that in a struggle to survive, it is again that you will be able to look and see things that are a part of a kind of ritual. Not ritual in a sense of following a set pattern, a form that can never vary, but ritual in a lighter sense that expands our senses. One should be able to see one's own life and lives of other beings as part of something very sacred and special. (Barnes 99–100)

If Silko intends that Chato should die, then his death itself is "not something nasty or awful or horrible or something to avert one's eyes from: look at it." To see his life as "part of something very sacred and special" would be the point.

As already noted, Silko does not have any problems with incorporating other Native cultures into her writing. Mixing Silko's personal views with traditional Navajo views, however, can result in contradictions. Chato's death of freezing in an alcoholic sleep does not necessarily coincide with the revered Navajo goal of death of old age or Silko's view that death is part of something sacred. Ayah, a woman associated with the Navajo Spider Woman and the Laguna Spider Woman, cannot truly be an empowered Navajo woman living an autonomous life when, in fact, she loses her children. Inconsistencies begin to appear if only the Navajo cultural and historical contexts are used to understand "Lullaby." Similarly, using just the Laguna cultural and historical contexts fails to offer a consistent reading. Using both Navajo and Laguna cultural readings also poses problems. Therefore, Silko's use of the Navajo characters to tell her story creates problems that she might not otherwise encounter if she were to limit herself to a purely Laguna Pueblo context. American Indian tribal cultures are specific and unique; they do not always smoothly overlap, no matter how similar they might appear to be on the surface.

Silko eliminates any previous problems of inconsistency by having Ayah sing the lullaby at the end of the story. In Navajo style, the lullaby speaks about two of the most important Navajo deities, Mother Earth and Father Sky, in addition to other elements of the natural environment. In discussing a prayer from the Navajo Night Chant, or Nightway, a healing ritual designed to cure an individual's illness in mind and body, Ruoff offers an insightful description that equally applies to Silko's lullaby:

> The prayer illustrates the emphasis on physical and spiritual harmony and on the sacredness of place so much a part of American Indian oral literatures. Among the elements of the prayer that are common in these literatures are the following: repetition, movement in time and location, progression from physical well-being to spiritual peace to ability to speak, and the comprehensiveness of the allusions to aspects of nature. (*Introduction* 21)

Silko offers a short lullaby that has varying degrees of these aspects; it completes the cyclic nature of life, birth and death, in a context that is connected to the people, land, and mythic time:

> *The earth is your mother,*
>   *she holds you.*
> *The sky is your father,*
>   *he protects you.*
>
> . . . .
>
> *We are together always*
> *We are together always*
> *There never was a time*
> *when this*
> *was not so.* (*Storyteller* 51)

Concluding with the lullaby connects Ayah not only to her deceased children but also to her grandmother and mother, who sang the song, and it emphasizes the continuity of tradition. Although Ayah cannot "remember whether she had ever sung it to her children" (51), now that she has told the story, the song will endure through Silko's voice. The positive theme of eternity in the lullaby creates a note of survival and hope for Ayah and her people.

For Silko, the political is involved in the very telling of her stories. Gloria Bird (Spokane) observes, "That we are still here as native women in itself is a political statement," and Joy Harjo (Muscogee Creek) adds, "We are still here, still telling stories, still singing whether it be in our native languages or in the 'enemy' tongue" (Harjo 30, 31). Indeed, Ayah's story is a political statement narrated in the "enemy tongue." However, her story also testifies not only to the ongoing survival of the Navajo woman but also to the survival of all Native women. In a foreword to Aaron Yava's *Border Towns of the Navajo Nation,* Silko describes how in her writing she tries to present an exposé on contemporary American Indian life:

> I think Aaron says with his drawings what I attempt to say with my stories—that Indian life today is full of terror and death and great suffering, but despite these tremendous odds against us for two hundred of years—the racism, the poverty, the alcoholism—we go on living. We live to celebrate the beauty of the Earth and Sky because the beauty and vitality of life, like the rainbow colored horses leaping, has never been lost. The world remains for us as it has always been, One with itself and us, death and laughter existing side by side as it does in Aaron's drawings. (Foreword n. pag.)

Ayah's story in "Lullaby" demonstrates continuity in the midst of "death and laughter existing side by side," and her power arises, in part, from the paradigm of gender complementarity, a vision of self as an equally important member in the communal tribal structure. Ayah never loses her sense of herself as an important part of the marriage relationship. Her role of caring for her husband and children, while she has them, carries as much weight as Chato's role of working for the rancher or cashing the welfare checks. She never complains about her domestic contributions to the partnership because she values who she is and what she does, as does her tribal community.

Laura Tohe writes how Navajo women have continued to survive despite any "story about 'those poor' Indian women who were assimilated, colonized, Christianized, or victimized":

> This is a story about how these women cling to the roots of their female lineage despite the many institutional forces imposed on Indian communities and how they continue to survive despite five hundred years of colonialism. The Diné women continue to possess the qualities of leadership and strength and continue to endure and ultimately to pass on those qualities to their daughters, even though there is no word for feminism in the Diné language. (104)

Ayah remembers her past and in doing so keeps the traditions alive in the telling. Although she will not have the opportunity to help her daughter give birth or to pass on the skill of weaving to grandchildren, by remembering and telling the story, she keeps the connection to her tribal identity alive. Her act of remembering the traditions of the past creates a future with her story that can be retold, a story of unemployment, government welfare checks, and alcoholism, but also a life of continuity, adaptation, and survival.

CHAPTER 5

"Women Are Strong, Strong, Terribly Strong"
Female Intellectual Sovereignty in the Works of Louise Erdrich

With numerous major awards and honors for her writing, which draws on her Ojibwe heritage, Louise Erdrich is undoubtedly one of the most important writers of American Indian literature today. An enrolled member of the Turtle Mountain Band of Ojibwe, Karen Louise Erdrich was born on June 7, 1954, in Little Falls, Minnesota, and grew up in Wahpeton, North Dakota.[1] Her mother, Rita Joanne Gourneau Erdrich of Ojibwe and French descent, and her father, Ralph Erdrich of German descent, were both teachers at the Indian school in Wahpeton. Her mother's father was Patrice Gourneau, a tribal chairman; his role is echoed in Erdrich's writing by the characters Nanapush, a tribal chairman in the novel *Tracks,* and Nector Kashpaw, a tribal chairman in the novel *Love Medicine.*

This chapter examines how Erdrich's depiction of strong female characters grows out of a tribal context of gender complementarity and intellectual sovereignty. Erdrich's fiction spans a period from as early as about 1847 in *The Birchbark House* to as current as 1997 in *The Last Report on Miracles at Little No Horse.* During that 150-year period, tribal customs and traditions may have changed because of adaptation to the dominant mainstream society, but the power, strength, and autonomy of the women remain constant throughout Erdrich's works. The ability of these female characters to endure and to succeed, despite the influence of external factors, such as disease, off-reservation boarding schools, Christian missionaries, and land dispossession, is politically significant in a history of cultural genocide.

Erdrich earned a B.A. in English from Dartmouth College in 1976 and a M.A. in the creative writing program from Johns Hopkins University in 1979. In 1981, she married Michael Dorris (Modoc), an anthropologist who at the time was the founding director of Dartmouth's Native American studies program. Dorris had already adopted three Native reservation children, whom Erdrich also adopted after they married. Together they had three more children of their own. Although the couple successfully collaborated on their joint and individual writing projects, they separated in 1995, and Dorris committed suicide in 1997. Erdrich added another child to her family in 2001 with the birth of a daughter.[2]

Erdrich has written and published poetry, short stories, novels, essays, and criticism. In 1982 her short story "The World's Greatest Fisherman" won the Nelson Algren Award, to be followed the next year by "Scales," which was included in *The Best American Short Stories 1983*. Her first novel, *Love Medicine* (1984), won the National Book Critics Award for best work of fiction. She is also the author of two collections of poetry, *Jacklight* (1984) and *Baptism of Desire* (1989). In addition, she has written three children's books: *Grandmother Pigeon* (1996), a picture book; *The Birchbark House* (1999), a novel for young readers and a finalist for the National Book Award; and *The Range Eternal* (2002), another picture book. Although Erdrich and Dorris admitted that they "agree[d] on every word" in their writings, both of their names appear on only two of their collaborations: *Route Two* (1991), a travelogue of a family trip along route 2 through Minnesota; and *The Crown of Columbus*, published in 1992 for the Columbus Quincentenary (Coltelli 50). In her novel *The Antelope Wife* (1998), Erdrich populates the setting of Minneapolis with contemporary urban Ojibwe characters, and in her novel *The Master Butchers Singing Club* (2003), she focuses on the European side of her heritage, creating German characters who live in the fictional town of Argus, North Dakota.

Erdrich's North Dakota cycle of novels includes *Love Medicine* (1984, revised 1993), *The Beet Queen* (1986), *Tracks* (1988), *The Bingo Palace* (1994), *Tales of Burning Love* (1996), and *The Last Report on the Miracles at Little No Horse* (2001). With multiple narrators and nonlinear plots, these six novels comprise a community of Ojibwe characters and non-Natives who live on or near a reservation in North Dakota, which critics generally have assumed is based on the Turtle Mountain Reservation. Erdrich, however, corrects that mistaken notion by adding an endnote to her most recent addition to the cycle, *The Last Report on the Miracles at Little No Horse*: "[T]he reservation depicted in this and in all of my novels is an imagined place consisting of landscapes and features similar to many Ojibwe reservations. It is an emotional collection of places dear to me, as is the town called Argus. It is not the Turtle Mountain Reservation, of course, although that is where I am proud to be enrolled" (357). Along with this setting, Erdrich's style of multiple points of view, tangled family relationships, and epic scale often has been compared to the novels and the creation of Yoknapatawpha County of William Faulkner, an author whose influence Erdrich acknowledges (Coltelli 49). Erdrich subverts the intentions of those who would like to pinpoint the geographical settings of her novels with definitive answers, a response fitting to the complexity of relationships and themes found in her novels.

In a recent interview, when asked whether Erdrich sees herself as a "'restorier' for Ojibwe—a reclaimer of narratives that were never written down or were drowned out by what was taught in school about Native Americans," she replies:

> I am just a storyteller, and I take them where I find them. I love stories whether they function to reclaim old narratives or occur spontaneously. Often, to my surprise, they do both. I'll follow an inner thread of a plot and find that I am actually retelling a very old story, often in a contemporary setting. I usually can't recall whether it is something I remember hearing, or something I dreamed, or read, or imagined on the spot. It all becomes confused and then the characters take over, anyway, and make the piece their own. (Bacon 6)

Erdrich describes the genesis of her storytelling process as "confused" and controlled by the characters; similarly, the intricacy and density of the works themselves defy simplistic and reductive explanations.

With a family background that includes an emphasis on education and politics, Erdrich's political position with regard to her fiction is not surprising:

> I think each of the books is political in its own way. I hope so. [...] There's no way to speak about Indian history without it being a political statement. You can't describe a people's suffering without implying that somebody's at fault. [...] you really can't write a book about Native Americans without being political. [...] Getting your teeth fixed is political. There's no way around it. I just don't want to become *polemical*. That's the big difference. (Schumacher 29)

Erdrich is aware that politics permeates every aspect of life, but as she states, she does not want her writing to be known as disputatious. Rather, she allows the characters to present differing viewpoints, and the reader has the responsibility for assessing the value of the political views expressed in the writing. "Erdrich speaks with an unquestionable authority," writes Peter Beidler, "about what it is to be a woman" (97). Although Beidler states the obvious about Erdrich's ability to speak as a woman, her female characters also tell their stories with authority. Their political views reflect an attitude that women are knowledgeable, capable, and experienced, all characteristics represented in the tribal concept of gender complementarity, which values the roles and work of women.

In *The Blue Jay's Dance* (1995), her nonfiction memoir about pregnancy, motherhood, and writing, Erdrich declares, "Women are strong, strong, terribly strong" (12). She cites this theme of strong women in the names of her own family ancestors. In her essay "The Names of Women," Erdrich discusses how traditional names that revealed personalities were lost and replaced with "the names of saints particularly beloved by the French":

> *She Knows the Bear* became Marie. *Sloping Cloud* was christened Jeanne. *Taking Care of the Day* and *Yellow Day Woman* turned into Catherines. Identities are altogether lost. The daughters of my own ancestors, *Kwayzancheewin*—Acts Like a Boy and *Striped Earth Woman*—go unrecorded, and no hint or reflection of their individual natures comes to light through the scatter-shot records of those times, although they must have been genetically tough in order to survive: there were epidemics of typhoid, flu, measles and other diseases that winnowed the tribe each winter. They had to have grown up sensible, hard-working, undeviating in their attention to their tasks. (393)

In addition to explaining how "those women lost their names through the erasing efficiency of the Catholic priests," Erdrich conflates the other historical events of disease that impacted the tribe and concludes that these women had to be strong in order to survive the loss of their identifying names and families (Pellerin 36). Interestingly, as a result of these experiences, Erdrich ascribes to these women personalities grounded in reason, industriousness, and persistence in the context of work. Again, within the framework of gender complementarity, the inherent idea of the worth of women's labor is valued.

Julie Maristuen-Rodakowski observes that Erdrich's writing is "solidly based in the facts of the Chippewa Indians of the Turtle Mountain Reservation" (15). She goes on to note: "The Chippewa originally were an Algonquian-speaking tribe that was driven west by the expanding Iroquois in the Great Lakes area. Many of these Chippewa settled in the Turtle Mountain area, where the reservation itself was established later by an executive order dated 21 December 1882" (15). This is the reservation where Erdrich's grandparents lived and where she visited while growing up, so Maristuen-Rodakowski rightly assumes that this reservation is Erdrich's source for her information on the Ojibwe. There are many Ojibwe reservation communities, and Erdrich moves fluidly among the diversity of Ojibwe cultures in her writing.

Helen Hornbeck Tanner notes the area and number of Ojibwe bands:

> The Ojibwas are spread over a thousand miles of territory from southeastern Ontario westward across the upper Great Lakes country of the United States and Canada as far as Montana and Saskatchewan. Although classed as one people in

the Algonquian linguistic family, they have several alternate regional names and are divided into about one hundred separate bands or reservation communities. (438)

Erdrich's writing is based in the historical and cultural contexts of the Ojibwe, and her settings easily range across Montana, North Dakota, and Minnesota.

Maristuen-Rodakowski lists several major historical and linguistic factors that have influenced the Ojibwe since the time of contact. First is the influence of the French and English traders who exchanged merchandise with the Ojibwe for furs, married the Native women, and introduced alcohol to the tribe (15). In the seventeenth century, the children of the French and Ojibwe marriages were called Métis (a Canadian term). The combination of French and the Cree language of the Turtle Mountain Reservation became a language referred to as Michif (an Algonquian pronunciation of the French word *Métis*) (21). Thus, in addition to the Ojibwe language, Cree, Michif, French, and English were learned by the Indians (23). Intermarriage and resulting language changes account for the mixed-blood characters and French names in Erdrich's novels.

Two other important historical influences that appear in Erdrich's treatment of the Ojibwe are the effects of the General Allotment Act of 1887 and the introduction of Roman Catholicism in 1817 (18, 19). The Allotment Act provided that each head of an Indian household was to receive 160 acres of land; single members of the tribe received various lesser amounts depending upon their age. Although the goal was that Indians would leave their own cultures behind and become "civilized," the project failed and resulted in a loss of 65 percent of Indian land. Because of the mixed ancestry of the Ojibwe, they had difficulty proving they should receive an allotment. Later treaties corrected this situation, so mixed-bloods became eligible, but by then there was not enough land close to where they lived, and they had to relocate to Montana if they wanted their share (18). In 1855, Father Belcourt opened a school on the reservation, and nuns soon followed to teach (19–20). The effects of both the Allotment Act and Catholicism on the Ojibwe are evident in Erdrich's writing, the former especially in the novel *Tracks* and the latter in most of her fiction and poetry.

Although the communal view of the tribe looks at the good of the whole group before anything else, in *The Ojibwa Woman*, Ruth Landes writes how the Ojibwe traditionally viewed the value of individualism: "The ideals of the Ojibwa, the ends toward which every person should strive [...] are knit into an internally consistent system. The keystone to their culture, the bias which molds all personal actions and reshapes the cultural details that have been borrowed from neighboring tribes, is individualism" (178). Erdrich creates female characters, both Native and non-Native, as distinct individuals in numerous roles, as shown, for example, by four of Jack Mauser's wives in *Tales of Burning Love,* a novel that covers a contemporary time span from 1962 to 1995: Eleanor Schlick is a college professor (36); Candice Pantamounty is a dentist (272); Marlis Cook is a blackjack dealer and would-be singer (166); and Dot Adare Nanapush is a bookkeeper (89). Erdrich's female characters manifest their strength in a variety of ways. Landes notes that there can be a wide range of behaviors among women, as well as variable behaviors in different periods in the lifetime of any one woman (xx). To show how women's independence and traditional roles as mothers have evolved over time, this chapter focuses on examples of women who live as singles, as mothers giving birth, as political activists, as businesswomen, and as a man in order to serve as a priest of the Catholic Church. That Erdrich's female characters fill so many different roles attests to their resiliency, resourcefulness, and creativity.

The epitome of an independent woman, living alone and providing for all her own needs in the traditional Ojibwe lifestyle, is found in the character of Old Tallow in *The Birchbark House.* Old Tallow's single lifestyle represents both gender complementarity and intellectual sovereignty. She has the indigenous knowledge to perform female- and male-gendered tasks for her survival as a single woman, and her contributions to the rest of the tribal members are valued. Also, according to Robert Allen Warrior's (Osage) definition of intellectual sovereignty, Old Tallow engages in a process of asserting the power she possesses as an individual to make decisions that affect her life and that of the community (124).

The protagonist of *The Birchbark House,* seven-year-old Omakayas (Little Frog), lives with her family on the Island of the Golden-Breasted Woodpecker in Lake Superior in 1847, a time when the whites were increasingly encroaching on their land. The novel spans one year, during which, among other things, Omakayas helps nurse and save her family from a smallpox epidemic that leaves eighteen Ojibwe dead (154), including her baby brother, Neewo.

Omakayas has a special relationship with Old Tallow, who helps her recover from the loss of her brother and explains to her why she survived the "scratching disease." Old Tallow saves Omakayas, a child less than two years of age when her family died in a smallpox epidemic on Spirit Island: "'[E]veryone but you died of the itching sickness—you were the toughest one, the littlest one, and you survived them all'" (233). Old Tallow believes that Omakayas was sent to Yellow Kettle, her new mother, to save them: "'Because you'd had the sickness, you were strong enough to nurse them through it. They did a good thing when they took you in, and you saved them for their good act. Now the circle that began when I found you is complete'" (235). Old Tallow acts as a wise elder who not only rescues Omakayas but also instructs her in how to recover from her deep depression by informing her of her origins and how she went to live with her adopted family.

"Contrary to many adoption practices elsewhere," writes Landes of the Ojibwe, "neglected children are often taken into the household of adoptive parents and there accorded the finest treatment" (138). Although there are other children in the family, certainly this adoption scenario is true in the case of Omakayas; she is treated well and as one of the family's own as Old Tallow tells her: "'They took you in as their daughter, loved you as their daughter, you are a daughter to them, and a sister to your brother, and to Angeline'" (*Birchbark* 234). Omakayas cannot understand, however, why Old Tallow gave her away although she is the one who found her and nursed her back to health (233). When asked, Old Tallow responds, "Count yourself lucky! What kind of life with an old bear hunter like Tallow? Nobody has ever stayed with Old Tallow. She drives them off. Eyah!" (234–35). Although the tribal custom of unconditionally adopting children is evident in the story, there is also an acceptable space for those women who choose not to raise children and who prefer to live alone.

Old Tallow lives by herself in town, and she never had any children although she had three husbands, all of whom "had slunk off in turn during the night, never to be seen again" (19). Erdrich describes her as "a rangy woman over six feet in height. She was powerful, lean and lived surrounded by ferocious animals more wolf than dog and fiercely devoted to her. Old Tallow could bring down a bear with her pack of dogs, her gun, or even the razor-sharp spear that she practiced throwing into the splintered base of a tree" (19–20). Women who choose to perform masculine tasks rather than live on the dole of neighbors are not atypical. "Those women who cross the occupational line and take up men's work, "asserts Landes, "do so casually, under the pressure of circumstances or of personal inclination. They [...] are forced to men's work through the exigencies of widowhood, desertion, illness of the husband, etc." (136). Old Tallow hunts, fishes, dresses the animals, and shares her catch with Omakayas's family when her father, who works for the fur trade company, is gone, paddling canoes and trapping animals (*Birchbark* 9). Without Old Tallow's contributions to the family's food supplies, they would have a difficult time. The grandmother, mother, and older sister stay at home to care for the three younger children and really do not have any interest in hunting the large animals. They are content to engage in snaring rabbits (82) and performing traditional food gathering activities, such as picking berries (26), ricing (95), and maple-sugaring (196).

Erdrich portrays Old Tallow as a brave woman with a temper whom others, including her third husband, Hat, fear: "He shivered a little as he thought of her. He couldn't help it. [...] sometimes she scared him with her temper. Other times, he was amazed at her courage. He grimaced in shame—unlike him, his wife was afraid of nothing" (2). Erdrich attributes the usually male-gendered qualities of courage and fearlessness to Old Tallow, and although this strong woman intimidates her husband, at the same time he is in awe of her. Having approved male qualities and/or occupations does not diminish Old Tallow's status as an acceptable woman. According to Landes, "They are designated by no special term, there are no alterations in costume or linguistic forms, they are never suspected of sexual irregularities even though some never marry, they have no privileges that do not pertain to the occupation they follow, they are never jeered at" (136). As an example of how she is esteemed by other males, Omakayas's father likes her and shows his affection by teasing her and "giving her little gifts, too" (*Birchbark* 52).

Despite her sometimes-cranky disposition, Old Tallow exhibits traditional nurturing behavior in her treatment of Omakayas and her family. She "loved them even more than she loved her dogs" (150), as she proves when she kills one for attacking Omakayas (180). Old Tallow is a woman who expresses herself in both feminine and masculine ways, depending on what her situation requires. "Women who prefer to live alone," surmises Landes, "in all probability enjoy, and even seize upon, this manner of life: they desire solitude, or wish to hunt and trap, or delight in complete self-reliance" (168–69). Old Tallow prefers to live alone and exemplifies the concepts of gender complementarity and intellectual sovereignty in that she has the necessary knowledge of survival skills and the autonomy to provide for herself and others.

In the North Dakota cycle of novels, Erdrich introduces a cast of characters who are related by blood, marriage, and friendship and who will reappear throughout the novels. Among those characters are several powerful women who illustrate the tribal concepts of gender complementarity and intellectual sovereignty. One of these strong female characters is Fleur Pillager (b. 1895–d. ca. late 1980s or 1990s), who has the necessary knowledge to live as a single woman at different times in her life. A respected and feared medicine woman and mother of Lulu Nanapush, she is a woman who has survived disease, famine, three near-death drownings, and land dispossession. As a political voice for the importance of holding on to the land, she works successfully to recover lost Pillager land and advises others about its lasting value. The novel *Tracks* contains three births, of which Fleur is the laboring mother in two. Birthing scenes in Erdrich's work reveal an evolution in her treatment of parturition, one that moves from a distanced third-person point of view to a first-person narration of the mother's experience.

Erdrich renders the earlier delivery scenes in a variety of ways with humor, traditional Ojibwe symbols, impotence of other people, and violence perpetrated on the mother and newborn child. The development in Erdrich's handling of birthing scenes ultimately speaks to the oppressive practices and attitudes of Western medicine, while privileging the Ojibwe customs and power of motherhood, ideas situated in gender complementarity and intellectual sovereignty. Bearing children, of course, is essential to the continuance and survival of the tribe. Therefore, a vast body of indigenous knowledge has passed down through the midwives who help pregnant women deliver their babies. These important roles for women—the laboring mother, the assisting midwife, and the nurturing mother—are valued by the community and represent intellectual sovereignty by the power and knowledge women need to perform them successfully.

As already noted, Erdrich and Dorris did not publish any work until they agreed on every word, an example of gender complementarity within their writing relationship. Although only one name may have appeared on the final copy, they described their work as a cooperative effort, "progressive, more than editor, less than coauthor, somewhere in between" (*Louise*). They called themselves "collaborators" on both their writing and their children (three older adoptive children and three younger daughters). Although Erdrich did not publish *Tracks* until 1989, the original manuscript was written in 1980 (*Louise*). *Tracks* has three birthing scenes that seem to represent less personal knowledge of the birthing experience because they are narrated from the third-person point of view. *The Beet Queen* (1986), *A Yellow Raft in Blue Water* (Dorris, 1987), and the new and revised edition of *Love Medicine* (1993) contain birthing scenes that illustrate not just changes peculiar to different texts, but changes that reflect a more intimate understanding of parturition and seem more closely related to personal experience.

During the period of *Tracks*, 1912–24, Erdrich recounts three births. The first involves Fleur. Fleur never speaks in the first-person voice, but instead is seen through one of the novel's two narrators, in this case, Nanapush. Although the birthing house is women's space and Nanapush does not see firsthand what Fleur experiences, he listens to the women talk: "I am a man, so I don't know exactly what happened when the bear came into the birth house, but they talk among themselves, the women, and sometimes they forget I'm listening" (60). Erdrich closes a difficult two-day labor with a comic incident. She introduces a drunk bear (totem animal of the Pillager) into the scene to help Fleur deliver: "[W]hen Fleur saw the bear in the house she was filled with such fear and power that she raised herself on the mound of blankets and gave birth" (60). The people attending the delivery have not helped Fleur; they are impotent to effect any change other than to become comical characters in their responses to the intoxicated bear that barges in on them. Fleur needs the symbolic help of her clan's power animal in order to bring the baby into the world.

Apart from Fleur's weakened condition, Erdrich offers no other specific details of her labor or delivery, just the aftermath, when Fleur's lifeless body responds to her baby's cry: "At that sound, they say, Fleur opened her eyes and breathed. That was when Margaret went to work and saved her, packed wormwood and moss between her legs, wrapped her in blankets heated with stones, then kneaded Fleur's stomach and forced her to drink cup after cup of boiled raspberry leaf until at last Fleur groaned, drew the baby against her breast, and lived" (60). Margaret Rushes Bear Kashpaw, the mother-in-law, helps Fleur with her home delivery, using traditional Ojibwe customs to care for the mother and newborn. Because Erdrich's great-aunt was a midwife, she says that she grew up with this heritage, which most likely included information about labor, delivery, and postnatal care (Interview McKosato). In effect, Fleur owes her life to time-honored Ojibwe healing traditions, a debt that reflects the valued role of women as midwives and their intellectual sovereignty.

Instead of humor, Erdrich treats the second birth in *Tracks* with perversion and violence. The mother, Pauline, is a mixed-blood—Puyat and white—who rejects her Native heritage for assimilation into the white culture and Catholicism.[3] To avoid the "taint of original sin" on the illegitimate child she carries, Pauline refuses to cooperate in her delivery and chooses death for herself and her baby: "I shook with the effort, held back, reduced myself to something tight, round, and very black clenched around my child so that she could not escape" (135). Bernadette Morrissey, who attends the delivery, must resort to violent measures in order to save the baby and mother:

> [S]he came back into the room with a coil of rope. She also brandished an instrument made of two black iron cooking spoons, wired together at the handles. [. . .] I was roped in place as tight as she could pull. And when the next pains, and the next, and the next pains threw me upwards, straining at the bindings, she managed to put the spoons to the child's head and wrench her into the world. (135)

Erdrich continues to place women together during birthing, but as the event moves a character closer to the white culture, the dynamics change dramatically. Wanting to become white, Pauline does not rely on traditional Native customs to help in the delivery of her child; nor does Bernadette, who has been educated by the French nuns in Quebec (64). Erdrich focuses on what Bernadette does to Pauline rather than the physical sensations that Pauline feels as she gives birth. Pauline's lithotomy position, with hands and legs tied to the bed, and the use of the "masculine 'hands of iron'—the forceps" resemble European-American medical practices for laboring mothers and not traditional Ojibwe ones (Rich 142). Thus, comparing the first and second birthing scenes in *Tracks*, Erdrich clearly privileges the former and criticizes the latter.

The third birth in *Tracks* returns to Fleur and the premature birth of her second child. For the second time, Fleur must "raise herself" to have her baby because the bystanders are ineffectual. Although Pauline is present in this scene, fear paralyzes her and prevents her from helping Fleur (157). Fleur must rely on her own strength to deliver the baby: "[S]he raised herself with vast effort and took the child from her own blood, then the knife from its sheath where it hung from the bedframe. She cut the cord and breathed into the child's mouth, rubbed its skin and changed its dead gray color. When it cried out she bound it tightly against her, into her shirt" (157). Despite Fleur's courageous efforts, in the end the baby dies, and Fleur would have also if not for the arrival of Margaret, who finishes what Fleur began, heating the medicine that will help her recover. Again, Erdrich has another woman present at the home delivery, but Pauline cannot help the mother in distress. The focus remains on Pauline, the narrator and the impotent one, and not on the mother's physical sensations of delivering a premature baby. In all three birth episodes in *Tracks*, Erdrich pays more attention to the events and characters surrounding the delivery than to the actual experience of the mother during her labor.

In the other novels, the birthing scenes take a different direction. Obviously different plots, characters, and periods affect the nature of these birthing scenes, but the focus also changes with more attention paid to the mother's experience. In *The Beet Queen*, a novel that spans the years 1932–72, Celestine James, the primary Ojibwe character of the novel, goes into labor during a snowstorm in 1954 and starts out for the hospital. When she drives into a snowbank, she makes her way to the house of Wallace Pfef, a closet homosexual who must help her deliver the baby. For the first time, Erdrich has a male assist the mother, but she still delivers in a home, not a hospital. Further, the male helping Celestine is of nontraditional masculine gender. On a spectrum with home births and female midwives at one end and hospital births and male doctors at the other, Celestine's birth scene lies somewhere in the middle.

While Wallace runs around gathering items to help Celestine, he narrates her labor pains through his eyes and ears. He describes her "whooping sound like bitterns" and her "tensing and rocking, sometimes kneeling" position (170). Even when Celestine wails loudly, saying she felt the head just for a minute, Wallace describes the look of "astonishment" on her face as one of strength (171). In the final moments before her baby enters the world, Wallace continues to report the events: "She closed her eyes and instead of the whooping sound she made a kind of low whine. It didn't sound to me like pain though, just effort. She roared when the head came. Then she pushed down again and held herself, pushing down, for a long time. The sound she made was a deeper one, of vast relief, and the baby slid into my hands"

(171). Erdrich still does not allow an internal perspective of the mother, but she does present more vivid details of the birthing process through Wallace. Furthermore, the birth happens inside the home, not in a hospital, and the male character works with the mother rather than telling her what to do, respecting her body's natural process.

In contrast, in Michael Dorris's *A Yellow Raft in Blue Water*, which takes place in the mid-1980s, Christine Taylor (Fort Belknap Reservation) gives birth in a hospital, a place she hates, causing the entire event to take on a totally different tone (197).[4] While in labor, Christine has "an idiot for a nurse, a woman who nagged, 'Don't bear down until the doctor comes'" (195). Narrating in the first person, Christine wants to tell the nurse "to go to hell, to shut her face," but her contractions prevent her from saying it: "I lost myself in the force of the contraction. I dug my chin into my chest, held my breath, and pressed so hard my eyes felt as though they'd burst from my skull. Alarm bells went off in my brain. The baby was too big for me, something was wrong. If I bore down again, even a little, my body would rip apart" (195). The nurse ignores the natural rhythms of the mother's labor pains and admonishes her not to do what comes naturally but instead to wait for the doctor as if the woman cannot deliver her baby without a male physician present, an idea in direct contradiction to gender complementarity.

When the doctor arrives and gives his approval for Christine to bear down, she resents his arrogance, thinking, "[W]hat did he know?" and tries not to follow his order (195). He subtly threatens her with the possibility of using forceps if she does not cooperate, and the stupid nurse says, "'Just get *mad* at the baby,'" [...] "'Just say 'Bad baby, bad baby,' and shove it out'" (195). In defiance, Christine finds the strength to oppose the nurse: "I could have killed her at that moment. The force of my hate almost wrenched me off the table, and it gave me strength. When the next contraction came I put common sense away, tightened and loosened everything I could feel. I held my eyes on the nurse's face. 'Good baby,' I managed. 'Good baby, good baby, good baby'" (195–96). Christine may have to deliver her child in a hospital, but she will not participate in ideology that works completely against the power of the mother during labor. In the last seconds before her baby enters the world, her mind focuses on only the pain: "There was nothing but my pain. I gave myself to it, drowned in it. My thoughts were a white screen in a black room," and then her baby daughter arrives (196).

Erdrich would have been quite familiar with Christine's birthing scene because she and Dorris edited their writing together, as Dorris notes: "We go over every word and achieve consensus on every word; basically we agree on every word when it's finally finished" (Coltelli 50). That Dorris should be the one to have his name on the novel with the birth scene in the hospital is curious in light of Erdrich's birth scenes, which all take place in home deliveries.

The Christine birthing scene demonstrates what Adrienne Rich discusses so eloquently in *Of Woman Born: Motherhood as Experience and Institution*, the medical establishment's marginalization of the woman's birth experience. Rich cites Brigitte Jordan's description of routine hospital delivery in the United States, which involves "a complex of practices which are justified, on medical grounds, as being in the best interest of mother and child [...] the separation of the laboring woman from any sources of psychological support, surgical rupturing of the membranes, routine episiotomy, routine forceps delivery, and the lithotomy position for delivery, to name just a few" (177). Drawn as flat characters, the disinterested doctor and a stupid nurse are totally out of touch with the mother's feelings; therefore, they function as somewhat comic foils to the mother's pain and anger. In moving the mother out of a home environment to a sterile hospital to give birth, Dorris comments on how the natural event of parturition changes to a medical procedure that, according to Rich, takes the power away from the woman (182). Unlike Fleur, who is connected to tribal knowledge and practices, Christine is detribalized. Although the author includes more of what Christine feels during her delivery, he also continues to increase the interference of outside forces that take the focus away from the mother's experience. Again, Dorris critiques the Western medical practices that diminish the natural power of the woman's ability to give birth.

Perhaps Erdrich responds to this issue that the medical establishment creates when one of the chapters she adds to *Love Medicine: New and Expanded Edition* (1993) deals with a birth attended by two women in the privacy of the mother's home. In the original 1984 *Love Medicine,* there is no Part Two in the chapter "The Beads." In the new version, Marie Kashpaw (the same baby pulled with forceps from Pauline in *Tracks*) decides not to go to the hospital to deliver her baby: "The only thing that wouldn't cost money, I thought to comfort myself, was this baby, as long as she wasn't registered, as long as I did not go to the hospital, as long as I could have her in the house, she was free" (97). Although Marie bases her decision on economic concerns, she still privileges a home birth over one in the hospital. Even when her husband urges her to go to the hospital, she refuses because she "was afraid of that place" (100).

Marie's mother-in-law, Margaret Rushes Bear Kashpaw (who attended Fleur's first delivery in *Tracks*), and Fleur help Marie with the birthing. This particular birth brings together three women and traditional Ojibwe language and customs associated with having babies. Although the delivery is "hard enough for her to die," this birthing scene more than any other in the works of Erdrich and Dorris captures the mother's experience, told in her own words (104). Moreover, the language that Marie uses to describe her labor differs from that in the other birthings in its connotations of female body rhythms, "like small ripples," and the positive valence of pain in childbirth (101):

> Perhaps because of Rushes Bear [Margaret] or because of the thought of Fleur, the word that finally came wasn't English, but out of childhood, out of memory, an old word I had forgotten the use of, *Babaumawaebigowin.*
> I knew it was a word spoken in a boat, but I could not think how, or when or what it meant. It took a long time to repeat, to pronounce. Between times, the round syllables bobbed on my tongue. I began to lose track of where I was, in my absorption, and sometimes I saw myself as from a distance, floating calm, driven by long swells of waves. (102)

Marie describes the contractions and the pain without ever resorting to any of the negative connotations of the other birthing scenes discussed. In *A Dictionary of the Otchipwe Language*, R. R. Bishop Baraga defines *Babamiwebaognin* as "I am driven by the waves in a high sea" (61). Marie finds a way in language to think of her body as moving with the contractions, with the "waves" of pain. In other words, Erdrich writes through the body to discuss this particular birthing event. The pain does not disappear; Marie just works with it—not against it.

Not only does Marie have her Native Ojibwe language to help her during labor, but she also has the psychological support offered by Rushes Bear and Fleur. These two old Ojibwe midwives offer knowledge, comfort, and empathy that nobody else can give as well to her: "I put my hand out and Rushes Bear put her hand into it. I turned my face away when the next one came. She did not let go. Then I felt another person's hand [Fleur] come down, on my brow, and it was like the touch of peace, such mercy" (*Love* 102). Only women who have been through childbirth can empathize with what the mother experiences during labor. Marie cannot obtain this same kind of sensitivity from anybody else, male or female, and she definitely would not find it in a Western hospital setting, at least as portrayed in the Christine birthing scene. To find this kind of respect and encouragement, Erdrich creates an Ojibwe female support system through Rushes Bear and Fleur, women who have lived long enough to acquire the knowledge and wisdom necessary for successful midwifery, an example of female intellectual sovereignty.

The delivery concludes with a description that incorporates the Ojibwe language and customs, female support, and the mother's mental attitude of working with her body to deliver her baby:

> [W]hen I woke she [Rushes Bear] burned tobacco, sage, gave me some tea. I fell asleep again, and woke in darkness, laboring strong. Now I clung on to their voices, all I had, as they spoke to me in low tones, as they told me when to hold my breath and when to let it go. I understood perfectly although they spoke only

the old language. Once, someone used my word. *Babaumawaebigowin*, and I understood that I was to let my body be driven by the waves, like a boat to shore, like someone swimming toward a very small light. I followed directions and that way, sometime the next afternoon, my child was born. (103)

Marie's delivery does not begin to compare to Christine's in the hospital. Whereas Christine has interference from the white medical establishment in the name of helping her, Marie has the unobtrusive assistance of Rushes Bear and Fleur, who cooperate with her and follow her body's natural rhythms rather than trying to force her natural process. Whereas Christine resents any guidance from the stupid white nurse and arrogant white doctor, Marie welcomes the coaching from Rushes Bear and Fleur, which helps her find her way through the pain of the contractions.

The connection among Marie, Rushes Bear, and Fleur involved in this birth represents the maternal time of the birthing process: women continuously helping women to bear children. Rushes Bear and Fleur respect Marie's body and do not violate the mother's sense of power. They demonstrate this attitude of love and concern from beginning to end in their treatment of Marie: "I was washed and smoothed, put back underneath my covers in a fresh robe. The two women did all of these things so quickly, without wasting a motion, that I hardly knew that they were doing them. The tea made my eyes close, and I tried thanking them but those words came too slow" (104). This birthing scene captures the personal element that was missing from the earlier ones discussed. After having children of her own, Erdrich brings this richness of experience to fruition in writing this birthing scene, both the mother's personal expression of the experience and an appreciation for Ojibwe midwifery knowledge.

Erdrich's thoughts on the birthing process do not end in her fiction. In *The Blue Jay's Dance: A Birth Year*, she contemplates different aspects of her life: woman, mother, pregnancy, birthing, infant care, and writer. Because she does not separate these parts of her life, she observes their relationships and how they influence one another. Most notable is her list of literary mothers and their examples to her. She writes, "Women writers live rose nights and summer storms, but like the blue-eyed jumping spider opposite our gender, must often hold their mates and families at arm's length or be devoured" (143). That children are a concern of Erdrich's should be obvious from the numerous tellings of birthings in her writing. How she continues to deal with the responsibility of her own children and maintain her dedication to her writing presents a dilemma for which she seeks answers in the models of her literary mothers.

Erdrich wants and needs the same support that Marie receives from Rushes Bear and Fleur during delivery. Just as the midwives help the mother give birth to her child, Erdrich's literary mothers help her give birth to her writing by modeling how they manage to write and care for families: "I collect these women in my heart and often shuffle through the little I know of their experiences to find the toughness of spirit to deal with mine" (144). Erdrich knows these women understand the responsibilities of parenthood, the need to continue writing, and the inherent conflicts in those two arenas. Continuing with the "blue-eyed jumping spider" metaphor, she writes: "We are wolf spiders, carrying our babies on our backs, and we move slowly but with more accuracy. We learn how to conserve our energy, buy time, bargain for the hours we need" (143). From her "mother list," Erdrich finds the "toughness" she needs to give birth to writing that has a "savage coherence," the same kind of raw connection seen among the women during Marie's birthing scene (144, 147).

Toughness, not surprisingly, is a characteristic found in the makeup of Lulu Nanapush Lamartine, Fleur's daughter. In *Conversations with Louise Erdrich and Michael Dorris*, the editors Allan Chavkin and Nancy Feyl Chavkin characterize Lulu as "the central role" in *Love Medicine*, Erdrich's novel of contemporary life on and around the Ojibwe reservation on the North Dakota plains (xviii–xix). In an interview with Malcolm Jones, Erdrich describes Lulu as one of the "most compelling" characters in the novel, which spans fifty years, 1934–84, and follows the interconnected lives of the Kashpaw-Lazarre and Nanapush-Lamartine families. Jones comments on Lulu's function as a pivotal character: "Lulu Lamartine, part earth mother, part strumpet, is a human pivot round which much of the novel's action turns. As her complicated love life affects more than one household, so do the children from these households slowly uncover relationships of both blood and spirit that have their foundations in Lulu's actions" (Chavkin 7). In another interview, Shelby Grantham notes, "The wise and lusty Lulu is Dorris's favorite and has become for Erdrich 'one of the most real characters [she] know[s]'" (Chavkin 15). Although Erdrich and Dorris agree that Lulu represents one of the most interesting characters in the book, intentional fallacy discourages privileging Lulu's story over that of any of the other characters (Chavkin ix).

In fact, the novel's fourteen stories, some of which have been previously published independently as short stories, use multiple narratives and multiple points of view, which reflect an American Indian communal perspective rather than the singular first-person or omniscient point of view of a traditional protagonist. Erdrich elaborates on this storytelling technique as a "legitimate novelistic form":

> It also reflects a traditional Chippewa motif in storytelling, which is a cycle of stories having to do with a central mythological figure, a culture here [*sic*]. One tells a story about an incident that leads to another incident that leads to another in the life of this particular figure. Night after night, or day after day, it's

a storytelling cycle. It's the sort of thing where people know what they're going to say. They're old stories, but the stories have incorporated different elements of Non-Chippewa or European culture as they've gone on, so that sometimes you see a great traditional story with some sort of fairy tale element added to it. (Chavkin 4)

Therefore, although Lulu's may be a central role, her story fits into the cycle of stories and merits no more nor less attention than any of the others.

Although Erdrich finds Lulu an important character, when critics examine characters whose lives reveal the novel's themes of forgiveness and transformation, they tend to take a traditional Western approach and look at other characters who might seem more important in terms of plot development: June Morrissey, Marie Kashpaw's niece, whose death opens the novel; Lipsha Morrissey, Lulu's grandson and June's illegitimate son, who searches for his personal identity; Gerry Nanapush, Lulu's convict son and the father of Lipsha; Nector Kashpaw, lover of Lulu, husband to Marie Kashpaw, and adoptive father to Lipsha; and Marie Kashpaw, adoptive mother of Lipsha. Narrowing a discussion of the novel to one character must lie in the context of the way that particular person relates to the rest of the community. In looking at Lulu Lamartine as a strong woman, a model of tradition and survival, she must be seen as only one strand in a complex network of characters, stories, and themes.

Louise Flavin discusses female characters—June, Albertine, Marie, and Lulu—but she seems to see Lulu as only a vehicle through which Marie can achieve the status of sainthood: "Forgiving her husband's lover as she had forgiven her husband, caring for Lulu in her time of need, and sharing with her the loss of Nector make Marie a saint on earth" (62). Flavin seems to overlook that Lulu not only serves as a figure to be forgiven but, in fact, also needs to forgive others in her own life so that she, too, becomes transformed through the power of love.

James Ruppert, another critic who does not seem to offer a complete reading of Lulu, argues that Erdrich "is capable of satisfying two audiences at once, commenting on two cultural systems from a position of deep understanding and knowledge" ("Mediation" 229). He categorizes these two systems of differing cultural concepts of identity in the following ways: the white perspective reads the stories as psychological and social, whereas the American Indian perspective reads the stories as communal and "mythical." In the case of Lulu, Ruppert claims that Erdrich develops only her communal and psychological identities while ignoring her mythic or social story (238). On the contrary, Lulu is far more complex than Ruppert implies, and she has a mythic and social story.

Erdrich creates several allusions to Lulu's mythical identity. First, she is one in a continuing intergenerational family line of tricksters. Her mother,

Fleur, has trickster characteristics and so does her son, Gerry Nanapush (Velie 122).[5] Alan Velie describes the general characteristics of the trickster as one who "is amoral and has strong appetites, particularly for food and sex; [...] is footloose, irresponsible and callous, but somehow almost always sympathetic if not lovable" (122). Erdrich makes at least three references to the relationship between Lulu and food: savoring a hot salted potato (*Love* 79–80); remembering peaches, "sweet glowing crescents" that she ate at the school kitchen (83); and eating buttered bread sprinkled with sugar (113–14). Lulu's sensual relationship with food, especially sweets, reflects her trickster characteristic of a strong appetite for food to the point that she endures the pain of burning her fingers when eating the hot potato to satisfy her hunger.

In commenting on the stories about the mythological trickster, Catherine M. Catt notes that common Ojibwe tales include multiple and varied sexual adventures (73), and Lulu's "wild ways consist primarily of sexual liaisons with numerous men, a kind of greed that is typical of the Trickster" (77–78). Lulu certainly has the reputation of having sexual relations frequently and with whomever she chooses, as Beverly Lamartine notes when observing her eight children and wondering why they all look so different: "Some of them even had her maiden name. The three oldest were Nanapushes. The next oldest were Morrisseys who took the name Lamartine, and then there were more assorted younger Lamartines who didn't look like one another, either. Red hair and blond abounded; there was some brown. The black hair on the seven-year-old at least matched his mother's" (*Love* 109). Not only does Lulu have the physical evidence to prove that she is a sexually active and fertile woman who has had many different partners, but Erdrich also alludes to Chaucer's wife of Bath, known for her numerous husbands and overactive libido, when she describes Lulu's teeth as "the little gap-toothed smile" (115). Because the trickster has the ability to survive death, Catt characterizes him as a "metaphor for endurance or survival" (73). As a sexually active survivor, "Lulu is the bridge between the Nanapushes of *Love Medicine* and Old Man Nanapush of *Tracks*, linking the generations and carrying on the Trickster tradition" (78).

The Ojibwe story of "Naanabozho and the Gambler" establishes the precedent for tricksters to win in games of chance (Vizenor 129). Consequently, another trickster characteristic that Lulu displays involves her talents as a card player. Lipsha details his education in learning to cheat at the senior citizens center and credits Lulu with his knowledge: "The games were cheerfully cutthroat vicious, and the meanest player of them all was Lulu. She'd learned to crimp, that is, to mark your cards with little scratches and folds as you play, when she started losing her eyesight. It was just supposed to keep her even in the game, she said" (*Love* 348–49). Lipsha appreciates

Lulu's tutelage, especially when he meets his father, Gerry Nanapush, and watches him as he plays cards at King Kashpaw's apartment: "His fingers moved around the paper edges, found the nail nicks. His wolf smile glinted. There was a system to the crimping that he recognized. Those crimps were like a signature—his mother's. I'd only learned Lulu's system, not restyled it. 'She taught me,' I said" (354). Lulu passes on her card tricks to her son and grandson, an example of the knowledge that helps her survive even in recreational gambling.

Failure to acknowledge Lulu's numerous similarities to an Ojibwe mythical trickster figure denies her importance as a character steeped in tradition. According to Ruppert, American Indian readers can identify the "mythical" qualities of characters, and in the case of Lulu, they would see her trickster role as one that teaches moderation and what the appropriate behavior should be for the rest of the tribe/community. William Asikinack (Anishinabe) states that Ojibwe "stories were and continue to be told for a specific purpose: that is, to teach a lesson or moral to the listener/learner" (11). The women on the Ojibwe reservation would have been happier if Lulu had left their husbands alone. At a meeting of the tribal council, the people voice their feelings about Lulu: "'She's had the floor and half the council on it'"; "'All those Lamartine sons by different fathers'"; and "'Ain't the youngest Nector's?'" (*Love* 283–84). Lulu exemplifies a woman scorned by the community because she does not practice any self-control. As Catt notes, however, the trickster is powerful in a dual way:

> His lawless and anti-social behavior prohibits Trickster from belonging to the society of man, and although he propagates life, he is not a god in the sense of original creator. Because he is neither god nor man and may change shapes several times in the course of a story, Trickster's character will always remain ambiguous and paradoxical. His acts make all things possible—both good and evil; he will never represent only one thing to his observers. (75)

Despite the negative side of Lulu's sexual promiscuity, the resulting contempt and isolation she suffers from the other women in the community, the positive side is that she has many children. She not only has creative power to produce Ojibwe offspring but also has political power over the men, the fathers of her children, who are on the tribal council.

Because trickster characters are also humorous and lovable, Lulu has the final word at the tribal council meeting to discuss the government's money offer for the people to move off their land in order to build a modern tomahawk factory, which Lulu describes as "equipment of false value. Keepsake things like bangle beads and plastic war clubs" (*Love* 283). Not wanting to move off her land, Lulu threatens to name publicly the fathers of her children, a powerful ploy that results in a motion for a financial settlement for her: "'I'll name all of them,' I offered in a very soft voice. 'The fathers... I'll point them out for you right here.' There was silence, in which a motion was made from the floor. 'Restitution for Lamartine,' they said. 'Monetary settlement'" (284). Although Lulu's goal is not the settlement, her clever tactic is successful, an indication of her power, autonomy, and intellectual sovereignty. Single-handedly, she controls the entire room, and this power originates in her sexual relationships and the resulting children of those encounters.

Lulu's calculated behavior plausibly coincides with the traditional behavior of widows and frequent illegitimacy as described by Landes: "[Illegitimacy] is reprehensible and punished by the creditor sib, but the unconventional widow manages the situation with a coolness or a defiance that is never seen in the delinquent young girl. The widow, with her greater sexual sophistication, engages deliberately upon prospective illegitimacy, having decided that the personal satisfactions will outweigh institutional censure" (83). Lulu's sexual promiscuity is not necessarily an anomaly in the behavior of widows. As Lyman confirms, he was "the child of her wild grass widowhood and everybody knew it" (*Love* 305). She knows what she wants and does not concern herself with the consequences of public scorn but rather displays her autonomy, power, and intellectual sovereignty over her own sexual conduct. She knows how to respond to the community's criticism. Thus, there is a tension between her actions as an individual and the repercussions of those actions in the community. As Landes notes, the community would consider Lulu's behavior as "reprehensible," and they do.

Erdrich offers several elements that acknowledge Lulu's communal identity, and one of these overlaps into the area of mythical identity. Lulu is associated with the long ago Ojibwe "class of individuals known as tchissakiwinini, a person who knows spiritual magic, whose vocations and feats [are] similar to those of the eastern jugglers in such feats as rope-tying, knife-swallowing and fire-eating tricks" (Vizenor 81). Erdrich compares Lulu's domestic and culinary talents to those of a juggler/magician as she prepares dinner in the kitchen:

> She seemed to fill pots with food by pointing at them and take things from the oven that she'd never put in. The table jumped to set itself. The pop foamed into glasses, and the milk sighed to the lip. The youngest boy, crushed in a high chair, watched eagerly while things placed themselves around him. [...] by the time he [Beverly] looked up from dessert, they [the other children] had melted through the walls. The youngest had levitated from his high chair and was sleeping out of sight. [...] She turned to the sinkful of dishes and disappeared in a cloud of steam. (*Love* 119–20)

Lulu performs the ordinary tasks of preparing a meal, feeding the children, and cleaning up as a magician does in creating an illusion, complete with vanishing, levitation, and disappearing acts, and in the process she bewitches Beverly Lamartine, almost as if she has cast a spell to enchant him: "He had fallen" (120).

In addition, the tchissakiwinini had powers to communicate with the spirits and "bring tidings from departed friends" and know things "about absent friends or relatives, or whether a sick person would overcome sickness and live, or whether death would follow, and where one would find some lost and stolen articles" (Vizenor 82). Although people do not literally seek out Lulu for answers, they realize that she holds some kind of extrasensory perception. Lipsha knows that Lulu, "the jabwa witch" (*Love* 332), has the touch. He recounts her knowing what nobody else does, that the Defender girl was pregnant, that Old Man Bunachi had received an overpayment in his social security check, and that Germaine's commodity flour was worm-infested. Lipsha explains her talent for intuiting: "Insight. It was as though Lulu knew by looking at you what was the true bare-bone elements of your life" (332–34). Erdrich grounds Lulu's characterization in a strong base of Ojibwe legend and myth, and the association with the tchissakiwinini reinforces the importance of the communal heritage, intellectual sovereignty, that she portrays.

A second element of communal identity for Lulu resides in the traditional form of Ojibwe shame that surrounds her as a loose woman. Ojibwe custom dictates that to cut off a woman's hair means disgrace: "It was no uncommon occurrence among the women for a wife or rival crazed with love and jealous frenzy to seek an early opportunity to viciously attack the object of her hatred and if possible cut off her nose or her braids of hairs—the former object being to disfigure the face and the latter to disgrace the victim" (Vizenor 80).[6] Marie Kashpaw, the jealous wife who would have good reason to seek revenge on Lulu, her husband's mistress, does not act directly as the agent in the loss of Lulu's hair. However, in Nector's mind Marie watches as her unfaithful husband, in an ironic twist of fate, accidentally starts the fire that destroys Lulu's house (*Love* 144–45). Lulu loses her hair when she enters her burning house to save her son Lyman, and it never grows back (286, 116). Thus, in the context of Ojibwe tradition, Lulu's disgrace, result of her "wildness," remains with her always to remind her and others of what she represents (278).

A third communal element in Lulu's character lies in her role as a tribal elder who passes on knowledge to a younger person in search of personal identity. In "'homing' plots," William Bevis notes "a traditional tribal elder who is treated by the novel with great respect precipitates the resolution of the plot. [...] that elder is a relative—usually parent or grandparent—with whom the protagonist forms a new personal bond" (18). Similarly to *The Birchbark House*, in which the young Omakayas learns from Old Tallow her true parentage, in *Love Medicine* Lipsha learns from Lulu that his real parents are June Kashpaw and Gerry Nanapush (335). As a result, Lipsha forms a new relationship with Lulu: "I'll respect her from now on because her motives was correct in telling me. She made an effort. She told me about June in a simple way that let me know that grown-up business was meant" (333). Thus, Lulu plays an active role in Lipsha's survival because she helps him to connect with his roots and with his communal ties to the Ojibwe tribe. Once again, Lulu is powerful in her role of providing important information to her grandson.

Possibly more important than any of her other roles is Lulu's communal role as political activist but with the style of a libertine (Ruppert, "Mediation" 238). In her political activism with the American Indian Movement (AIM), she works to maintain respect for the tribe's traditions. Unlike those members who "grew out their hair in braids or ponytails and dressed in ribbon shirts and calico to make their point," Lulu refuses to give up her present-day style and continues to wear her "black spike heels and tight, low-cut dresses blooming with pink flowers. [...] her makeup, her lipstick, and what I used to call her 'Dear Abby' wig, a coal-black contraption of curls" (*Love* 303).[7] Lulu's style of dress represents an aspect of her sexuality that she never loses as she ages. Even when she is a grandmother, Father Jude Miller, a Catholic priest, falls in love with her at first meeting: "[I]t came clear to him because of a dream. Inside it—as at the school, where she wore her jingle dress of red and silver—Lulu stood with her lynx eyes and face of a hungry cat and her fan held rigid and upright like a weapon, like a shield. As she turned to him with an imperious and practical grace, he thought, So this is what it's like to fall in love" (*Last* 235). Lulu's power as a vibrant woman does not diminish with age, and she gives that same power to her political activism. She does not care about appearances of the past as if that alone will solve the problems facing the community today. She wants to make changes of substance that deal with contemporary issues of poverty and unemployment and still maintain a respect for the tribe's history. She cares as much for the land and for the future of the Ojibwe reservation as she does for days gone by; however, she will not give up her contemporary dress or her love life, autonomous choices that reflect her gender complementarity and intellectual sovereignty.

Lulu sees the project of a souvenir factory as an opportunity to produce "'museum-quality' artifacts" rather than "fake arrows and plastic bows, dyed-chicken-feather headdresses for children, dress-up stuff" (*Love* 303). When the tribal council first tries to force her off her land, she responds by telling them how superficial their plans are: "It was the stuff of dreams, I said. The cheap false longing that makes your money-grubbing tongues hang out. The United States government throws crumbs on the floor, and you go down so far to lick up those dollars that you turn your own people off the land"

(282). Erdrich does not seem to take sides in the debate between the traditionalists and the progressives, but she does offer a picture of the problems individuals face on the reservation today. Perhaps she simply suggests "the necessity of working out an identity in relation to one's past," as the novels of D'Arcy McNickle (Salish/Kootenai), N. Scott Momaday (Kiowa), Leslie Marmon Silko (Laguna Pueblo), and James Welch (Blackfeet) do (Bevis 43). Regardless, Lulu carries on a tradition of communal political activism that began with her "old uncle Nanapush who wrote the letters that brought [her] home" from the government school (*Love* 69), utilizing intellectual sovereignty as a means of survival.

Several incidents in Lulu's life help to explain her psychological identity. Ruppert posits that her childhood experience of discovering a dead body in the forest impacts her later adult personality ("Mediation" 238), which she describes as one of "wild and secret ways" (*Love* 276). Although that discovery may have contributed to the formation of her adult personality, there are other events equally important. Lulu believes that men and women come together to create a wholeness, life itself: "She [Rushes Bear] said the woman is complete. Men must come through us to live" (82). Lulu seems to create life through her sexual relations to avoid the death that she saw as a child. When she visits Moses Pillager to become pregnant, she lies and tells him that she is looking for her mother (78). At the time, Lulu does not realize the implications of what she says, but what she seeks may be her own mothering experience, a child of her own to love. Her journey and relationship with Moses Pillager demonstrate both intellectual sovereignty and gender complementarity.

Lulu's large family gives her the opportunity for a great deal of mothering. Having many children seems to assure Lulu that somebody will always love her and give her affection. Thinking about her sons in terms of the future, she says, "Those boys will always put meat on my table" (117). Of course, that does not happen in *Love Medicine* because Henry Junior dies, Lyman fights with his mother over the tomahawk factory, and Gerry leaves to avoid capture by the law. In fact, in old age Lulu does not have anyone to fulfill the role of provider or companion, except her grandson, Lipsha. Her rival Marie Kashpaw becomes a surrogate mother when she volunteers to assist Lulu after her eye operation. As Marie administers the eyedrops, Lulu "sees" the new relationship: "She swayed down like a mountain, huge and blurred, the way a mother must look to her just-born child" (297). In what appears to be a baptismal scene, a rebirth of sorts, Lulu becomes the child as Marie mothers her in this new mother-child relationship.

Another event that has far-reaching psychological effects in Lulu's adult life is her experience at the government boarding school. She claims that when she left home to go to school, she cried her last tear: "It was on that bus that Lulu Lamartine cried all the tears she would ever cry in her life. I don't know why, but after that they just dried up" (280–81). Lulu thinks that she does not become a "passionate, power-hungry woman" until later in life, but the truth is, she wants control from the time she leaves home (70). In school she runs away repeatedly, is punished, and longs to hear "the old language in [her] mother's mouth" (68). In order to assimilate and acculturate the American Indians, the boarding schools during this period cut the children's hair and forbade them to speak in their native tongues.[8] As a result, Lulu's efforts to gain control in her life evolve, in some degree, from having no power while at the boarding school.

Perhaps seeing the dead man in the forest does carry the most importance in the way Lulu's psychological identity develops, but leaving home for the government school and motherhood also contribute to Lulu's adult personality: "I loved what I saw. And yes, it is true that I've done all the things they say. That's not what gets them. What aggravates them is I've never shed one solitary tear. I'm not sorry. That's unnatural. As we all know, a woman is supposed to cry" (277). Erdrich makes the comparison between Lulu and cold metal: "[S]he had a mind like a wedge of iron" (135). To survive, Lulu has steeled herself against more pain. To release any sadness in her life, Lulu needs to feel the emotions that she has blocked. Only then will she be able to heal.

Moreover, Lulu needs to forgive Nector Kashpaw, who she believes deliberately set fire to her house. She admits that Nector is the one grudge in her life that she cannot let go, and she questions why people must endure such pain: "How come we've got these bodies? They are frail supports for what we feel" (281, 287). When Nector goes to her in the laundry room and in his senility asks for forgiveness, Lulu cannot refuse (293). After Nector dies, Lulu is ready to express her grief, but she still needs Marie Kashpaw to help her mourn with tears and to understand that her actions have affected another member of the community in a painful way. After Lulu's eye surgery, Marie volunteers to take care of her, and despite Lulu's claims that she has "no regrets," Marie responds, "Somebody had to put the tears into your eyes'" (296–97). No longer blind to another's feelings, Lulu finally understands "how another woman felt" (297). As Marie Kashpaw forgives Lulu, Lulu also learns forgiveness; she absolves those she holds responsible for some of the misfortune in her life. As Marie puts the eyedrops into Lulu's eyes, Lulu becomes new again and sees the world as a newborn does (297).

Lulu's social story deals with two images: the loose woman, or whore, and the traditional earth mother who bears children. From a white perspective, Lulu may seem to be promiscuous and to have no redeeming qualities. However, that would oversimplify her character because as an Earth mother, she perpetuates the race, an action that involves continuance and survival for the Ojibwe tribe. Beverly observes the tribal quality of Lulu's boys: "They moved in dance steps too intricate for the noninitiated eye to imitate or understand. Clearly they were of one soul. Handsome, rangy, wildly various, they were bound in total loyalty, not by oath but by the simple, unquestioning belongingness of part of one organism" (118). The boys' individual mixed-blood relationships are not what matters; the most important point is their sense of community.

Also, through the creative powers of bearing her children, Lulu has survived and flourished: "It was just that I kept my youth. They couldn't take that away. Even bald and half blinded as I am at present, I have my youth and my pleasure. I still let in the beauty of the world" (278). The women who survive in *Love Medicine* do so, in part, because of the mothering experience. Concerning motherhood, Paula Gunn Allen (Laguna Pueblo/Sioux) claims: "Maternity was a concept that went far beyond the simple biological sense of the word. It was the prepotent power, the basic right to control and distribute goods because it was the primary means of producing them. And it was the perfect sign of right spirit-human relationship" (*Sacred* 255). Thus, through the very nature of their bodies to create life, women like Lulu and Marie are able to cope with the sometimes-harsh realities of life on the reservation: alcoholism, unemployment, poverty, adultery, and suicide.

In *The Blue Jay's Dance: A Birth Year,* Erdrich writes about continuation while she awaits the birth of her daughter: "Perhaps it is odd to contemplate a subject grim as suicide while anticipating a child so new she'll wear a navel tassel and smell of nothing but her purest self, but beginnings suggest endings and I can't help thinking about the continuum, the span, the afters, and the befores" (8). Just as the storytelling cycle exists in spherical and cyclical dimensions, birth and death fit the circular concept. Motherhood provides the beginnings that help balance the endings in the never-ending circle of life. Lulu tells Lyman that he is her artistic creation: "'You're a work of art. You're my baby'" (*Love* 305). For Lulu, babies allow her to create and to continue life. Making babies helps assuage the pain of separation, abandonment, and death. Erdrich comments on the connections among mothers, daughters, and granddaughters: "Not only do I feel how quickly they are growing from the curved shape of my arms when holding them, but I want to sit in the presence of my own mother so badly I feel my heart will crack" (*Blue* 69). Lulu uses similar language to describe her separation from her mother: "I never grew from the curve of my mother's arms. I still wanted to anchor myself against her. But she had tore herself away from the run of my life like a riverbank. She had vanished, a great surrounding shore, leaving me to spill out alone" (*Love* 68). Children seem to cushion the separation from the mother as they continue a cycle of the mother-child relationship from one generation to the next.

As an example of how all the stories in *Love Medicine* connect, Lulu's story moves in and out of other characters' lives, sharing the problems and joys that affect all those who live on the Ojibwe reservation. Just as Lulu learns to forgive and is forgiven, she is transformed and reborn as other survivors in the novel go through transformations. Her characterization is complex with no simple explanations for everything she says and does. Nevertheless, her story is one of gender complementarity, one among the storytelling cycle; "A globe of frail seeds that's indestructible," a tribute to a woman's power, autonomy, and intellectual sovereignty (258).

Lulu continues her political activism in *The Bingo Palace*, a novel in which Erdrich resists the U.S. government's interference with the tribal sovereignty of the Ojibwe through the characters' legal actions, business ventures, education, and traditional ceremonies. She again allows different narrators to relate their stories but ends the novel the same as she begins, with the first-person plural voice—"we"—indicating the importance, continuity, and authority of the tribal communal voice and identity. Erdrich underscores Ojibwe intellectual sovereignty through the central role that females play in the community and the tribal economic ideologies as put forth by both female and male characters, a dual focus that provides a contemporary example of gender complementarity.

In the first chapter, "The Message," Erdrich makes clear the relationship among the power structures of the federal and state governments and the Ojibwe nation: "Lulu entered the post office beneath the flags of the United States, the Great Seal of North Dakota, and the emblem of [the] Chippewa Nation" (2). The signifiers of power structures all claim jurisdiction over the Ojibwe, in this case over the handling of the mail by the federal institution that controls how, when, and where written messages are sent. Lulu must work through the dominant culture to contact her grandson, Lipsha Morrissey. The reader must assume that she wants him to return to the reservation in case his father, Gerry Nanapush, contacts him for help, as he later does in the novel. Lulu mails him a photocopy of an out-of-date wanted poster of his father, a piece of government property that she has stolen from the post office. She does not, however, write anything on this copy or include any other already written words. Although she uses the mail system, she does not use written language but a picture to communicate her message. And her tactic is successful because Lipsha responds by returning home to the reservation. Lulu achieves her goal through her own design, a strategy that she knows will succeed. Therefore, she uses the government mail system in such a way that she does not totally abide by the conventional standards of communication but subtly challenges them. From an oral tradition, Lulu's undermining of a system of literacy, in effect, privileges other forms of communication.

Erdrich describes Lulu as a woman who "took on the day's business of running the tribe" (1). In this sense, Lulu's job description seems to be resisting, challenging, and undermining the U.S. government, as demonstrated by her manipulation of the mail service. In addition, she proudly displays the wanted poster in "a brass and crystal picture frame" in her home (4). Lulu's "message" to the government seems to be a mocking one; rather than feeling shame about her son's convict status, she takes great pride in displaying his wanted poster.[9]

Utilizing the government's own paperwork system, Lulu also manages to have Gerry transferred to "Minnesota's new maximum-security facility" (224). Taking advantage of the Indian Religious Freedom Act (1978), Lulu arranges for Gerry to be "near his medicine advisors" (224). En route Gerry escapes, and afterward Lulu dons her traditional clothes and calmly waits for the federal marshals to arrive, almost as if she has orchestrated this whole drama from the beginning when she stole the wanted poster at the post office and knew in advance what the outcome would be.

Just as there are competing signifiers of authority at the post office, there are similar jurisdictional issues when the federal authorities arrest Lulu and the Ojibwe police arrive (264). Whose jurisdiction should reign? Erdrich empowers the tribe to resist the U.S. government, when in front of all the media—reporters, photographers, rolling cameras—Lulu lets forth "the old-lady trill, the victory yell," which inevitably invites the rest of the tribe to join in with her (265). Lulu has learned what Warrior describes as "The Battle to Define 'Red Power'" during the period 1960–73: "[B]y defying state law in full view of media and law-enforcement personnel, these Natives were among those initiating a new way of bringing their political struggles to the attention of the United States and the world. The series of events in Washington and other places continues to affect Native politics and intellectual discourse to the present day" (26). Lulu employs the same tactics as Red Power activists: put one's face and cause on camera in front of the nation. As she plays a cat and mouse game during her interrogation, the communal narrator explains that the Ojibwe know without a doubt that Lulu has designed the whole scenario, intentionally exhibiting her intellectual sovereignty: "[T]hey finally take her in, arrest her, cart her off but with a kind of ceremony that does not confuse a single one of us, for she has planned it. And all so perfectly!" (*Bingo* 264). Tellingly, her "victory yell" reverberates with her conviction that she has successfully influenced the scenario between her and the agents of the government exactly as she intended.

Lulu's behavior indicates the important role played by Ojibwe women in a matriarchal society. In *We Have the Right to Exist*, Wub-e-ke-niew (Ojibwe) defines "matriarchial" [*sic*] as "a political system in which women hold political authority. *Ahnishinahbaeotjibway* [Ojibwe] society was and remains an egalitarian harmony of Sovereigns; I write of our political system as matriarchial because women elders, roughly translated into English as Clan Mothers, were accorded great respect and were thus quite influential" (252). Wub-e-ke-niew depicts how the concept of gender complementarity functions politically among the Ojibwe; women and men play equally important roles. As an elder of the Ojibwe tribe, Lulu has enormous power, and her struggle for sovereignty is a process to assert the power she possesses as a member of her community and as an individual who can make decisions that will affect all those on the reservation (Warrior 124). In her senior years, "she is full speed into politics" (*Bingo* 129). Her goal is to reclaim the reservation, which at one time was six times larger (129). Lulu deals with issues of "community and land as central categories," which Warrior claims contribute to an understanding of intellectual sovereignty (xxii–xxiii). Erdrich presents Lulu as an active elder who works tirelessly for the benefit of her family and community, a woman who accomplishes what others cannot and who, through her own intellectual sovereignty, earns the admiration of her tribe.

Lulu is not the only woman whom the community watches. Even the young women, who do not yet have a great deal of political power, display the beginnings of what they will become. Shawnee Ray Toose, for example, has the ability to dance the traditional dances at powwows and design clothing "with a Chippewa flair" (*Bingo* 73). Drawing on her heritage, she plans to earn money for her college education by going into business and selling her traditional clothing designs (67). Displaying her loving maternal side, Shawnee Ray also cares for her son, Redford, and makes traditional clothing for him (17). Shawnee Ray loves her family, and she trusts her sisters' deep affection for Redford enough that she leaves him in their care despite their admitted alcoholism.

When the authorities arrive to take Redford away, the aunts, Mary Fred and Tammy, do all they can to protect him. Their alcoholism, however, stands in the way; the authorities will not accept their return to traditional ways of healing. Since "receiving Jesus, they had not attended a single AA or Assembly of God meeting" (119). Shawnee Ray supports her sisters, who, turning away from the mainstream and Christian options for treating alcoholism, try their own tradition, reaffirming their intellectual sovereignty: "Mary Fred started going to sweat lodge with Uncle Xavier. He's been studying with an old man up north. He knows a lot about old-time medicine, and he's helping them out, maybe curing them" (120). Yet, in an act that challenges their intellectual sovereignty regarding healing rituals, tribal officer Leo Pukwan, social worker Vicki Koob, and Zelda Kashpaw arrive at the aunts' place with a warrant and court papers to take Redford from them. By drawing a detailed picture of the "benchmarks of alcoholic dependency within the extended family of Redford Toose" (175), Erdrich shows the reader how the dominant discourse works against Ojibwe intellectual sovereignty. The social system does not recognize the value of Redford's extended family nor the traditional healing knowledge for addiction; its only concern is with the symptoms of alcoholism. Rather than work with the family, the dominant institutions of law, social work, and medicine work against them.[10]

Still, the sisters do not quietly hand Redford over to the authorities without resistance. Erdrich never implies the child has been neglected or is in any danger. In fact, the two women are fearless in the face of authority in their efforts to protect their nephew. Tammy vehemently challenges the group—"You've got no business here"—and Mary Fred physically assaults Officer Pukwan by hitting him "flat on the chin with the butterfly buckle" (174, 177). They believe that their right to keep Redford should be judged on their blood relationship to the child and the fact that their sister left him in their care. They base their intellectual sovereignty in that knowledge: "'Redford loves me, loves us,' Tammy said. 'His mother's our fucking sister'" (174). There can be no doubt that these two aunts love Redford and would never let any harm come to him despite the fact that Redford might receive better care from Zelda.

Although Zelda is a controlling woman, perhaps as a result of her maternal heritage from Marie, she also is a powerful woman who the community agrees deserves much credit for her good works: "Zelda is the author of grit-jawed charity on the reservation, the instigator of good works that always get chalked up to her credit" (14). Discussing the value of powerful women to the health of the community, Gunn Allen states, "[T]he centrality of powerful women to social well-being is unquestioned" (*Sacred* 3). Clearly, the community recognizes the key role that Zelda plays in its own well-being. She works in the tribal office and has access to the records that indicate blood quantums; hence, she can arrange for Redford to be enrolled as a full-blood (17). This is an important act because of Redford's uncertain parentage, and one that will entitle him to tribal membership regardless of tribal and/or federally required blood quantums. Official tribal membership in addition to cementing his relationship to the community also will ensure that Redford is eligible to receive any benefits due the members of the tribe. Zelda helps Redford because she wants his mother to marry her half-brother, Lyman Lamartine.

In contrast to helping, Zelda also can hinder the social well-being of others in the community if she chooses. Lipsha wants to obtain a band card to prove that he is the son of Gerry Nanapush and June Morrissey and to settle his enrollment and entitlements, but Zelda stands in his way (128). Because Lipsha wants to be with Shawnee Ray, thus disrupting Zelda's plans, she works against him. Thus, working according to her own idea of what is best for Redford and Shawnee Ray, Zelda can help or hinder the social well-being of the community.

In helping Redford, Zelda arranges for him to have a naming ceremony. Maintaining connections with Native names carries importance for the Ojibwe, and Redford is not the only character who participates in this tradition. Zelda's daughter, Albertine Johnson, who is "going to be a doctor," takes a traditional name of a healer, Four Soul (118). Not only does Albertine find a way to move between both cultures in a lucrative profession, she also recognizes her past and the power of her gendered act in taking the name of a healer. In recognizing her ancestor, she exercises her power in resisting the power of those who supplanted Native names with Anglo names in boarding schools and on tribal rolls. Another instance that emphasizes the significance of names occurs when Fleur Pillager tells Lipsha to call himself what he is, not what the dominant culture says he must call himself according to its patriarchal and legal naming conventions: "If you're a Pillager then claim so. Don't say Morrissey" (133). In effect, Fleur encourages Lipsha to claim the other half of his legitimate heritage through his paternal grandfather, Moses Pillager. The importance of naming weaves itself throughout the novel and suggests another example of the intellectual sovereignty of the Ojibwe, one that attaches significance to tribal historical and cultural connections to names.

In addition to arranging the naming ceremony for Redford, Zelda practices another norm for her community, that of caring for its members. Although Zelda might be a domineering and interfering character, within the ideology of a tribal structure, her actions speak to the well-being of the whole group. She takes Shawnee Ray into her home and cares for her child, Redford. Erdrich writes about children in the context of tribal dynamics, about those whites normally would refer to as illegitimate children. Erdrich continues to see the children in terms of the Ojibwe attitude—intellectual sovereignty—that they are part of the community.

Zelda's mother, Marie Kashpaw, is another woman who has taken in motherless children and has raised them as her own; she has cared for June Morrissey and then June's son, Lipsha. As another powerful woman in the tribe, Marie also passes on knowledge and tradition to the younger generation. She gives the ceremonial pipe of her deceased husband, Nector Kashpaw, to Lipsha for two reasons: First, Marie has always "grant[ed] Lipsha extra"; and second, Nector taught Lipsha how to use it (27, 29). Erdrich continually points out how the Ojibwe value the children in the community by the way they raise them in an extended family, by the way they instill in them a sense of who they are through traditions and customs, and by the way they draw them back to the reservation and their connection to place.

In these ways, she resists any attempts by the dominant culture to weaken their self-image and worth. By focusing on the love, concern, and care that the community gives these children, Erdrich repeatedly stresses the validity of Ojibwe intellectual sovereignty and the way this ideology works to value this group.

Erdrich emphasizes the significance of the Ojibwe female when she uses the metaphor of the mother and child attached by the umbilical cord to illustrate the connection of the tribe to its past: "The red rope between the mother and her baby is the hope of our nation. It pulls, it sings, it snags, it feeds and holds" (6). The present generation is connected to the people in the past who came before, as the people in the present will be connected to those who arrive in the future. The knowledge that is carried from one generation to the next is in the blood of the mother, "the red rope," and that heritage nourishes the people with the notion of sovereignty. Traditions necessary for the survival and continuance of the Ojibwe can be found in that heritage that "pulls," "sings" "snags," "feeds," and "holds" the people together with their past. The entire community is imbued with this knowledge; Lipsha claims that Shawnee Ray represents "the best of our past, our present, our hope of a future" (13). She connects to the past through the traditional dances and the Ojibwe influence on her clothing designs, and she plans to continue that path in the future as she attends college and raises her son: "Her idea is to go into business. To pay for college, she wants to sell her original clothing designs, of which she has six books" (67). Shawnee Ray exercises Ojibwe intellectual sovereignty in her economic aspirations, and she has found a way to mediate successfully between both cultures, her own and the dominant mainstream. Lipsha predicts a bright future for her and imagines that she will earn graduate degrees and be brilliant in the arts or politics (152). Shawnee Ray is a concrete example of the younger generation connected to its past and moving forward into the future as educated individuals with unlimited possibilities in the arts, politics, and law.

Lipsha knows the assets of the Ojibwe women, and he defines those aspects when he thinks of Zelda: "When women age into their power, no wind can upset them, no hand turn aside their knowledge; no fact can deflect their point of view" (13). Lipsha describes, yet again, the intellectual sovereignty that the women possess. In true gender complementarity, the elder women have power that no one can deny or challenge; their knowledge cannot be ignored. Their ability to wield power can be seen in Lipsha's description of a typical setting of Indian men sitting together at a table in the bingo palace with the occasional presence of a woman who "through the force of her quiet, runs the entire show" (42). Even the power of a dead woman, June Morrissey, manifests itself throughout the novel. One night as a ghost she visits Lipsha at the bingo palace and offers him bingo tickets that will eventually help him win the van (54–55). Conveniently, she also appears during Gerry's getaway to chauffeur him away in her blue Firebird (258). Erdrich consistently affirms the importance of Ojibwe women through nothing less than the tradition of Ojibwe intellectual sovereignty.

Fleur is another example of how an influential female who possesses tribal knowledge can hold the responsibility for instructing a younger person from the next generation. Despite the community's disappointment over Fleur's choice of Lipsha as a successor, no one dares challenge her because she is an elder. Erdrich contrasts Fleur's lifestyle, living alone in "an old-time place, a low, long house of sawed beams tamped smoothly between with yellow gumbo clay, dug up from underneath the top soil," distanced from others on the reservation, with that of Lipsha, who has been "back and forth to the city," which has "weakened and confused" his "touch" (134, 7). Erdrich makes clear that Fleur, who "own[s] herself," has personal sovereignty; therefore, her ability to survive to such an old age seems to be, in part, due to her conscious detachment from the influence of the mainstream culture (140). Even after living in Minneapolis with all the materialist trappings of the dominant culture, she lets go of those things when she returns to the reservation (*Last* 265). Father Damien describes Fleur as having a "fierce intelligence," and her intellectual sovereignty serves her well. She is content to leave a life of luxury in the city and return to the reservation to a familiar lifestyle of camping, wearing men's overalls, and tying her hair back while she builds a cabin of poles and mud on her land (262).

Fleur had an agenda of revenge, and her work is now done in the city. She went there with the intention of finding John James Mauser, who through his lumber company managed to buy her land through payment-due notices. Fleur knows that she is capable of recovering her land through her own intellectual sovereignty: "Yes, these hands were clever. [...] She would find the ghost man, the thief, and be nothing around him. She would watch him, learn everything about him, and from the knowledge ascertain just how she could destroy him and restore her land" (187). Fleur is successful in that she finds Mauser, marries him, spends his money, has a son by him, leaves him, and returns to the reservation with the boy: "This son she brought home was the visible form of that revenge" (262).

Fleur manages to move between the two cultures and take what she wants. When the lumber company finished clearing the trees on Pillager land, it was put up for sale and bought by the former Indian agent, Jewett Parker Tatro, who "cheated so carefully and persistently" (*Bingo* 142). Fleur recovers Pillager land around the lake by playing cards with Tatro: "Fleur was never one to take an uncalculated piece of revenge. She was never one to answer injustice with a fair exchange. She gave back twofold. When the Agent got up from his chair she would have what he owned" (145). Fleur recovers land that originally belonged to the Ojibwe. In doing so, she sets an example for the rest of the community and highlights the importance of keeping the land with which the Ojibwe and their identity are entwined. Additionally, she accomplishes the reacquisition through her own intellectual sovereignty, an act that flies in the face of the U.S. government, which tolerated those who through questionable means acquired the Indian lands in the first place.

As the elder who instructs Lipsha and Lyman, Fleur represents the wise woman who can instill in the younger generation the wisdom and knowledge needed for future economic ventures, particularly any involving land and community. Gender complementarity involves the balanced contributions of both genders to the community, and to discuss the female characters in Erdrich's work, it is helpful to look at them in relation to the male characters. These male characters deal well with strong powerful women and are not intimated by them but learn from them. Lipsha goes to Fleur, asking for a love medicine to secure the love of Shawnee Ray Toose, and in a vision Lyman receives instructions from Fleur about investing in land. Both Lipsha and Lyman court Shawnee Ray, but she also is a strong woman who has plans of her own. She wants to go to college, design Ojibwe-accented clothing, and dance at powwows to earn money for school. Lipsha and Lyman have no choice but to stand by and defer to Shawnee Ray's plans. The male characters must respect and work with the independent female characters who lead autonomous lives.

Lipsha needs Fleur as a role model because he does not occupy a particular political or economic position in the social structure of the tribe. When Lipsha attends a winter powwow, Erdrich describes his role in terms of negatives, what he is not:

> He was not a tribal council honcho, not a powwow organizer, not a medic [...].
> He was not a member of a drum group, not a singer, not a candy-bar seller. Not a little old Cree lady [...], not one of us. He was not a fancy dancer [...], not a traditional, not a shawl girl [...]. He was not our grandfather, [...]. He was not even one of those gathered at the soda machines [...]. He was not the Chippewa with rings pierced in her nose or the old aunt with water dripping through her fingers or the announcer [...]. (9–10)

If the Ojibwe are to continue building a community based on their intellectual traditions, perhaps Lipsha needs to take a more active role by assuming responsibility for a contribution to his people. What can he offer the tribe? Lipsha notes that his "one talent in this life is a healing power [he got] passed down through the Pillager branch of [his] background" (64). If his gift is his "touch," then how can he nurture his talent and support the health of his community? Perhaps Lipsha's quest is not to find a way to make Shawnee Ray love him or to win the bingo van, but to find a way to make his people love him again, for they are disappointed with his accomplishments to date: "We have done so much for him and even so, the truth is, he has done nothing yet of wide importance" (7). Reestablishing connections with the women on the reservation, such as Fleur, who can teach him, might be exactly what Lipsha needs to help him rekindle his healing power.

Lipsha learns from his grandmother, Lulu Lamartine, how to concentrate when playing bingo and how to be "one-minded in [his] pursuit of a material object" (63). But he begins to think only of himself and buys into the greed of capitalism, charging for his healing ability and consequently losing his "touch" (64). Lipsha must do his part to ensure the welfare and continuance of the tribe. He knows he belongs to the community, but he has not discovered his place within that structure. He says, "I am [...] back where I belong without a place to fit" (11). Lipsha must find his niche because he realizes that place is important in the whole picture of his life; he will always be connected to his home, and this knowledge is part of his intellectual sovereignty. He states, "I have this sudden knowledge that no matter what I do with my life, no matter how far away I go, or change, or grow and gain, I will never get away from here" (21). Knowing the importance of returning home and the connection to place indicates an aspect of Lipsha's maturing process. As William Bevis notes, "'[I]dentity,' for a Native American is not a matter of finding 'one's self,' but of finding a 'self' that is transpersonal and includes a society, a past, and a place. To be separated from that transpersonal time and space is to lose identity" (19). In order to use his "touch" appropriately, Lipsha will have to reconstruct himself again in relationship to his community, not as an isolated individual. Any economic gain from his talents must benefit the community.

Unlike Lipsha, Lyman Lamartine, Lulu's youngest son, represents the way the Ojibwe exercise their intellectual sovereignty and still accommodate the dominant power structure. Lyman has learned the language of dealing with non-Natives. He is "a dark-minded schemer, a bitter and yet shaman-pleasant entrepreneur who skipped money from behind the ears of Uncle Sam, who joked to pull the wool down, who carved up this reservation the way his blood father Nector Kashpaw did, who had his own interest so mingled with his people's that he couldn't tell his personal ambition from the pride of the Kashpaws" (5). The Ojibwe need people like Lyman who can maneuver in both cultures; he has "a nose for scams and schemes" (15). Lyman is the kind of entrepreneur who has transformed a small bingo operation into "something bigger, something [they] don't know the name of yet, something with dollar signs that crowd the meaning from [their] brain"

(15). Even though Lyman may be thinking of his own financial interests, his development of the bingo palace (and the tomahawk factory in *Love Medicine*) benefits the community because, in addition to money from the residents on the reservation, it draws in money from outside sources, that is, non-Natives. Instead of the whites' exploiting the American Indians, as history has shown is usually the case, the Ojibwe can legally take money from the whites.

Business-minded people like Lyman are necessary for the economic growth of the Ojibwe because there are other problems that the Indians must deal with, as Lipsha explains: "From day one, we're loaded down. History, personal politics, tangled bloodlines. We're too preoccupied with setting things right around us to get rich" (17). Just trying to attend to other pressing and important issues requires a great deal of energy, and Lipsha rightly appraises the situation by noting that dealing with current problems on the reservation does not necessarily leave enough time to focus on the economics of the community. Yet, Lyman's bingo palace "is doing bigger business and contributing to the overall economic profile of [their] reservation, as it says in his brochures" (103). Lyman sees himself as "an ID picture composed of economic tribulations and triumphs," as "drive" and "necessity," because there is no other person who can "plan his plans, lift his voice, scheme, and bring the possibilities into existence" (148).

Lyman exemplifies survival. Already, he survived the river when his older brother, Henry Lamartine, Jr., drowned (*Love* 193). So when he has a vision of Fleur's talking to him about how to invest his money in land, he can only foresee success and survival for himself and the community. In matriarchal fashion of gender complementarity, Fleur, the Old Lady, *Mindemoya*, has the wisdom that results from living a long life, one filled with dealing with the U.S. government; she knows the importance of holding on to the land, how easily one can lose it, how difficult it can be to recover it. Fleur tells Lyman, "*Land is the only thing that lasts life to life. Money burns like tinder, flows off like water, and as for the government's promises, the wind is steadier*" (*Bingo* 148). She goes on to warn him, "*This time, don't sell out for a barrel of weevil-shot flour and a mossy pork*" (148), and finally she details how to use the government and federal trust land to his own advantage: "*Put your winnings and earnings in a land-acquiring account. Take the quick new money. Use it to purchase the fast old ground*" (149). Fleur advises with intellectual sovereignty, and Lyman has exactly the kind of business mind that can carry out Fleur's instructions. Lipsha reasons that Fleur wants "a clever operator who can use the luck that temporary loopholes in the law bring to Indians for higher causes, steady advances" (221). Lyman shows his talent for acquiring investors in his business projects when he convinces Lipsha to let him handle the saving and investing of his bingo winnings (101). Lyman is a man who can outmaneuver the U.S. government, and he has skills that benefit the tribe.

As Lyman receives Fleur's counsel about land, Lipsha gleans advice about land in his vision quest from the "mother of all skunks," who says, "This ain't real estate" (200). Although the scene is rendered in a comic fashion, the message still carries a cautionary warning: The Ojibwe "reservation is not real estate" (221). Lipsha realizes that a casino would provide the economy with money that the reservation needs: "You have to stay alive to keep your tradition alive and working" (221). Nevertheless, he also can see beyond the initial success of a casino; he sees the possible problems that could evolve from "the low of bingo life" (221). Lipsha knows from experience how he lost his "touch" when he started to charge for it. The same could be true of a casino: "[L]uck fades when sold. Attraction has no staying power, no weight, no heart" (221). The real heart of a casino—the core that is left after the superficial glitz fades—has "no substance, there's nothing left when the day is done but a pack of receipts" (221). Lipsha's concerns temper the confidence that Lyman has in his business venture, and his foresight also deserves critical consideration by the tribe. By acknowledging the visions of both Lyman and Lipsha, another version of complementarity, the Ojibwe can plan for the possible consequences of such a successful operation, including any unforeseen problems. In this way, the Ojibwe can hope to prevent potential interference from the U.S. government and continue to exert their own intellectual sovereignty, of which they are quite capable.

Jeanette Armstrong of the Okanagan Nation describes the *enow'kin* process as one in which all tribal members have a voice and must have an opportunity to express their ideas in all tribal decision making. She maintains that

> [t]he underlying principle is respect of each other and caring for one another. That means taking responsibility for listening to the other, hearing the other from their perspective, and understanding why it is important for them and then seeing how it comes up against your perspective. Where those two things come into conflict, you take the responsibility to find a way to make it more comfortable for the other person. (Thorpe 237)

Similarly to the *enow'kin* process, Erdrich writes, "We do know that no one gets wise enough to really understand the heart of another, though it is the task of our life to try" (*Bingo* 6). She creates a dialogue among the Ojibwe in which each person has a voice that must be heard. Thus, the reader hears the characters' different opinions about reservation lands and the proposed casino resort, the pros and cons of developing new economic interests that have the potential for both positive and negative results. "There's lots of ways to make money," Lyman concedes, "and gambling is not the nicest, not the best, not the prettiest. It's just the way available right now" (103). Only after considering all the issues will the tribe have the necessary information to make the best possible economic decisions for the community. Warrior discusses the importance of American Indians' establishing a criticism based on a framework of intellectual sovereignty to examine their own culture. He argues that this criticism must be open-ended with connections to the land and community and be capable of flexibility, much like an ongoing process, in order to accommodate the many different kinds of American Indian writing being produced today (44). Erdrich permits the reader to observe this critical process advocated by Warrior, one tied to the land and community.

In *The Bingo Palace* Erdrich suggests that the Ojibwe can survive and enact their own intellectual sovereignty, particularly in their economic dealings, whether those are fashion designing, healing, or gambling. That intellectual sovereignty seems to include critical self-reflection. Hence, Lipsha concludes, "To stay awake in life as much as possible—that may be the point!" (99). In other words, the Ojibwe must maintain self-awareness, a deliberate consciousness, of their internal situations (Warrior 97). As Lulu asserts about Lipsha's generation, the "young Indians of today are living on a different planet" (*Bingo* 130). To survive with the dominant culture continually attempting to marginalize the American Indians and to interfere with their economic ventures, the Ojibwe can base their community on their intellectual sovereignty and an understanding of their ties to the past, tradition, and place. "[T]he newly built tribal mall, a complex erected to keep cash revenues in local hands," illustrates an example of cash flow taken into and kept on the reservation, the result that Lyman hopes to realize with a casino (29). These examples show how the Ojibwe can maintain control of their own economics, knowing what will work best for their own situation in terms of earning income. Erdrich offers her characters economic survival and continuance in the face of sometimes overwhelming challenges, and she does so on the basis of the dynamics of gender complementarity and Ojibwe intellectual sovereignty.

In Erdrich's most recent publication in the North Dakota cycle of novels, *The Last Report on the Miracles at Little No Horse,* the narrative spans the life of Agnes DeWitt during the years 1910–97, as she reconstructs herself into Father Damien Modeste, a Catholic priest who ministers to the Ojibwe on the remote reservation of Little No Horse. Although Father Damien is a white woman, looking at how Erdrich deals with issues of gender construction sheds light on how she sees the roles of strong, powerful women. Because there is no other way for Agnes to minister the sacraments of the Catholic Church, she has no choice but to disguise herself as a man for the major part of her life, some 84 years, and live the "most sincere lie a person could ever tell" (61).

Agnes begins her transformation when she changes places with the deceased Father Damien Modeste (The First) and dresses in his clothing: "his cassock, and the small bundle tangled about him, a traveler's pouch tied underneath all else, Agnes put on in the exact order he had worn them. A small sharp knife in that traveler's pocket was her barber's scissors—she trimmed off her hair and then she buried it with him as though, even this pitiable, he was the keeper of her old life" (44). Her conversion begins from the outside with the accoutrements of the priest and the cutting of her hair. As the title of this section, "The Exchange," suggests, Agnes makes an equal trade: her former identity for the priest's. Appropriately, she buries her past along with Father Damien (the First) and is resurrected as the new Father Damien II. Agnes maintains her female sexuality, but cross-dresses, or changes her outward physical appearance with male clothing and hairstyle.

As people respond to Agnes-as-a-priest, she soon realizes the different ways women and men are treated. Kashpaw drives her to the reservation, and she notices that he treats her better than she has ever known: "[T]he driver treated her with much more respect as a priest than she'd ever known as a nun. He was deferential, though not uncomfortable. [...] So this is what a priest gets, heads bowing and curious respectful attention! Back on the train, people also had given Father Damien more privacy" (62). Even as a nun, Agnes never experiences the kind of deferential treatment that the power and authority of the office of a priest yields her. She rationalizes that she thoroughly enjoys the newfound importance because as a human being, she deserves this kind of consideration. She feels comfortable on the receiving end of such thoughtfulness, as if it were perfectly natural for all human beings to treat one another this way. Erdrich implies that in an ideal world both women and men would have the power and authority enjoyed by those in positions like that of a priest, and they would also be treated as equals, at least as they would be in a relationship structured by gender complementarity in which both genders are valued. Thus, after the initial change of costume, Agnes learns that as a priest, she can behave as though people will take her seriously; that results in the beginning of her mental adjustment, an internal one, to accompany her new external identity.

This change of thinking happens quickly and naturally, and by the time Agnes leaves Kashpaw to finish walking to her new vocation and home, she has undergone a complete metamorphosis in her view of her new identity in relationship to her future and surrounding environment: "[S]he was essential to a great, calm design of horizonless meaning" (65). Anything is possible, for there are no restrictions on how Agnes can construct herself. Any insecurity that she might have felt about her decision to become Father

Damien is put to rest once and for all: "In that period of regard, the unsettled intentions, the fears she felt, the exposure she already dreaded, faded to a fierce nothing, a white ring of mineral ash left after the water has boiled away. [...] Father Damien Modeste had arrived here. The true Modeste who was supposed to arrive—none other. No one else" (65). Agnes has no doubts about her new skin that houses the true spirit of Father Damien, a priest who wants to attend to the spiritual needs of the Ojibwe. So convinced is she of the rightness of her reembodiment, the stamp of approval from a higher power seems to be implied. In her self-description as the "true Modeste who was supposed to arrive," Agnes proclaims a truth that is predestined.

Although Agnes has committed herself totally to her new identity, she still needs to convince the community, to prevent any scandalous discoveries of her impersonation. She makes a list of gendered behaviors with which she must conduct herself in a masculine style in order to make believers of those around her:

Some Rules to Assist in My Transformation
1. Make requests in the form of orders.
2. Give compliments in the form of concessions.
3. Ask questions in the form of statements.
4. Exercises to enhance the muscles of the neck?
5. Admire women's handiwork with copious amazement.
6. Stride, swing arms, stop abruptly, stroke chin.
7. Sharpen razor daily.
8. Advance no explanations.
9. Accept no explanations.
10. Human occasional resolute march. (74)

In verbal exchanges with others, body language, attitude, and daily rituals, Agnes views the priest's life as one that creates an hierarchy with him in the superior position of knowledge and power. For example, rule number five suggests that any handiwork that women do must be complimented profusely as if to compensate for the women's subordinate position in life, or lack of knowledge and power. Obviously, the work of the women is not valued nearly as much as the work of the men. The Western view of relations between men and women, grounded in the Christian context of the Catholic Church, dictates the way Agnes sets up her rules to assist in her transformation, a system contrary to that of gender complementarity.

Agnes comes to understand that all identities involve the construction of gender politics. She has to ask herself, If she can so easily create a new masculine identity for herself, then how real was her previous identity of Sister Cecilia? "Between these two, where was the real self? It came to her that both Sister Cecilia and then Agnes were as heavily manufactured of gesture and pose as was Father Damien. And within this, what sifting of identity was she? What mote? What nothing?" (76). Agnes understands that the true core of a person does not necessarily have anything to do with inherent gender traits but rather is more of an androgynous entity that she can construct however she chooses. This epiphany leads to her realization that she can contain a multitude of personalities, and moreover, she can choose how she will construct them: "She decides to miss Agnes as she would a beloved sister, to make of Father Damien her creation. He would be loving, protective, remote, and immensely disciplined. He would be Agnes's twin, her masterwork, her brother" (77). Agnes wants to create a priest who includes more feminine qualities of nurturing, thereby creating a man of God who represents a more balanced construction of both gender traits, a personality that more closely resembles the structure of gender complementarity.

Agnes's combination of gender traits becomes clear in looking at her sense of fearlessness and her menstrual cycle. First, she believes that because she has survived "the robbery, the chase, the bullets, and the flood, then transformed herself to Father Damien, she could not be harmed. That inner assurance would make her seem fearless, which would in turn increase the respect she won among the Anishinaabeg" (78). Agnes's experiences contain valued masculine traits of adventurousness and courage, which lead to her acquiring a sense of boldness due to surviving such catastrophic events. She knows that her inner confidence emits an aura of courage that she might not have gained had she not lived through her previous escapades. Second, in dealing with the "misery of concealing the exasperating monthly flow that belonged to her past but persisted into the present," Agnes is constantly reminded of her female sexuality (78). In order to simplify her life and ease the difficulty of hiding her menses, allowing her to continue her work, she prays for an end to her monthly "affliction." Whether God answers her prayers or mind predominates over body, her periods end. When Agnes receives her wish, however, she feels ambivalent about losing a most female reminder of herself: "[S]he felt a pang, a loss, an eerie rocking between genders" (78). A sense of both gender constructions, Agnes and Father Damien, is always present. Agnes successfully negotiates both personalities, no small feat, knowing that she will always be a woman but needs to be a man in order to do the public work of a priest.

Perhaps the most significant example of Agnes's handling of both genders takes place when she prays: "Agnes and Father Damien became one indivisible person in prayer" (109). The complete union of her two personalities demonstrates the androgyny at her core, or more precisely, her spirit, which is neither female nor male, but pure essence of her being. In communion with God, Agnes rises above her outward appearances and her hidden identity to move closer to a more perfect state of grace: "Sorrows, confusions, pains of flesh and spirit, all melted into the sweet trance of the moment" (110).

Although Agnes exercises extreme measures to hide her female characteristics—binding her breasts and no longer having a monthly flow—there are people who either suspect or know that she really is not a man. Agnes assumes that Fleur knows: "Nothing slipped by her, so he accepted that she'd known his secret from the beginning, and it hadn't mattered" (264). The Ojibwe call a woman-man an *ikwe-inini*, but they do not use the term with any ridicule or disrespect, and perhaps this explains why Fleur never mentions Agnes's secret (153). When Agnes takes medication to numb the pain of the end of her relationship with Father Gregory Wekkle and sleeps for days, Mary Kashpaw also discovers the truth about her by noticing that she has no whiskers growing on her face. Rather than ignore the truth, Mary goes to great lengths to keep it hidden, watching over Agnes and pretending to shave her, so nobody will suspect: "Every morning after that she heated a kettle of water, readied the mug of shaving soap, dipped in the brush, stropped the razor, and was seen ostentatiously, to be putting these things aside just as Sister Hildegarde arrived" (212). Once Mary knows, she goes beyond not caring about Agnes's deception and becomes even more devoted to her. In fact, of all those who know her true identity, only Sister Leopolda threatens to expose Agnes for who she really is: "I know what you are. And if you banish me or write to the bishop, *Sister* Damien, I will write to him too" (273). Nothing comes of Sister Leopolda's accusation, and she is the only character who ever threatens Agnes's reputation.

In Agnes's initial contact with the Ojibwe, Kashpaw, her driver, "sensed something unusual about the priest from the first":

> Something wrong. The priest was clearly not right, too womanly. Perhaps, he thought here was a man like the famous Wishkob, the Sweet, who had seduced many other men and finally joined the family of a great war chief as a wife, where he had lived until old, well loved, as one of the women. Kashpaw himself had addressed Wishkob as grandmother. Kashpaw thought, *This priest is unusual, but then, who among the zhaaganaashiwug is not strange?* (64)

If Kashpaw perceives Agnes as strange because she does not have the typical characteristics of a male priest, he does not necessarily think less of her for that but instead explains it away as just another quirk of white people. According to his understanding of effeminate men, there is a socially accepted place for them within the tribal community. His attitude represents that of most of the Ojibwe who know Agnes's true identity and accept her for who she is.

Although Father Gregory Wekkle knows Agnes's secret and even makes love in their youth to the "skin that covered the body that housed two beings," on his return visit years later, he eventually treats her with subtle condescension, resorting to deeply ingrained socialized hierarchical behaviors among priests and women (208, 303). Agnes realizes that he is unaware of his patronizing attitude even though he is still attracted to her: "Practice had perfected her masculine ease, and age had thickened her neck and waist so that the ambiguity which had once eroticized her now was a single and purposeful power that, heaven help him, he found more thrilling" (301). Despite his sincere feelings for Agnes, she resents his assumption that he is entitled to a private part of her that "only she was meant to possess" (303). In other words, Agnes will not allow any other person to have power over her as if she is less than he.

Unlike Father Wekkle, Nanapush, an established tricksterlike character, knows that Agnes is a woman, but he does not care that she wants to live her life as a man. He only uses his knowledge of her true identity when he wants to distract her enough so that he can win at a game of chess. He startles Agnes by bolding asking why she has spent her life acting as a man, and once the truth is out in the open, Agnes actually feels relieved as the heavy burden of deceit that she has carried for years lifts (230–32). Nanapush explains that he has known all along, but he still wonders why she has chosen this path: "'Are you a female Wishkob? My old friend [Kashpaw] thought so at first, assumed you went and became a four-legged to please another man, but that's not true. Inside that robe, you are definitely a woman'" (231). What most impresses Agnes is that her unveiling does not really matter to Nanapush; he merely has used it to remove her bishop:

> "You tricked me, old man."
> "Me!" said Nanapush. "You've been tricking everybody! Still, that is what your spirits instructed you to do, so you must do it. Your spirits must be powerful to require such a sacrifice."
> "Yes," said Agnes, "my spirits are very strong, very demanding, very annoying." (232)

The Ojibwe embrace Agnes as who she is, reflecting an attitude of acceptance embedded in gender complementarity, valuing people for themselves and the work they do, unlike the Western Christian attitude evinced in Father Wekkle's treatment of Agnes, one of hierarchy and possession. As one trickster to another, Nanapush understands that Agnes had no choice but to obey her spirits and live as a priest, exercising her own form of independence.

From 1847 in *The Birchbark House* to 1997 in *The Last Report on the Miracles at Little No Horse*, Erdrich writes consistently about strong female characters. Whether the female is seven-year-old Omakayas, who survives smallpox and recovers from the death of her baby brother, or Old Tallow, who rescues her and assists in her recovery, the characters are steeped in Ojibwe tradition, gender complementarity, and intellectual sovereignty, which all contribute to their survival. When the characters are mothers surviving difficult births, such as Fleur, Pauline Puyat, Celestine James, Christine Taylor, or Marie Kashpaw, they depend on the toughness of spirit that Erdrich ascribes to the power of laboring women and in many cases to the intellectual sovereignty associated with traditional midwifery. Whether the woman is a widowed mother such as Lulu Lamartine or a Catholic priest such as Father Damien, the political implications are that women can live autonomous lives and succeed in whatever kind of work they choose. Erdrich creates no limitations that strong women cannot overcome but instead provides them with a "great, calm design of horizonless meaning" (*Last* 65), allowing them to engage in an endless number of possibilities for their lives.

CHAPTER 6

"'I'm Talking Like a Twentieth-Century Indian Woman'"

Contemporary Female Warriors in the Works of Sherman Alexie

Sherman Alexie, who is of Spokane and Coeur d'Alene descent, has laughingly described himself as the "Indian du jour" because of his current high-profile status and popularity as an acclaimed American Indian writer, but he acknowledges that someday someone else will replace him (Interview Chato). His immodesty does not reflect an overactive ego but rather a realistic assessment of his position among contemporary Indian authors. In the June 1999 summer fiction issue of *The New Yorker,* Alexie's name was among the "twenty best young fiction writers in America today" (Buford 65), and in 1996, he was picked as one of *Granta* magazine's "Twenty Best American Novelists under the Age of Forty." Alexie's writing is known, for among other things, portraying the realities of life for contemporary reservation and urban Indians—unemployment, poverty, alcoholism, death, humor, popular culture, history, and anger, to name just a few of the themes.

Alexie also writes strong women into his works. In an interview with the brothers John Bellante and Carl Bellante, Alexie presents his views on the importance of the role of women in culture when asked "Precisely what about white culture makes [him] so angry":

> Pretty much everything patriarchal. [. . .] There used to be a sense of matriarchal power [among Indian societies]. That's not the case anymore. Not in my tribe

anyway. We've resisted assimilation in many ways, but I know we've assimilated into sexism and misogyny. [...] As with anything else, women always have power. Women are the creators. We get into trouble when we try to deny that. So I'm angry toward this patriarchal country that creates an environment totally hostile toward women. (Bellante 15)

By critiquing a U.S. patriarchal culture that subordinates and devalues women, Alexie privileges the inherent power in women's roles as creators. His attitude of valuing the role of women and their power and seeing the negative consequences of ignoring their contributions to the culture represents the ideology of gender complementarity, in which there is no hierarchy of the genders but rather an equal regard for the roles and work of each other. Alexie further states, "Indian women are the reason Indian cultures have survived" (Interview Chato). Unlike Leslie Marmon Silko (Laguna Pueblo) and Louise Erdrich (Ojibwe), who prefer to let their writing make political statements, Alexie openly acknowledges his political position with regard to the way women are treated in the United States. This chapter examines how Alexie portrays strong Native female characters, both within and beyond the boundaries of traditional heterosexual roles, as transmitters of culture, marriage partners, college students, and political activists.

Sherman Joseph Alexie, Jr., was born on October 7, 1966, in Spokane, Washington, to Sherman Joseph Alexie, a Coeur d'Alene, and Lillian Agnes Cox Alexie, of Spokane, Salish, Kootenay, and Colville (all are Salish tribes) descent. Alexie grew up on the Spokane reservation in Wellpinit, Washington, where he is an enrolled member through his mother. While attending the Wellpinit School, he was assigned a textbook in which his mother's name was written. After that discovery, he chose to attend the high school off the reservation in Reardan, Washington, where he was convinced that he would receive a better education; the theme appears repeatedly in his work. He went on to Gonzaga University in Spokane on scholarship from 1985 to 1987 and transferred to Washington State University (WSU) in Pullman, where he studied from 1988 to 1991. In 1995, WSU awarded Alexie his degree in American studies and an Alumni Achievement Award although he had left the program in 1991, three credits short of a degree. Alexie began writing poetry in a workshop, in which he was encouraged by his teacher, Alex Kuo, at WSU. Soon after leaving WSU, Alexie received the Washington State Arts Commission Poetry Fellowship in 1991 and the National Endowment for the Arts Poetry Fellowship in 1992. Numerous literary nominations, honors, and awards would follow as Alexie began a prolific writing and publishing career.[1]

Alexie soon published his first collections of poetry, *The Business of Fancydancing* (1992) and a limited edition of *I Would Steal Horses* (1992), which won Slipstream's fifth annual chapbook contest. These were followed by a collection of short stories in *The Lone Ranger and Tonto Fistfight in Heaven* (1993), for which he received a PEN/Hemingway Award for Best First Book of Fiction, the Great Lakes College Association Best First Book of Fiction Award, and a Lila Wallace–Reader's Digest Writers' Award. In that same year, he also published two more volumes of poetry, *Old Shirts and New Skins* (1993) and *First Indian on the Moon* (1993); he later published two more limited editions of poetry, *Seven Mourning Songs for the Cedar Flute I Have Yet to Learn to Play* (1994) and *Water Flowing Home* (1995). For his novel *Reservation Blues* (1995), Alexie received the Before Columbus Foundation's American Book Award, and he also ventured into songwriting. Song titles double as the titles of the book's ten chapters, and song lyrics begin each chapter. Jim Boyd (Colville, Lakes Band) collaborated with Alexie, setting his lyrics to music. Alexie not only wrote some of the music but also joined in some of the singing, and the results were released as *Reservation Blues: The Soundtrack* (1995). Susan Brill notes that chapter 7's song, named after one of the characters, "Big Mom," focuses on "the strength of Indian women, especially grandmothers" (9).

In 1996, Alexie published another volume of poetry, *The Summer of Black Widows,* and in the same year, the novel *Indian Killer.* In 1998, he published the limited edition of poetry *The Man Who Loves Salmon,* followed by *Smoke Signals: The Screenplay* (1998). This work is adapted from the short story "This Is What It Means to Say Phoenix, Arizona," from the collection in *The Lone Ranger and Tonto Fistfight in Heaven.* "Billed as the first Indian-produced, Indian-directed, Indian-acted, and Indian-written feature film" (Cline 201), when it was released at the Sundance Film Festival in January 1998, the movie won two awards: the Audience Award and the Filmmakers Trophy. After wide release, the film received a Christopher Award, for an artistic work that "'affirm[s] the highest values of the human spirit'" (Rani).

In 2000, Alexie published another collection of poetry, *One Stick Song,* followed by another collection of short stories, *The Toughest Indian in the World* (2000). In 2002, Alexie wrote and directed the independent film *The Business of Fancydancing* which won numerous film festival awards. In an interview with Jennifer Niessen, Alexie comments on the need for women to work in filmmaking: "Creation, you know even the creation of a baby, you need a man and a woman. So if we think about art as creation of life, a film should be as close to equally male and female as possible. So I wanted to do that. I wanted to make sure that we hired a lot of women to work on the film. Because moviemaking is a boys, boys club" (Interview Niessen). Clearly, Alexie advocates gender complementarity in his art. His collection of short stories *Ten Little Indians* was published in 2003, and he has plans to adapt his novel *Indian Killer* for film.

Alexie wears many hats as a poet, short story writer, novelist, stand-up comedian, songwriter, screenwriter, director, and producer. In addition to his many writing talents, he won the Taos Poetry Circus World Heavyweight Championship for four consecutive years from 1998 to 2001. He also has served on the Presidential Panel for the National Dialogue on Race (1998) and on the board of directors for the American Indian College Fund. Alexie was a 1999 O. Henry Award juror and was one of the judges for the 2000 inaugural PEN/Amazon.com Short Story Award. He was also a member of the nominating committee for the 2000 Independent Spirit Awards, the awards for independent film. When asked what keeps him grounded and on the right path, Alexie answers that he has a "strong Indian wife" (Interview McKosato).[2] Obviously, he admires and understands the value of her strength, an example of gender complementarity within marriage and the role that the wife plays.

Beyond gender complementarity, published information does not specify whether the Spokanes are patriarchal/matriarchal, patrilineal/matrilineal, or patrilocal/matrilocal to explain Alexie's worldview about gender dynamics. Historically, there is no evidence that the Spokane tribe was either patrilineal or matrilineal in its social structure. Elkanah Walker, a missionary who spent nine years among the Spokane Indians, 1839–48, wrote the following description of marriage customs among the Spokane people in a letter dated September 12, 1839, and addressed to the Reverend David Greene, a secretary for the American Board of Commissioners for Foreign Missions: "'You might as well trace out the relation existing among a band of wild horses as to trace out the connection of families [...] They are continually changing their wives—throwing away one and taking another'" (Drury 113). This observation not only indicates the difficulty for an outsider in determining the lineage of the Spokane Tribe, but also illustrates the kind of Christian-based ethnocentric perspective that many whites exercised in their assessment of the morals of American Indians. Without knowing the reasons for which the Spokanes might justify the termination of a marriage, there is no way of understanding their decisions.

David C. Wynecoop does not shed much more light on the matter of family descent in his *Children of the Sun: A History of the Spokane Indians*. The author comments in general on family ties: "The social and political organization of the Spokanes was influenced by ties of blood, mutual interests, and dialects" (9). In *A Concise Dictionary of Indian Tribes of North America*, Barbara A. Leitch notes the following concerning the social and political structure of the Spokane Tribe:

> They were composed of three geographical divisions, Upper, Lower, and Southern (or Middle) Spokane. These were further subdivided into bands, composed of several related families who camped together. Each band was led by a chief

> and an assistant chief, selected on the basis of wisdom, influence, bravery and other leadership qualities. Often a number of bands would winter camp together, forming a village and selecting a village chief. There may have been a few hereditary chiefs in earlier times. There was also a tribal chief who with the band chiefs made up the tribal council. In later years, as tribal authority became more centralized, band chiefs became less important, eventually being replaced by tribal sub-chiefs and "small" chiefs. (444)

Families who were related *in some way* were joined in bands, but the author does not offer any suggestion of how this decision was determined. Similarly to the overlapping of characters and families in the works of Erdrich, Alexie's characters also reappear in different works, much as the historical families who were somehow connected in bands do.

In *Indian Reservations: A State and Federal Handbook,* the Confederation of American Indians makes no distinction about the custom of family descent among the Spokane Tribe: "Having no clans, Plateau Indians counted descent on both sides of the family. There was little formal organization" (288). Robert Sherwood (Spokane), the director of the Culture Department at the Spokane Tribal Headquarters in Wellpinit, Washington (1996), confirms, "Descent is determined on both sides of the family." Of that tradition he says, "It's a common thing." Thus, in order to know a particular person's kinship ties, one would need to know whether the family in question claims patrilineal or matrilineal descent.

Finally, there is a reference to matriarchy in Alexie's short story "Saint Junior" from his collection *The Toughest Indian in the World.* Grace Atwater says to her Spokane Indian husband, Roman Gabriel Fury, "'[Y]ou grew up in a matriarchy. You should vote for a woman'" (155). Thus, according to Alexie, the Spokane Tribe is matriarchal; that characterization helps explain Alexie's recognition of women's power.

Alexie grew up with his mother's tribe on the Spokane Reservation, but his father is Coeur d'Alene. The two tribes are linguistically and historically connected:

> The Spokane Indians are of the Interior Salish group that has inhabited northeastern Washington, northern Idaho, and western Montana for centuries. The native language spoken by the Spokanes is common to other Salish tribes with only a slight variation in dialect. Generally speaking, the Spokanes can converse easily in their native tongue with the Kalispels, Coeur d'Alenes, and Flatheads. ("History" 1)

Alexie's parents are both fluent in Salish, but they did not teach their children the language (Interview Highway). Although Alexie can understand Salish, he cannot speak it. Alexie makes use of both his personal heritage and the close connections among the Salish tribes in his writing. In *Reservation Blues,* for example, Chess and Checkers Warm Water, the keyboardists and singers in the Coyote Springs band, are Flathead Indian sisters. In the short story "Indian Country," from *The Toughest Indian in the World* collection, Low Man Smith, the protagonist, is Coeur d'Alene. Although Alexie does not believe in writing about tribes other than his own, he draws on his linguistical, historical, and cultural knowledge of the connections among the Salish tribes (Interview Chato). Furthermore, Alexie utilizes certain ideas that are Pan-Indian, for example, a history of warfare and reservations, and, among contemporary Native peoples, mainstream education (Hafen, "Pan-Indianism" 7).

A historical event that connects the Salish tribes and appears in Alexie's writing is the uprising in 1858 in which the Spokanes joined the Coeur d'Alenes, Yakimas, Palouses, and Paiutes (*Lone* 96–103). Usually referred to as the Coeur d'Alene War, it is also called the Spokane Plains War (Waldman 232). The Interior Salish tribes had extensive contacts with whites after the Lewis and Clark Expedition in the early 1800s and were generally peaceful, trading furs for guns, ammunition, and other goods. Because of treaty violations, however, in the 1850s the Coeur d'Alenes joined in an uprising against settlers. The Coeur d'Alene War of 1858 grew out of the Yakima War of 1855–56. In May 1858, about one thousand Coeur d'Alenes, Spokanes, and Palouses attacked and routed a column of 164 federal troops under Major Edward Steptoe at Pine Creek in the western part of Washington Territory. Next, about 600 troops under Colonel George Wright rode into the field to engage the Indians. When the Indians and whites met in September at Spokane Plains and Four Lakes, the Indians, who were not as well armed as the whites, suffered heavy losses (Waldman 67).[3] After the war, the Spokanes settled on various reservations, including the Spokane Reservation near present-day Wellpinit, Washington, and the Colville Reservation near present-day Nespelem, Washington. Others joined the Flatheads on their reservation near present-day Dixon, Montana (Waldman 232).

One of the specific events in the Spokane War that appears frequently in Alexie's writing deals with Colonel Wright's destruction of eight hundred ponies. This memory, along with that of Wright's command to execute Indians charged with inciting attacks, hung over the Spokanes and prevented them from ever again trying to oppose the whites with the use of arms (Prucha 407–8). Alexie makes use of the images of horses in his early poetry in *The Business of Fancydancing*. In the poem "Grandmother," for example, he associates the grandmother's body with the strength of horses:

> she would be hours in the sweatlodge
> come out naked and brilliant in the sun
> steam rising off her body in winter
> like a slow explosion of horses (4–7)

The simile compares the "steam" of the grandmother's warm body with the supposed cloud of dust that a herd of horses might make when galloping, an image of their raw power and grace. There is also, however, with the word *explosion* an echo of the horses that Wright ordered shot and killed in 1858. The association of the grandmother's participating in traditional customs and the history of Wright's killing the ponies reappears in *Reservation Blues* in the figure of another grandmother figure, Big Mom, but before that Alexie narrates the historical events of the Spokane War from a Native perspective in the short story "The Trial of Thomas Builds-the-Fire" from *The Lone Ranger and Tonto Fistfight in Heaven.*

Telling the stories, Thomas Builds-the-Fire takes on three different first-person voices: one of the ponies that somehow was spared in the massacre; Qualchan, one of the Yakima warriors who had started the Yakima War in 1855 and was later tried, sentenced to death, and hanged (Waldman 67); and a sixteen-year-old warrior named Wild Coyote, who killed two soldiers in the attack on Major Steptoe's troops (*Lone* 96–103). In retelling the pony's story, Alexie frames it as an event of survival, resistance, and continuance rather than one of death and destruction, a curative metaphor for the "vanishing" American Indian: "'It was a nightmare to witness. They were rounded into a corral and then lassoed, one by one, and dragged out to be shot in the head. This lasted for hours, and that dark night mothers cried for their dead children. The next day, the survivors were rounded into a single mass and slaughtered by continuous rifle fire'" (*Lone* 97). Colonel Wright believes that by exterminating the band of horses, which represents the Spokane chief Til-co-ax's "entire wealth," he is doling out retributive justice to a hostile chief who "has been sending his young men into the Walla Walla valley, and stealing horses and cattle from the settlers and from the government" (96–97). What Wright fails to acknowledge, of course, is that the Indians were initially upset because white settlers were encroaching on their lands. To emphasize the Native point of view, Alexie renders the pony's account of the massacre in language that could easily be mistaken for a human voice recounting the deaths of his or her tribal members.

To counter this devastation and sense of defeat, Thomas Builds-the-Fire continues the story, relating how the soldiers saddle him to ride him, as if he has passively surrendered to their victory. The pony rebels and bucks every rider who tries to break him, thereby reasserting his will: "'Another man tried to ride me, but I threw him and so many others, until I was lathered with sweat and blood from their spurs and rifle butts. It was glorious. Finally they gave up, quit, and led me to the back of the train. They could not break me. [. . .] I lived that day, even escaped Colonel Wright, and galloped into other histories'" (98). Alexie turns the previously conquered pony into the winner, a voice that again sounds like that of the Spokanes who have refused to be beaten by someone else's version of history. "The event resonates in Alexie's work," as James Cox notes, "as a signifier of the cruelty of the Army and the attempt by white culture in general to destroy the Spokane" (62). Similarly to the way the pony prevails, however, the Spokanes have survived, endured, and continue to tell their stories, emphasizing their existence as a sovereign nation.

In Thomas Builds-the-Fire's retelling of Qualchan's hanging, Alexie includes his wife's role, that of a traditional female warrior: "My wife also fought beside me with a knife and wounded many soldiers before she was subdued. After I was beaten down, they dragged me to the noose and I was hanged with six other Indians, including Epseal, who had never raised a hand in anger to any white or Indian" (*Lone* 98–99). Although Alexie does not name the wife and devotes only one sentence to describe her actions, she is not insignificant. Plainly, she acts as an independent woman, exercising her own power to be a warrior, an example of gender complementarity. Her response does not surprise anyone and is not condemned by tribal members. This example of a strong female warrior, who fearlessly attacks soldiers, fighting alongside her husband in an attempt to prevent them from hanging him and successfully wounding "many" of them before they can restrain her, paints a picture of a woman who is not limited by her gender but who is valued for her fierce loyalty, courage, and bravery. Additionally, Qualchan's wife points to the contemporary version of a female warrior in the characters of Marie Polatkin in the novel *Indian Killer,* Norma Many Horses in the short story "The Approximate Size of My Favorite Tumor," and Sara Polatkin in the short story "Indian Country," all of whom are addressed later in this chapter. The idea of physically powerful and mentally keen women, who are grounded in the context of gender complementarity and valued for their strengths, spans 150 years in Alexie's works, much like the historical span covered in Erdrich's novels.

In a recent interview, Alexie talks about strong women in television and film. He attributes the success of a television series like *ER,* in part, to the "powerful women," and he argues, "Ninety percent of feature films—bad movies—could be saved by a simple thing: Give the woman in the movie a little bit of power at a key moment of the film, and it would have been saved" (Interview Torrez 7–8). Alexie has stated that he is working with Shadow Catcher Productions and Miramax Films, the companies involved with the production of *Smoke Signals,* on the film project for *Reservation Blues.* If this novel is adapted to the big screen, it is hoped that the screenplay will remain faithful to the text, because Alexie has said that the "women represent the strength in the book" (Interview Chato).

Of particular interest is the character Big Mom, who Alexie says represents the grandmother, fertility, and goddess on the mountain: "Big Mom is the spiritual strength of the tribe [...] the strength of the feminine" (Interview Chato). This spiritual strength is evident in the second chapter of *The Lone Ranger and Tonto Fistfight in Heaven*, "A Drug Called Tradition," when the narrator sees his grandmother walking across Benjamin Lake, echoing Jesus' walking on water (Matt. 14.26): "Big Mom was the spiritual leader of the Spokane Tribe. She had so much good medicine I think she may have been the one who created the earth" (*Lone* 23). With Christian allusions to the miracles of Jesus and to God's omnipotence in creating the world, Alexie implies that for the Spokane Tribe, Big Mom represents a Native feminine spirituality of tremendous power. When asked about the continuity that Big Mom provides in Alexie's writing and on whom she is based, Alexie answers, "Well, in the most basic sense, she's based on my grandmother, who was also Big Mom. But, because of her name, she also takes on this larger weight. She's sort of the goddess of all things, this huge fertility figure, somebody up on Olympus, God. God itself. She's this creative force" (Jaffe-Notier 10–11). This view of creative power associated with the feminine underlies Alexie's other female characters, privileging a matriarchal culture rather than the dominant mainstream's patriarchal culture, and illustrates the power sharing of gender complementarity.

Big Mom presents an imposing figure, one who not only matches her name but also impresses the band members: "Big Mom was over six feet tall and had braids that hung down past her knees. Her braids themselves were taller than any of the members of Coyote Springs and probably weighed more, too. She had a grandmother face, lined and crossed with deep wrinkles. But her eyes were young, so young that the rest of her face almost looked like a mask" (*Reservation* 202). Similarly to the striking figure of Old Tallow in Erdrich's *The Birchbark House*, Big Mom's face contains features that signify the wisdom of age—"lined and crossed with deep wrinkles"—and the exuberance of youth—"her eyes were young" —more concrete evidence of her mythic status as she contains all ages. Perhaps her stature emphasizes the weight of her teaching and the influence she has over people. After all, "there were stories about Big Mom that stretched back more than a hundred years" (200), and to match such a long-standing reputation, she would require the matching equivalent in her physical bearing.

In *Reservation Blues*, Big Mom sees and hears Colonel Wright's soldiers slaughter the horses in 1858 from the vantage point of 1992, where "she saw the future and the past" (10). She transcends time to be able to see this historical event: "She saw the Indian horses shot and fallen like tattered sheets" (10). Because she communicates with the horses, teaching them songs, hearing their singing screams, and listening to the silences, she understands how history repeats itself in the songs of those who suffer: "With each successive generation, the horses arrived in different forms and with different songs"

(10). Big Mom honors the memories of those horses that died, preserving tribal history.

In chapter seven, "Big Mom," Alexie opens with lyrics that call attention to the importance of her role to tribal knowledge. The song speaks about a grandmother, Big Mom, who is singing songs and stories that the listener has been missing, and the singer reassures the listener that she will "always come back for" her (197–98). The message is a communal one of encouragement that restores confidence in the singer and the listener, in this case, the Coyote Springs band. Big Mom mentors Coyote Springs, just as she has helped other singers and musicians, and perhaps one of her most important lessons to her students is that they can always go back to the reservation and connect with what she represents: positive tribal knowledge that will help them survive. As P. Jane Hafen (Taos Pueblo) notes, "Big Mom instigat[es] tribal and communal support of Thomas, Chess, and Checkers as they embark on a journey of survival" (74). Through Big Mom, Alexie privileges reservation connections, history, survival, and sovereignty.

After meeting Big Mom, Checkers Warm Water writes her impressions in her journal. She realizes that Big Mom has special talents, and after they take a sweat together, an episode reminiscent of the sweat in the poem "Grandmother," Checkers believes, "Big Mom sang better than anybody [she] ever heard, even Aretha Franklin" (205). As with any powerful woman, Checkers also fears Big Mom's ability to read minds, and this leads her to wondering about the origins of Big Mom's godlike qualities: "I looked at Big Mom and thought that God must be made up mostly of Indian and woman pieces. Then I looked at Father Arnold's and thought that God must be made up of white and man pieces" (205). Karen Jorgensen argues that Alexie uses doppelgangers in *Reservation Blues,* a "series of Native American characters who are shadowed by representative non-Indian doubles" (19). Thus, Jorgensen sees Big Mom's double as the Catholic priest (23). Rather than Father Arnold's shadowing Big Mom, the relationship between the two characters represents gender complementarity, in which Big Mom is the feminine spiritual aspect that complements the masculine spirituality of the priest, thereby creating a more holistic belief system of equally valued contributions from both parties. This relationship of gender complementarity is most apparent at the end of the novel when Big Mom and Father Arnold attend the funeral for Junior Polatkin. Big Mom tells Father Arnold: "'[Y]ou cover all the Christian stuff; I'll do the traditional Indian stuff. We'll make a great team'" (*Reservation* 280). Again, a team effort, or gender complementarity, acknowledges the importance of each player's participation.

As other aspects of Big Mom's character do, her role as a teacher takes on mythic proportions. When she demonstrates to the Coyote Springs band how to play the "loneliest chord," she explains, "'All Indians can play that chord.' [...] 'It's the chord created especially for us'" (206–7). Big Mom's knowledge of music and history represents her intellectual sovereignty. As Hafen notes: "Big Mom's chord is the genetic memory that unites diverse Indian peoples. It is the narrative chord that escapes specific musicality, yet is heard through regenerative storytelling. The chord has the particular contemporary overtones that reverberate through mythic time and Spokane sensibilities" (75). Big Mom not only has knowledge about music and the history of the Spokane Tribe but also has indigenous knowledge that reaches across time and tribal specificity to touch all Indians who hear her. After all, the Coyote Springs band represents two different Salish Indian tribes. Thomas Builds-the-Fire, Victor Joseph, and Junior Polatkin are Spokane Indians, and Chess and Checkers Warm Water are Flathead Indians. Big Mom's chord affects them all: Thomas says, "'I can play that chord.'" Victor shouts, "'Enough!' [...] 'I can't hear myself think!'" Junior faints, and Chess says, "'Please,'" because "she didn't know if she wanted Big Mom to please, quit playing, or please, don't stop" (*Reservation* 207). In this case, Big Mom's music is merely a metaphor for her power. Whether teaching, mentoring, or connecting her students to their tribal sovereignty, heritage, and knowledge, she always exists as an autonomous female, doing valuable work for the tribe, an example of gender complementarity. As indicated by the musicians' intense responses, undoubtedly Big Mom's indigenous knowledge and her role as a teacher are important issues for Alexie.

In fact, the importance of education for American Indians has been a major theme in both Alexie's life and his writings. When he participated on the Presidential Panel for the National Dialogue on Race (1998), he had the following to say about education: "'With the establishment of the American Indian College Fund and the 29 American Indian colleges on reservations in the Indian communities throughout the country, I think we have begun that process of understanding that education can be just as traditional, just as tribal as a powwow or any other ceremony, that education should become sacred'" ("Dialogue" 6). Alexie raises issues about education that unquestionably merge in the character of Big Mom: education, tribal traditions, and sacredness. Although these characteristics might tend to a more traditional understanding of education for American Indians, Alexie also takes a contemporary view of the issue in the character of Marie Polatkin in his novel *Indian Killer*.

Writing in the mystery genre, Alexie offers a critique of the academy in *Indian Killer* through the character of a Spokane Indian, Marie Polatkin, who is a political activist and a University of Washington college student. In chapter seven, "Introduction to Native American Literature," Marie questions the syllabus for a course taught by Dr. Clarence Mather, a white male anthropologist and wannabe Indian who "wear[s] a turquoise bolo tie, and his gray hair tied back in a ponytail" (58). As Brill notes, "Dr. Mather's syllabus, lectures, and interpretations of Indian literature demonstrate his erroneous and disturbingly romanticized misconceptions about Indians and their cultures and literatures" (10). During the first ⟨   ⟩ Marie engages Dr. Mather in a debate about the reading list he has chosen for the course, making an argument for the kinds of texts and authors that *should* be taught in a course titled Native American literature. As an example of a contemporary female warrior, Marie feels empowered "to harass a white professor who [thinks] he [knows] what it [means] to be Indian" (*Indian* 61). Also, through the issues that Marie raises, she offers an opportunity to explore what Alexie proposes beyond his critique of Dr. Mather's reading assignments, texts that Marie believes are neither authentic nor the most appropriate examples of Native American literature.

In *Tribal Secrets: Recovering American Indian Intellectual Traditions*, Robert Allen Warrior (Osage) writes that possibilities open up to American Indians when they remove themselves from the dichotomy of "a death dance of dependence, on the one hand, abandoning [themselves] to the intellectual strategies and categories of white, European thought and, on the other hand, declaring that [they] need nothing outside of [themselves] and [their] cultures to understand the world and [their] place in it" (123–24). He goes on to state, "[T]he struggle for sovereignty is not a struggle to be free from the influence of anything outside [themselves], but a process of asserting the power they possess as communities and individuals to make decisions that affect [their] lives" (124). Marie Polatkin perfectly illustrates the possibilities that can open up to a Native woman who refuses an "either-or" detrimental model such as the one that Warrior describes.

Marie exploits mainstream education and political activism to her own advantage and that of urban Indians. An English major in her senior year, she is also the "activities coordinator for the Native American Students Alliance at the University" (*Indian* 34, 31). Although she grew up on the reservation, she feels somewhat isolated from her Spokane Tribe because she neither speaks Spokane nor dances nor sings traditionally, elements often attributed as signifiers of authentic Indianness (33). Still, she remains firmly grounded in her tribal connections, as evidenced by her surprise visits home to see her parents and her welcome to Reggie Polatkin, her distant urban cousin, whom she has not seen in over a year (34). Marie willingly shares her dinner of Apple Jacks cereal and allows Reggie to spend the night on her couch (90–91, 95). Additionally, through her involvement in protests over Indian issues and her work with the Seattle downtown homeless shelter, Marie builds community among urban Indians (38–39). Marie's intellectual sovereignty resides in the contexts of her Spokane and urban tribal connections, her academic involvement, and her political and social activism, all aspects of the process of asserting the power she possesses as a member of a community and as an individual to make decisions that affect her life (Warrior 124).

As with his other Native female characters, Alexie sees Marie as a powerful woman within the context of tribal gender complementarity, not in the traditional European-American patriarchal paradigm of subordination. Further evidence of Alexie's critical views on women's roles in labor and religion in a patriarchal culture is found in two poems in his collection *One Stick Song*. In the poem "Water," he comments on both women's and men's working as airport security: "I'm pleased this airport has progressed / beyond an antiquated notion of gender roles." In the poem "Why Indian Men Fall in Love with White Women," he describes a woman working in a doughnut shop as "a blessed and gifted woman who wanted to be a priest, a Jesuit / an Ignatian, of all things, but was turned back by the Catholic / Church / and its antiquated notions of gender" (66, 75–76). Clearly, Alexie does not limit the possibilities for women on the basis of their gender, in work or religion, and Marie is evidence of his vision.

According to Ron McFarland, Marie's "family name associates [her] with Chief Polatkin, one of whose daughters was married to Qualchan, who led the Spokane, Palouse, and Coeur d'Alene tribes in 1858 against Colonel Wright" (34). Perhaps this daughter is the model for the wife of Qualchan, discussed earlier, whom Alexie constructs as a female warrior in *The Lone Ranger and Tonto Fistfight in Heaven*. About Marie, Alexie has said, "She's the strength in the book," a description similar to that of Big Mom in *Reservation Blues* (Interview Chato). Answering an interviewer's question about the characterization of Marie, Alexie responds: "I wanted to write [. . .] an Indian woman character [. . .] who was like *most* of the Native women I know [. . .] a very intelligent, very ambitious, very dedicated, very politically active Indian woman" (emphasis added, Exclusive Interview). Alexie connects his view of strong Native women to those he knows, presumably both those on the Spokane Reservation and those in an urban environment.

Enrolling in Dr. Mather's course gives Marie the opportunity to demonstrate her power. She challenges "[his] role as the official dispenser of 'Indian education' at the University," thereby privileging her Native knowledge and authority (*Indian* 58). Mather's attitude perfectly illustrates what educator Paulo Freire describes as the "'banking' concept of education," in which

> knowledge is a gift bestowed by those who consider themselves knowledgeable upon those whom they consider to know nothing. Projecting an absolute ignorance onto others, a characteristic of the ideology of oppression, negates education and knowledge as processes of inquiry. The teacher presents himself to his students as their necessary opposite; by considering their ignorance absolute, he justifies his own existence. (58–59)

Marie enters Mather's classroom, however, refusing to participate in the academy's patriarchal narrative or to accept the role of receptacle that Mather assigns to her; she will not allow him as narrator to fill her with his narration, one that she knows is false (Freire 58). As she so eloquently surmises after seeing his reading list, "Dr. Mather [is] full of shit" (*Indian* 59). She aggressively confronts the basis of Mather's knowledge: "You think you know more about being Indian than Indians do, don't you? Just because you read all those books about Indians, most of them written by white people" (247). Marie decenters his teacher-centered classroom, subverts his role of authority, and resists the idea of a knowledge hierarchy, one in which dominant mainstream knowledge is considered more valuable than other knowledge. In sum, Marie promotes an agenda of tribal intellectual sovereignty.

Marie identifies herself as a fighter, someone who believes that "being an Indian [is] mostly about survival" (34, 61). Therefore, her right to confront Mather stems mainly from the personal level, the fact that she is a Spokane Indian, a cultural insider, who understands the importance of working for the continuance of all Indian peoples. Moreover, with her educational background and political protest experience, she has the intelligence and self-confidence to defy Mather's oppressive ideology, one that claims superior knowledge not only over students but also over Indians. Although she recognizes that some people, such as the white student David Rogers, see her only as the exotic Other, as like Pocahontas, another brown female minority to colonize by sleeping with her, Marie does not limit her possibilities because of her ethnicity or gender (61, 69). In fact, her political work allows her to create lines of communication that mediate between the communities of Native students, homeless people, and urban Indians and mainstream institutions of power represented by the university, the police, and the press. She is a powerful contemporary female warrior, fighting with words, who says, "'I'm talking like a twentieth-century Indian woman. Hell, a twenty-first-century Indian'" (247–48).

Examining Marie's objections to Mather's reading list provides insights to Alexie's philosophy of what instructors should teach in a Native American literature course. First, Marie criticizes Mather's selection of *The Education of Little Tree* by Forrest Carter, pointing out that the author's claims of Cherokee ancestry are fraudulent (59). Thus, rule number one for instructors compiling Native American literature reading lists would be to select those books authored by people with legitimate claims of Indian identity. The issue of what constitutes legitimate claims of Indian identity, at least according to Alexie, would best be left as a topic for a Native scholar to examine. However, suffice it to say that within the context of *Indian Killer*, Alexie uses Marie, a Spokane woman who was raised on the reservation, as his mouthpiece. So, in this case, a person with reservation origins qualifies as one with legitimate claims of Indian identity.

The second objection that Marie raises deals with the issue of autobiographies cowritten by white men, such as *Black Elk Speaks* (1932), as told to John G. Neihardt; *Lame Deer: Seeker of Visions* (1972), by John Fire/Lame Deer and Richard Erdoes; and *Lakota Woman* (1990), by Mary Crow Dog and Richard Erdoes (58). Perhaps the fact that publishers categorize these books as "autobiographies" as opposed to "told-to-" or "told-through-white-men" books is what most annoys Alexie. His attack implies that he would continue to oppose inclusion of these books on a Native American literature reading list even if instructors were careful to inform students about the inherent problems of filters involving white recorders. Therefore, Alexie argues that any book cowritten by a white man should not be taught in a Native American literature course.

Finally, Marie makes basically the same observation about the rest of Mather's reading list, books all associated in some way with white people: "The other seven books included three anthologies of traditional Indian stories edited by white men, two nonfiction studies of Indian spirituality written by white women, a book of traditional Indian poetry translations edited by a Polish-American Jewish man, and an Indian murder mystery written by some local white writer named Jack Wilson, who claimed he was a Shilshomish Indian" (58–59). Marie protests books classified as Native American literature that are edited, translated, or written by white people and argues that they do not meet the criteria of Native American literature. She also takes exception to authors who claim to be Indian but cannot prove membership in a tribe, thereby exploiting questionable Indian identity connections to further their literary careers (67). Marie argues that for texts to be classified as Native American literature, the author must truly be Native American, and when called into the department chair's office, she goes further by asking, "Why isn't an Indian teaching the class?" (312). Thus, Alexie strongly objects to what the academy teaches in Native American literature courses and even questions who teaches it.

Craig Womack (Muskogee Creek/Cherokee) shares Alexie's concerns regarding Native American literature and makes a similar argument when he writes, "[O]ne can teach courses on Native lit, and now even on Native literary criticism, assigning as texts, books authored exclusively by Native people. [. . .] the minimal requirement for a Native studies course should be that every classroom text is written by a Native author; otherwise, how can we possibly lay claim to presenting Native perspectives?" (10). For both Alexie and Womack, then, the determining factor for a Native American literature reading list is that the text represent an "authentic" Native American perspective, one that only "authentic" Indians can have.[4]

Alexie's critique of the academy and white professors and writers in *Indian Killer*, his complaint of white people's speaking with authority for and about Indians, appears frequently in his work. In his review of Ian Frazier's *Off the Rez*, Alexie writes, "Frazier's formal use of 'the rez' marks him as an outsider eager to portray himself as an insider, as a writer with a supposedly original story to tell and as a white man who is magically unlike all other white men in his relationship to American Indians" ("Some of My Best Friends"). Alexie rejects white writers who believe they understand the lives of American Indians, and by writing about Indians, white writers perpetuate the colonizing act of telling the reading public what Indians are "really" like.

In his short story "Dear John Wayne," Alexie skewers the white anthropologist Spencer Cox, who wants to interview the 118-year-old Spokane Etta Joseph, born on the Spokane Indian Reservation and now a resident of the Saint Tekawitha Retirement Community in Spokane, Washington. Currently, Cox is working on a "study on the effect of classical European ballroom dancing on the indigenous powwow," but Alexie has Etta control the interview, subvert Cox's agenda, tell her story about her love affair with John Wayne, and good-naturedly poke fun at the ridiculousness of Cox's self-importance (*Toughest* 193). Cox considers himself more of an expert on the Salish than the Salish themselves as he cites the qualifications that identify him as an authority in academic circles: "I am a cultural anthropologist and the Owens Lecturer in Applied Indigenous Studies at Harvard University. I'm also the author of seventeen books, texts, focusing on mid- to late-twentieth-century Native American culture, most specifically the Interior Salish tribes of Washington State" (190). Again, Alexie makes his point that no matter how many books Cox has published, he never will be able to speak authentically about Spokane Indians' lives. Etta tells him that his books are filled with lies and he will never know about her. To survive, she has had to live her life in a white world for "fifty-seven minutes of every hour," and when Cox asks about the other three minutes, she responds, "That, sir, is when I get to be Indian, and you have no idea, no concept, no possible way of knowing what happens in those three minutes" (194). As a strong female elder, Etta is a powerful woman who does not allow Cox to colonize her life: "Those three minutes belong to us. They are very secret. You've colonized Indian land but I am not about to let you colonize my heart and mind" (194).

In his short story "One Good Man," Alexie blasts another white professor at Washington State University, Dr. Lawrence Crowell, not because he is a wannabe who spent time at the 1969 Alcatraz occupation and the 1973 Wounded Knee occupation but "because he thought he was entitled to tell other Indians what it meant to be Indian" (*Toughest* 227). In these examples, Alexie seems to object most to the arrogant attitudes of whites who think that because they study, research, write, publish, and teach about Indians or their literatures, they become experts on what it means to live one's life as an Indian, contrary to the intellectual sovereignty that Alexie uses in his own writing.

Alexie voices a familiar and legitimate complaint when he says, "Indians rarely get to define our own image, and when white people do it, they often get assigned all this authority, and I guess that's what my problem is, that Indians are never even allowed the authority to self-define" (Barnes & Noble.com 2). This theme appears again in the poem "The Unauthorized Autobiography of Me," where he notes, "Successful non-Indian writers are viewed as well-informed about Indian life" (*One Stick Song* 22). In the same poem, Alexie goes on to discuss the economics of publishing when he critiques the whites who write about Indians: "A book written by a non-Indian will sell more copies than a book written by either a mixed-blood or an Indian writer," and "Most non-Indians who write about Indians are fiction writers. Fiction about Indians sells" (21, 22). Alexie has suggested that white authors who write fiction works about Indians at the very least should donate 10 percent of their royalties either to the American Indian College Fund or to the tribe about whom they write (Interview Highway). He admits, "I'm resentful that there are many writers out there making careers off Indians and [. . .] doing absolutely nothing in return. [. . .] People ask me and I give hard-core answers. You're making money, give it back" (Interview Highway). Consequently, Alexie's objections to whites' writing about Indians can be attributed not only to their arrogance and their sense of authority to define Indians but also to the profits they gain from their fiction.

By introducing the general reading public to the issues surrounding how whites teach Native American literature in the academy, Alexie raises their awareness. This is the first step in effecting change, but Alexie does not seem to offer anything beyond his critique of white-man arrogance. Nothing can be inferred as a solution to poor choices by either unknowingly or willfully ignorant professors. He does not offer any suggestions for white scholars. His only advice recommends deferring to Native scholars and writers because they have the authority of cultural insider status. In an interview for *Indian Killer*, he expresses the following wish: "I would like to reach a larger audience and using a popular form like the mystery might enable me to do that" (Exclusive Interview). He also has said, "First and foremost, writers like to get attention" (Purdy 11). Alexie's desires to reach a larger audience, get attention, and at the same time realistically expect that white scholars will not write about his works as they teach them in Native American literature classes call for changes that seem unlikely to happen simultaneously in the near future. Alexie chooses the character of Marie Polatkin in *Indian Killer* to voice this political discourse on education, writing, and publication in

Native American literature, which demonstrates her resistance to the politics of power.

According to Alexie, non-Native scholars have no entry into the criticism of his work because they cannot speak with authority as cultural insiders. True, they are limited by their position, but at the same time, not all of them attempt to speak with the authority of cultural insiders. There are white scholars who consciously listen to what the Native scholars and critics prescribe in terms of approaches to the literature, whether they are tribal-specific cultural and historical contexts, issues of sovereignty and connections to the land, and/or literary criticisms developed from the literature of the tribe in question. On October 21, 2000, my research assistant attended the book fair in Seattle, Washington, and presented Alexie with the question "What would he recommend for white scholars who want to study Native American literature?" Alexie never responded.

In a more constructive fashion than Alexie, Womack briefly addresses the roles of white critics through one of his characters who asks, "How can white Lit Critters become helpers, rather than Indian experts? How can they promote the work of Native people over their own, and still was [sic] keep us their own good efforts at contributing to Native literary development?" (127). In writing about American Indian history, Angela Cavender Wilson (Wahpetonwan Dakota) suggests that white scholars consult American Indian sources for the cultural insiders' perspectives and, if they do not, acknowledge the limitations of their white perspective in their work (26). In the same way, perhaps white scholars writing about Native literatures should consult Native sources or admit the limited perspective of their work.

White scholars observing all these caveats about teaching Native American literary texts in an academic climate that demands expertise, knowledge, and authority in their specialization may encounter problems. Negotiating the academic culture and the requests from Native writers and scholars that white scholars observe the most basic considerations of the field can be difficult. Duane Champagne (Chippewa) argues that "there is room for both Indian and non-Indian scholars within American Indian studies," but he also remarks that those involved in American Indian studies experience difficulties because their "academic colleagues operate from different values and cultural perspectives" (181, 188), or as Elizabeth Cook-Lynn (Crow Creek Sioux) says, "[T]he esoteric language of French and Russian literary scholars [...] has overrun the lit/crit scene" ("American" 137).

Sherman Alexie maintains a sense of personal identity with connections to his Spokane tribe while engaging in a critical dialogue with the academic and larger community. In *Indian Killer*, he accomplishes this task, in part, through the character of Marie Polatkin. Alexie has argued, "[T]here are no models of any success in any sort of field for Indians. We don't have any of that. So there is no idea of a role model existing" ("Dialogue" 5). Without a doubt, Alexie creates the role model of a successful Spokane Indian woman in the character of Marie Polatkin. She is a strong, powerful, autonomous, intellectually sovereign woman who, among other things, challenges the academy about who teaches Native American literature and what that person assigns to be read. As a female voice, Marie's challenge develops from a context of gender complementarity in which she knows that her community will value her role as a contemporary female warrior of words.

Alexie continues the theme of education in his short story "Saint Junior" in his most recent collection, *The Toughest Indian in the World*. Saint Junior is the nickname for Saint Jerome the Second University, the Catholic liberal arts college of which both main characters in the story are graduates. In this story, however, unlike the single college student Marie Polatkin, the female coprotagonist is Grace Atwater, a Mohawk Indian from a matriarchal tribe. Married to Roman Gabriel Fury, a Spokane, Grace is described as "more Spokane than anything else" because she has lived on the Spokane Indian Reservation for so long (161). When Roman proposes that he would vote for a woman if she had a jump shot and believed in the socialization of medicine and education, Grace answers, "'Well, then, I guess that means I'm running for president'" (155). Although Grace's announcement to run for office is couched in humor, again, Alexie constructs an educated Native woman who has a political conscience, cares about the social issues of medicine and education, and visualizes herself holding the highest political office in the United States, all of which immediately create an image of a strong, powerful, and autonomous woman.

Further, Grace has a marriage in which the husband has no reservations about the ability of a woman to run the country, additional evidence of a relationship based in the context of gender complementarity. Roman values Grace for whatever contributions she makes to their union, and she affirms his support of women: "'[Y]ou grew up in a matriarchy. You should vote for a woman'" (155). Roman's parents both died before he finished high school, his mother of a pulmonary-related disease when he was three years old and his father in a head-on car accident on Reservation Road when he was fifteen years old (168). As Roman's legal guardian, Grandmother Fury has raised him, so Grace presumably refers to the Spokane Tribe as a matriarchy. With his understanding that women are powerful and autonomous, Roman tells Grace that he expects to see her announcement on television soon, and she responds with the revelations she would make in her press conference: "'I will begin my press conference by announcing that yes, I have smoked pot, and yes, I have had sex, lots of sex. In fact, I will introduce the seven men and one woman I have slept with and let them answer all the questions regarding my campaign and political philosophies'" (155). Grace holds nothing back regarding her history of illegal drug use and her bisexual partners, topics that typically make headlines and often destroy politicians' careers. With this kind of forthrightness and confidence, Roman predicts, "'[Grace] will be a hero to all women and men'" (155).

Grace is a fourth-grade teacher at the Spokane Tribal School, and she has subsumed the nurturing role of mother as caretaker with the role of teaching young children. Although she has no children of her own, she views her professional life as an extension of motherhood: "What about the maternal instinct? Well, for eight hours a day, over the last eight years, within the four walls of a fourth-grade classroom, she'd loved one hundred and thirty-six Spokane Indian boys and girls, had loved them well and kept them safe, and had often been the only adult in their lives who'd never actively or inactively broken their hearts" (162). Much as the character of Marie Polatkin in *Indian Killer*, who helps urban Indians, or the character of Big Mom in *Reservation Blues*, who as nurturer tries to help young people learn to choose for themselves a path of integrity (Jorgensen 22), Grace functions as teacher, nurturer, and salvation—a saving grace—for her students.

Despite Grace's awareness of the vital role she plays in the lives of the Spokane children, she does not think of her work as any more or less important than anybody else's in the community, another example of gender complementarity: "Still, Grace had never thought of herself as any kind of saint. More likely, she was just a good teacher; nothing wrong with that, but nothing uncommon or special about it either. She'd often wondered if she was doing everything she could to ensure the survival of the Spokanes, the Mohawks, of all Indian people" (*Toughest* 162). Grace's teaching is simply what she does, but when she claims that she is not a saint, an implied connection resonates between her and Saint Junior—the title of the story. If there is an association between the education that she gives children on the reservation and the education that Indians receive at institutions of higher learning, such as Saint Jerome the Second University, the difference is that she cares not only about the education of children but also about their very survival. Survival is not automatically included in the curriculum for Indian college students. Grace's concern for the education and survival of all Indian people reflects Pan-Indianism issues, which transcend tribal specificity.

As a high school student, and despite "an undiagnosed case of dyslexia," Grace had earned a perfect score on college boards, the CAT, which Roman defines as the culturally biased Colonial Aptitude Test (172, 165). In writing her personal essay for application to Saint Jerome the Second University, Grace imagines that she has already been accepted and cleverly composes what she expects to hear as the invocation from the president, Father Arnold. Incorporating all the dismal statistics that colleges usually offer to incoming first-year students, she makes clear her understanding of the reality that not everybody will survive college life:

> I am here to tell you that twenty-five percent of you will not make it through your freshman year. I am here to tell you that more than forty percent of you will not graduate from this university. I am here to tell you that all of you will engage in some form of illicit activity or another. [...] Most of you will fall in love and all of you will not be loved enough. And through all the pain and loneliness, through all the late hours and early mornings, you will learn. (173)

Not only does Grace survive college and learn, but while at school she also meets and falls in love with Roman.

Roman has his own personal experience with obstacles to entering college. Having scored "'in the ninety-ninth percentile in the verbal section'" of the CAT and scoring "'a ninety-nine on the math section [...] the second-highest score ever for a Native American,'" Roman is called into the office of Mr. Williams, the president of the Colonial Aptitude Testing Service, as a result of the assumption that "'there were certain irregularities in [Roman's] test-taking process,'" which must account for his unusually high scores (168–69). Despite the institutionalized racism that Roman encounters, he has the last word when he accuses Mr. Williams of trying to deprive him of the right to enter college: "'[Y]ou want to take my score away from me? You want to change the rules after I learned them and beat them? Is that what you really want to do?'" (171). Several of the pitfalls of college life, which Grace includes in her invocation, resemble problems often associated with life on Indian reservations: crime, drugs, and alcohol abuse. Both she and Roman, however, share a story of triumph that avoids those pitfalls and includes college graduation and a solid eighteen-year marriage. They complement each other to survive, and their own intellectual sovereignty helps them in that endeavor. Grace and Roman endure an educational system that does not seem to promote success stories for Indians, yet education is crucial to intellectual sovereignty for them.

Critics of the colonialist model of education believe that changes must be made if American Indians are to benefit from higher education and achieve self-determination. Educational counselor and scholar Jorge Noriega (Mestizo) summarizes the current status of college education for American Indians: "Altogether, the higher educational dimension of American Indian education serves at present as little more than the capstone to the whole colonialist system of indoctrinating and thus dominating indigenous peoples of North America perfected by Euroamerica over the past three centuries" (392). Noted American Indian studies scholar Vine Deloria, Jr. (Standing Rock Sioux), responds to this issue in his essay "A Redefinition of Indian Affairs" by asserting that major changes to the educational system would benefit more people than Indians: "Education must also be revamped; not to make Indians more acceptable to white society, but to allow non-Indians a greater chance to develop their talents. Education as it is designed today works to destroy communities by creating supermen who spend their lives climbing the economic ladder. America is thus always on the move and neighborhoods rarely have a stable lasting residency" (*Custer* 240). Deloria notes that the current educational system promotes an individualistic approach to life, the opposite of a tribal worldview in which the whole community's welfare is considered.

Despite the criticisms of the current educational system in the United States, Indians such as Roman Fury and Grace Atwater need those college degrees in order to gain credibility in the mainstream culture. Succeeding by the college's standards allows Indians access to economic opportunities and positions of power and leadership they might not otherwise have, and they then have the means by which to exert their own intellectual sovereignty and to challenge oppressive conditions for Indians controlled by local, state, and federal agencies. As Deloria observes: "Ideologically the young Indians are refusing to accept white values as eternal truths. [...] Accommodation to white society is primarily in terms of gaining additional techniques by which they can give a deeper root to existing Indian traditions" (239). Appropriately, the issue of education in the short story "Saint Junior" is framed with an introduction and conclusion steeped in tribal tradition and ceremony: the opening with the Cold Springs Singers singing the indigenous blues on top of Lookout Mountain, and the closing with Roman and Grace joining together in a physical ceremony of their bodies (*Toughest* 150, 188). They have returned to the Spokane Reservation, where the community benefits from their educational experiences.

In Grace's physical description, Alexie alludes to the size and weight of Big Mom, another indication of the connection between the two women and their strength. Once again, her size matches the weight of her other qualities as nurturer and teacher: "She was a big woman with wide hips, thick legs, large breasts, and a soft stomach. She was deep brown and beautiful"; "She had never been a skinny woman, not once, and was growing larger every year. She was beautiful, her long black hair dirty and uncombed" (163, 186). Alexie creates an image of an Earth mother, a maternal woman with "wide hips" who could bear many children even though she has not. In "growing larger every year," Grace takes on not only physical weight but also the essence of one whose other qualities continue to grow in comparable size: nurturing, teaching, and loving. In effect, Grace is another version of Big Mom. Finally, in privileging the characteristics of large, dark-skinned, and brunette women, Alexie counters the typical white, Barbie Doll standards of beauty for women in the dominant society: thin, fair-skinned, and blonde. Rather than denigrate the white standards, however, Alexie expresses the comparison in terms of equality: "Standards of beauty were much more egalitarian on the rez, and Roman was an egalitarian man" (156).

The lyrics to "Big Mom" in *Reservation Blues* assure the listener that she "will always come back" (198). In "Saint Junior," the story opens with a narration about the now-deceased six Spokane drummers who are the sons of "six Indian mothers who'd sat together at their own drum—Big Mom's Daughters—and sung their own songs" (*Toughest* 150–51). Once again, here is an example of gender complementarity in which both the men and women enter into the activity of singing and drumming. Whether the name of the women's drum group signifies that the members are actually the biological daughters of Big Mom or merely functions as a tribute to her is not clear. More important are the tangible presence of her memory through the generations and the fact that the ghosts of all these ancestors always accompany Roman: "He was the only Fury left alive in the world, but he was not alone. He had his basketball, his ghosts, and an Indian woman named Grace Atwater asleep at home" (154).[5] The conflation of the three companions converges in a refrain heard throughout the chapter: "*I'm back*" (157).

The words "*I'm back*" first appear as part of the basketball superstar Michael Jordan's comeback speech, but there is also an echo of Big Mom's song lyrics, as if she also "will always come back." Big Mom's spirit as a feminine nurturer and teacher seems to have returned in the form of Grace. Big Mom's spirit also seems to influence Roman. She always tells the Coyote Springs band members that they have the ability to map their futures: "'You make your choices'" (*Reservation* 216). Roman repeats this same philosophy in describing his love for Grace: "Of course you chose who you loved. If you didn't choose, you ended up with what was left—the drunks and abusers, the debtors and vacuums, the ones who ate their food too fast or had never read a novel. Damn, marriage was hard work, was manual labor, and *unpaid* manual labor at that. Yet, year after year, Grace and Roman had pressed their shoulders against the stone and rolled it up the hill together" (*Toughest* 177–78). Big Mom's words echo throughout Roman's discourse on the implications of "choice." Much as Roman and Grace's survival of the pitfalls of college life was, he sees the survival of his good marriage as a daily effort to avoid the saboteurs of relationships: alcoholism, domestic violence, financial problems, lack of consideration for each other, and lack of common interests. In an endeavor to maintain a healthy marriage, Roman acknowledges the "hard work" required and compares the couple's joint efforts to a ceaseless Sisyphean task, another example of gender complementarity. Unlike Sisyphus's labor, however, theirs is not fruitless for they have the rewards of a deep, meaningful, and lasting marriage.

Alexie takes a more humorous tone about marriage in his short story "The Approximate Size of My Favorite Tumor" in his *The Lone Ranger and Tonto*

Fistfight in Heaven collection. He still focuses on the responsibility of partners to do their part to make the marriage work, as in gender complementarity, but this relationship takes on an entirely different dynamic.

Novelist and poet Paula Gunn Allen (Laguna Pueblo/Sioux) writes in *The Sacred Hoop* that "the interesting thing about the use of humor in American Indian poetry is its integrating effect: it makes tolerable what is otherwise unthinkable" (159). Gunn Allen makes this observation in her discussion of American Indians' awareness of the historical impact of genocide and argues that American Indian writers always deal in one form or another with the question "How does one survive in the face of collective death?" (156). In "The Approximate Size of My Favorite Tumor," Alexie narrows the focus on this cultural theme and deals with the imminent death of just one person. Using humor, he "makes tolerable what is otherwise unthinkable."

James Many Horses, the narrator of the story, who has learned that he has "cancer everywhere inside of [him]" (*Lone* 157), jokes about dying in order both to cope with telling his wife, Norma, and to deal with his own mortality. Alexie grounds the humor in the literary techniques of contradictions, reversals, language games, and omissions that subvert assumptions about what would probably happen in a situation involving terminal disease. These humor-creating strategies, which begin with the title and continue throughout the story to the conclusion of the narrative, are also embedded in the tribal-specific cultural context of the Spokane Indian Reservation.

Several material examples that support Alexie's intellectual sovereignty, a tribal-specific cultural way of looking at the world, are associated with reservation life: The opening sentence of the story mentions the Department of Housing and Urban Development (HUD) house in which James and Norma Many Horses live, setting up an economic relationship with the government department (154). "A dinner of macaroni and commodity cheese" refers to the food supplies usually doled out through government assistance programs on Indian reservations, and the Powwow Tavern on the tribal highway calls to mind those who exploit Indians and problems associated with alcoholism by setting up business close to reservations (156). Finally, an incident in which a Washington state patrolman illegally harasses and extorts one hundred dollars from James and Norma Many Horses exemplifies the continuing racism and antagonistic relations between Spokane Indians and law enforcement agencies. Alexie creates a setting of economic, social, and legal problems familiar to Spokane Indians in which to portray a married couple who are dealing with cancer and ultimately with death. Cultural survival humor is necessary to cope with this scenario.

James Many Horses should not be happy about having a tumor that eventually will end his life, yet, in contrast to the commonly expected notions about tumors, the title refers to the approximate size of his "favorite" one, as if he would actually prefer one tumor to another. Furthermore, the "size" of the tumor should not matter. James Many Horses has a malignant tumor, and it will eventually cause his death no matter what the size. The "approximate" size of the favorite tumor is "just about the size of a baseball, shaped like one, too. Even had stitch marks," and this comparison is why size matters (157). It allows James Many Horses to establish a pattern of images and metaphors built around the sport of baseball, and in the process he reappropriates a part of American popular culture. He sets up a relationship between himself and famous ball players, such as Babe Ruth, Roger Maris, and Hank Aaron, all home-run record holders: "I told her [Norma] to call me Babe Ruth. Or Roger Maris. Maybe even Hank Aaron 'cause there must have been about 755 damn tumors inside me. Then, I told her I was going to Cooperstown and sit right down in the lobby of the Hall of Fame. Make myself a new exhibit, you know?" (157). The image of "755 damn tumors" becomes a metaphor for the way humor ameliorates pain. Hank Aaron's Major League career record of 755 home runs resonates with the power of those baseballs flying through the air. With every additional humorous piece of dialogue and action in the development of the plot, Alexie hits the reader with a home-run laugh and mediates the pain of knowing that the inevitable death of James Many Horses and Norma's loss of her husband cannot be averted.

James Many Horses turns himself into a hero worthy of display in the Cooperstown Baseball Hall of Fame. Traditionally, American Indians have resented scientists and anthropologists who have displayed the remains of Native ancestors and artifacts in museums, and currently, the Native American Graves Protection and Repatriation Act of 1990 mandates that all Native artifacts and remains be returned to the tribes. Rather than make himself the tragic victim of a terminal disease, however, James Many Horses reappropriates not only the idea of Native remains on exhibit in museums, as relics of the past, but also the great American national pastime. He valorizes himself, thereby reversing the negative and positive descriptions usually associated with losing the game of life and winning in sports.

In addition, Alexie reassigns the historical roles in American Indian-white relations—Indians lose; Americans win—so that James Many Horses becomes a winner through a white cultural symbol, the game of baseball, and will survive as an exhibit in the Cooperstown Hall of Fame. He does so, however, within the framework of an African-American ballplayer who plays for a team with a name usually associated with negative stereotypes of American Indians, the Braves. James Many Horses aligns himself with a famous Braves player, known for breaking records and racial barriers, and consequently, stacks the odds in his favor. The imagery is rich and multilayered with irony.

In the story's opening paragraph, James Many Horses sets up the polarizations of losing and winning but finds a way to maneuver between the two by devising a new strategy—survival humor:

> After the argument that I had *lost* but pretended to *win*, I stormed out of the HUD house, jumped into the car, and prepared to drive off in *victory*, which was also known as *defeat*. But I realized that I hadn't grabbed my keys. At that kind of moment, a person begins to realize how he can be fooled by his own games. And at that kind of moment, *a person begins to formulate a new game to compensate for the failure of the first*. (emphasis added 154)

After losing the first battle, James Many Horses realizes that just pretending to win the argument with Norma will not suffice, and as a solution to deal with the loss, he must discover another way to continue. Of course, the same conditions hold for dealing with his cancer. He finds that reconciliation through humor. Although the focus seems to be on James Many Horses's thoughts and actions, the controlling position that his wife, Norma, holds is of major importance in understanding her power within the marriage relationship. In other words, they complement each other. In fact, since their first meeting when Norma went home with him, she had lived with James Many Horses until the day he told her that he had terminal cancer (160). This is not a superficial relationship, as evidenced by the lengths to which James Many Horses will go to make light of his health and, at the same time, work out matters with his wife. If he did not care so much about her, he would not be so concerned with whether or not she is angry.

Another indication of Norma's power is her physical bearing. Norma is introduced early in the short story collection in "This Is What It Means to Say Phoenix, Arizona": "Norma was a warrior. She was powerful. She could have picked up any two of the boys and smashed their skulls together. But worse than that, she would have dragged them all over to some tipi and made them listen to some elder tell a dusty old story" (65). Not only is Norma's strength impressive, but she also acts as an intermediary, ensuring that the young people are directed toward those who are the keepers of cultural knowledge. Later in the collection, in "Somebody Kept Saying Powwow," Junior Polatkin fittingly describes her as a cultural lifeguard, watching out for those of [them] that were so close to drowning" (199).

When Norma and James Many Horses meet, Alexie describes her as an "Amazon," similarly to the way he describes other strong female characters in his writing, such as Big Mom and Grace Atwater: "Norma was over six feet tall. Well, maybe not six feet tall but she was taller than me, taller than everyone in the bar except the basketball players" (159). Humor is what first attracts Norma to James Many Horses, so its importance in the context of their relationship cannot be overstated. Norma's size is what first attracts

James Many Horses to her. Even though in fact she may not be six feet tall, her carriage gives the impression that she is. Further, comparing her statuesque figure to that of the Amazon women, tall, strong, often masculine female warriors, conjures up an image of not only Norma's size but also her strength and female warrior characteristics. Norma's size follows in the tradition of Big Mom, Alexie's prototype for female strength and power.

Norma also resembles Alexie's other strong female characters in other ways. Similarly to Big Mom, Norma has the respect of the tribal community: "She was really young, [...] but everybody called her grandmother anyway, as a sign of respect" (199). Like Grace Atwater, Norma has no children, and she worries about the future for Indians: "Don't know if I want to raise kids in this world. It's getting uglier by the second. And not just on the reservation" (207). Although she does not teach in the same way that Big Mom and Grace do, she is gifted with a talent for writing and "used to write stories for the tribal newspaper" (205). Like all of Alexie's strong female characters, Norma does not drink or smoke (200). She has athletic abilities associated with male-gendered behaviors, but they are simply more examples of gender complementarity at work: "She was a rodeo queen, but not one of those rhinestone women. She was a roper, a breaker of wild ponies. She wrestled steers down to the ground and did that goofy old three-legged knot dance" (202). She also could play basketball: "I always wished we could have suited Norma up. She was taller than all of us and a better player than most of us. [...] she could have played college ball if she would've gone to college" (206–7). Also, like Grace Atwater, Norma has been with both men and women sexually: "Norma took a woman home with her once in a while, too. Years ago, homosexuals were given special status within the tribe. They had powerful medicine. I think it's even more true today, even though our tribe has assimilated into homophobia. I mean, a person has to have magic to assert their identity without regard to all the bullshit, right?" (203). Again, Norma is a powerful woman who lives her life as an autonomous person, making her own decisions. Finally, when Junior Polatkin connects Norma to the past in his dreams, she takes on mythic status, much like Big Mom's: "I dreamed her a hundred years ago, riding bareback down on Little Falls Flats. Her hair was unbraided and she was yelling something to me as she rode closer to where I stood" (201). Norma is a smart, talented, athletic, strong, powerful woman, respected by the tribal community for all that she does and is, a true complement to James Many Horses. As Junior Polatkin says, "She was probably the most compassionate person on the reservation but she was also the most passionate" (209).

Immediately after the introductory paragraph, James Many Horses begins to deliver dialogue that disrupts the typical behavior of a husband and wife arguing by drawing on 1950s television situation comedies like *Leave It to*

Beaver and *Father Knows Best*, while still playing on the baseball language of "home" base: "Honey, I'm *home*," I yelled [...]. My wife ignored me, gave me a momentary stoic look [...]. "Oh, what is that?" I asked. "Your Tonto face?" [...] "Honey," I called after her. "Didn't you miss me? I've been gone so long and it's good to be back *home*." [...] "And look at the kids," I said [...]. "They've grown so much" (emphasis added, 154–55).

Implying that he has made the home run and arrived back at home base, Alexie uses irony to state the opposite of the actual conditions in order to make light of a serious situation and ease the tension. The husband has not been gone a long time, knows that his wife is angry with him for treating his impending death so lightly, and does not have any children. Perhaps knowing that he will die with no heirs to carry on his family name can be dealt with only in a humorous way to undermine the stereotype of the vanishing American Indian. In any case, only James Many Horses speaks. Refusing to say a word, his wife merely makes obscene gestures and annoyed facial expressions.

Saying nothing gives Norma even more power because her silence frightens James Many Horses: "She pretended to ignore me, which I enjoyed. But then she pulled out her car keys, checked herself in the mirror, and headed for the door. I jumped in front of her, knowing she meant to begin her own war. That scared the shit out of me" (155). Norma is a woman who means business, and her husband knows when he has gone too far in provoking her. Norma is not amused and knows how to control the situation. Immediately, James Many Horses tries to apologize, saying he was "just kidding" and "didn't mean anything"; he promises to "do whatever" Norma wants, but he is too late with his "I'm sorry" (155). James Many Horses sees his wife as a contemporary female warrior when he realizes that she "meant to begin her own war": "She pushed me aside, adjusted her dreams, pulled on her braids for a jumpstart, and walked out the door. I followed her and stood on the porch as she jumped into the car and started it up" (155). Saying only one sentence as she drives off into the sunset, Norma threatens her husband: "'I'm going dancing'" (155). With the threat of going to the Powwow Tavern to find another dancing partner, Norma basically wins the second battle, and her husband is left standing in her dust.

With Norma's reputation for dancing, she implies that if James Many Horses will not be her partner, she can find someone else to complement her. She is not interested in dancing alone: "[S]he could spend a night in the Powwow Tavern and dance hard. She could dance Indian and white. And that's a mean feat, since the two methods of dancing are mutually exclusive" (200). According to Junior Polatkin's description, Norma can do it all. Before she married James Many Horses, she usually "would dance with everybody, not choosing any favorites. She was a diplomat" (201). One night, however, she danced only with Junior Polatkin, and that was the night he dreamed about her. Because of her reputation for being able to dance, James Many Horses knows that Norma means business when she tells him that she is going dancing. As a metaphor for gender complementarity within marriage, he knows he had better worry about her finding a new dancing partner.

Alexie plays his own game with language and changes James Many Horses's name as the story progresses. The name moves through a variety of alterations just as the character's status changes focus from husband to abandoned spouse to man with no offspring to dying patient. A friend of James Many Horses, Simon, calls him Jimmy Sixteen-and-One-Half-Horses, Jimmy One-Horse, and Jimmy Zero-Horses. There is a minibiography in the devolution of the name; the variations emphasize different degrees of the character's diminishing status. Toward the end of the story, however, the narrator refers to himself as James Many Horses III, reestablishing himself as a member of a family line with longevity. The structuring of the names parallels the relationship between James Many Horses and Norma. They are together at the beginning of the story, separated, and rejoined at the end, just as his name is reestablished. In other words, James Many Horses needs his wife to complement him and make him more whole.

The James Many Horses III version of the name appears after the hospital has released James Many Horses to go home and die in the comfort of familiar surroundings: "And there I was, at home, writing letters to my loved ones on special reservation stationery that read: FROM THE DEATH BED OF JAMES MANY HORSES, III. But in reality, I sat at my kitchen table to write, and DEATH TABLE just doesn't have the necessary music. I'm also the only James Many Horses, but there is a certain dignity to any kind of artificial tradition" (168). Even as James Many Horses writes his deathbed letters, he maintains a sense of survival humor and adapts the Anglo custom of adding the ordinal number to his surname, indicating his place in his family line. He notes the artificiality of his constructed identity by using this naming practice, but he also questions the authenticity of the tradition, implying that the superficiality of the name does not guarantee the notion of progeny; nor does it reflect a tradition that is necessarily grounded in any other aspect of life, thereby connecting it to the larger community.

Alexie also changes the typical direction in some of the action for comic effect. Simon drives his car in "his only gear, reverse" (156). Besides the implications of reservation economics of having a vehicle that only operates in reverse, facing backward in order to move forward comments on the issue of progress. Mythic time conflates the past, present, and future; therefore, American Indians remain connected to their heritage as they continue to push forward. While rendering a comic scenario of driving a car, this change of direction also notes the importance of remembering the culture's history as the Spokane Tribe continues to endure as a sovereign nation in the twenty-first century.

Alexie uses omissions as another device to create humor. The reader is not privy to the first argument between James Many Horses and Norma because the story opens as he leaves the house. One can only imagine the conversation they have. In another instance when Alexie excludes the reader from hearing dialogue, James Many Horses has Simon drive him to the Powwow Tavern, where his wife has gone dancing. Once inside the tavern, he tries to apologize for the second time to his wife: "'Norma,' I said. 'I'm sorry. I'm sorry I have cancer and I'm sorry I'm dying.' [. . .] 'Are you going to make any more jokes about it?' she asked. 'Just one or two more, maybe,' I said and smiled. It was exactly the wrong thing to say. Norma slapped me in anger, [. . .]. 'If you say anything funny ever again, I'm going to leave you,' Norma said. 'And I'm fucking serious about that'" (158–59). Norma is still angry about James Many Horses's attitude toward his cancer. Even though their relationship began in a context of humor and continued with humor as an important part of the marriage, at this moment Norma cannot laugh about her husband's condition. She even resorts to physical violence by slapping him and threatening to leave him, acts that do not resemble those of a loving and caring spouse. Still, Norma has the strength and power to strike her husband, and she must know him well enough to realize that he would never return the abuse. Instead, his weapon of choice is humor.

Despite Norma's threat, James Many Horses can neither change who he is nor resist the temptation that she dangles in front of him: "I lost my smile briefly, reached across the table to hold her hand, and said something incredibly funny. It was maybe the best one-liner I had ever uttered. Maybe the moment that would have made me a star anywhere else. But in the Powwow Tavern, which was just a front for reality, Norma heard what I had to say, stood up, and left me" (159). Perhaps James Many Horses must respond to his wife with humor because she simply cannot laugh at his impending death. Although he calls her "a warrior in every sense of the word," he has seen how she reacts when an elder dies: "Norma would weep violently, throw books and furniture" (167). Norma cares so much because she realizes that the future of the Spokane Indians is uncertain: "'Every one of our elders who dies takes a piece of our past away.' [. . .] 'And that hurts more because I don't know how much of a future we have'" (167). As Big Mom does, Norma cares about connections to the reservation and tribal community. Norma shows the same kind of compassion for non-Natives, too, when she comes upon a car accident: "[S]he held a dying man's head in her lap and sang to him until he passed away. He was a white guy, too" (168). James Many Horses introduces humor to the situation; Norma introduces seriousness. Maybe it would be too painful for him to acknowledge her pain, so all he can do is make jokes. Alexie builds the tension in this scene so that the reader cannot wait to hear the joke, but then, he thwarts those expectations. The reader must *imagine* what the funniest one-liner could be. By not including it, Alexie magnifies the humorous effect. For Alexie, imagination is a powerful tool.

In another short story in the same collection, "Imagining the Reservation," Alexie writes a meditation on this topic: "Survival = Anger × Imagination. Imagination is the only weapon on the reservation"; "Imagination is the politics of dreams"; "Imagine a spring with water that mends broken bones. Imagine a drum which wraps itself around your heart. Imagine a story that puts wood in the fireplace" (*Lone* 150–53). Perhaps James Many Horses just imagines that he has uttered the funniest one-liner of his life. Perhaps he imagines that humor will mend his diseased body. Perhaps he imagines that a story will prevent him from dying. Regardless, the reader is also free to imagine that James Many Horses actually delivers the funniest one-liner of his life. Despite his success with the one-liner, he loses the third battle with his wife because Norma follows through with her threat and leaves, showing her commitment to what she warned she would do.

In an appropriate Native American structure of spherical space and cyclical time, balanced in gender complementarity, the couple ends where they began when Norma returns home and continues the joke with which the story opened: "'Honey,' she said. 'I'm home.' [...] 'Honey,' she said. 'I've been gone so long and I missed you so much. But now I'm back. Where I belong.' [...] 'Where are the kids?' she asked. 'They're asleep,' I said, recovered just in time to continue the joke" (168–69). Despite Norma's strength, she previously was not ready to accept James Many Horses's disease. After finally coming to terms with the reality of his cancer, she realizes that she belongs at home, where she can take care of him. This is her role in the marriage, and she is responsible for nurturing him. The kindest act that she can perform at this moment is to join James Many Horses in his humor, keep the fifties sitcom dialog running, and let him know that she loves him. After striking out three times, James Many Horses at last has won a battle with his wife and hit a homerun. Winning is part of the balance, part of the gender complementarity, in their marriage.

Norma confesses her infidelity while away from James Many Horses, and he admits his disappointment: "Believe me: nothing ever hurt more. Not even my tumors which are the approximate size of baseballs" (170). Because he has already noted, "Humor was an antiseptic that cleaned the deepest of personal wounds," he ends the story with another funny one-liner (164). James Many Horses has already recounted how Norma excels at making fry bread and helping people die (163). Now he suggests that Norma is good at only one of those two things, but he does not specify which, another case of omission. Norma might be good only at making fry bread because her confession of infidelity has deeply hurt her husband, and that obviously cannot be of any help to him while he dies. Norma, however, is still good at helping people die simply because she has returned to the reservation. This act alone supports the idea of endurance and survival for the Spokane Tribe. As Big Mom does, Norma goes back.

Gunn Allen claims, "Humor is a primary means of reconciling the tradition of continuance, bonding, and celebration with the stark facts of racial destruction" (*Sacred* 159). In the case of James Many Horses, humor becomes his only weapon in the face of death, and at the same time, it provides him with a way to bond with Norma and celebrate her return to the reservation, the community, and their marriage. When James Many Horses asks Norma why she left the man with whom she had been living and went back to him, "[s]he turned stoic, gave [him] that beautiful Tonto face, and said, 'Because he was so fucking serious about everything *Lone* 170). Like the tumors the approximate size of baseballs—circular shapes—James Many Horses and Norma find continuance even in the agents of death. The important point is not that James Many Horses has cancer and is dying or that Norma left him for a while. The important point to remember is that she returns. The political implications of Norma's returning to her husband and the reservation cannot be overlooked. Norma is most powerful in her act of accepting her husband's cancer and going back to help him die. As she says, "'[S]omeone needs to help you die the right way.' [. . .] 'And we both know that dying ain't something you ever done before'" (170).

Making people laugh, Alexie claims, is his greatest accomplishment: "'That's the only way people will listen to me and not run away screaming, or not get angry or not turn off because they don't want to hear what I'm saying, is if I'm funny. People listen to anything if you're funny'" (Assuras). And ultimately, Norma listens to James Many Horses because he is funny. In his essay "Indian Humor," Deloria writes about the significance of a culture's humor: "One of the best ways to understand a people is to know what makes them laugh. Laughter encompasses the limits of the soul. In humor life is redefined and accepted. Irony and satire provide much keener insights into a group's collective psyche and values than do years of research" (*Custer* 146). Through the metaphor of baseball, James Many Horses redefines his cancer and helps Norma learn to accept it. Through his humor, he contains all the pain and suffering that both he and Norma must endure. The Spokane Indians have survived colonialism and continue to exert their intellectual sovereignty, even through their humor. As Deloria concludes, "When a people can laugh at themselves and laugh at others and hold all aspects of life together without letting anybody drive them to extremes, then it seems to [him] that that people can survive" (167). James and Norma Many Horses can laugh at themselves and hold their marriage together without allowing anything but death to part them.

Other Native authors share Alexie's attitude toward humor. Erdrich agrees, "[T]he most serious things have to be jokes. Humor is the way we make our life worth living" (Moyers 144). Certainly, James and Norma Many Horses use humor in the most serious of situations: his terminal cancer. For whatever time James Many Horses has left, humor is one way in which he will make his life as worthwhile as possible. Erdrich extends the idea of survival humor to all tribes: "It may be that the one universal thing about Native Americans from tribe to tribe is survival humor—the humor that enables you to live with what you have to live with. You have to be able to poke fun at people who are dominating your life and family" (144). Erdrich notes that survival humor has grown out of a history of colonialism, the dominant culture's dictating how Natives live their lives. With that historical and cultural background, James Many Horses has the necessary survival humor to deal with the cancer that now dictates his life. Believing that humor is very important in American Indian life and literature, Erdrich challenges the stereotype of the "stoic, unflinching Indian standing, looking at the sunset," and claims that the opposite is closer to the truth: "Indian people really have a great sense of humor and when it's survival humor, you learn to laugh at things. [...] It's just a personal way of responding to the world and to things that happen to you; it's a different way of looking at the world" (Coltelli 46). And James Many Horses certainly has his own unique way of looking at his world of terminal cancer, as a tumor the approximate size of a baseball.

In the short story "Indian Country" in *The Toughest Indian in the World* collection, Alexie does not deal with the same kinds of female characters who have filled the pages of his previous works. Instead, he introduces lesbian characters. When asked in an online chat whether he was making a political statement with the addition of homosexuality in his writing, he had the following to say: "It's a personal and political statement. As my life has become more urban and more diverse, so have my friends become more urban and diverse. I think the hatred I am most upset with in the world is homophobia. It's the only hatred that has absolutely no basis in reality. Every other group of people has oppressed every other group of people—except the gays and lesbians" (Barnes & Noble.com 3). Alexie takes a strong position about the discrimination that gays and lesbians have suffered. Claiming that his position is both political and personal, he critiques the dominant culture's attitudes about and treatment of gays and lesbians because he argues that there is no rational basis for that kind of hatred. Noting that there would be much less art produced were it not for gays and lesbians, Alexie points out the hypocrisy of homophobia: "You get rid of all the gay art in the world, and you'd have two auto-repair manuals and three albums by John Tesh, and do you really want to live in that world?" (Barnes & Noble.com 3). In the same way that Alexie critiques the illogical bias of people who discriminate against lesbians, he examines how painful and damaging that attitude can be for both the lesbian characters and their families and friends in the short story "Indian Country."

Low Man Smith, a Coeur d'Alene writer, travels to Missoula, Montana, from his hometown of Seattle, at the invitation of Carlotta, a Navajo poet who teaches English at the Flathead Indian College. Going with the intention of asking Carlotta to marry him, he learns upon his arrival that Carlotta has already married an old flame, Chuck, and left for Flagstaff, Arizona. Broken-hearted, confused, and at a loss for what he should do next, Low Man looks for a used-book store where he can read a good book and drink coffee. Through a series of misunderstandings, he lands in jail. Because of his disoriented condition, the police officers want to release him to someone who can look after him. Low Man learns that an old college lesbian friend, Tracy Johnson, works at the local Barnes and Noble bookstore and is earning her M.F.A. at the University of Montana. He calls her, and she agrees to pick him up at the police station on her way to meet her Spokane partner the law school student Sara Polatkin, whom she plans to marry.

Riding in Tracy's 1972 half-ton Chevrolet pickup, Low Man appraises her physical looks since he last saw her: "Forty pounds overweight, she was beautiful, wearing a loose T-shirt and tight blue jeans. Her translucent skin bled light into her dark hair. [. . .] 'You're lovely,' said Low" (*Toughest* 136–37). Even some of Alexie's white women, who are drawn as large and beautiful physical presences, go against the dominant culture's standards of Barbie Doll beauty: thin and blonde. Tracy's partner, Sara, is the opposite, or complement, of her in stature: "She was short, thin, very pretty, even with her bad teeth and eccentric clothes—a black dress with red stockings, and Chuck Taylor basketball shoes with Cat in the Hat socks. [. . .] Her black hair hung down past her waist" (138). What Sara lacks in height and weight, she makes up for in her aggressive personality. She immediately third-degrees Low Man about his feelings for Tracy and their past relationship, wanting to know whether he still loves her and whether he ever had sexual relations with her (138–39). As the jealous and protective partner, she lives up to her family name, much as Marie Polatkin does, and resembles the warrior wife of Qualchan who attacks her husband's enemies. In this case, however, Sara is a lesbian protecting her interests in her soon-to-be wife.

The conflict in "Indian Country" is not that Carlotta has jilted Low Man but that Sara's parents, Sid and Estelle Polatkin, object to her plans to marry Tracy. They are traveling from the Spokane Reservation with the intent to change their daughter's mind. Alexie characterizes them with histories that might belong to any number of people living on the reservation:

> He was president of the Spokane Indian Reservation VFW. [...] Sid's hair was pulled back in a gray ponytail. So was Estelle's. Both of their faces told stories. Sid's: the recovering alcoholic; the wronged son of a wronged son; the Hamlet of his reservation. Estelle's: the tragic beauty; the woman who stopped drinking because her husband did; the woman who woke in the middle of the night to wash her hands ten times in a row.
> Now they were Mormons. (140).

Together, this couple has survived military service, alcoholism, and obsessive-compulsive syndrome, a lot to be said for the gender complementarity within their own marriage. Alexie uses the shorthand of Mormonism for the parents' homophobia because of the Mormons' well-known role as a primary political force behind antihomosexual issues and their position supporting the traditional family structure. Their antilesbian stance stems mainly from their Mormon conviction that homosexuality is a grave sin and from their fear of losing their daughter's presence in their heavenly and eternal family for committing such acts (145). Not being with the eternal family is a Mormon version of hell. Concerning the attitude toward gays and lesbians on Indian reservations, Alexie states: "Tragically, I think the homophobia in minority communities is greater than in the dominant culture. That whole lateral violence thing" (Barnes & Noble.com). To make this point, Alexie resorts to using the Mormons' stance associated with homosexuality. The parents enter in the spirit of love with intentions of forgiving Sara, but matters do not work out as they had hoped (*Toughest* 142).

Over a salmon dinner at the Holiday Inn, tempers flare as the five characters argue over Christianity, lesbianism, and who has the right to sit at that table defending Tracy and Sara's lifestyle. With Estelle's weeping, Sara's begging her mother not to cry, Tracy's telling Low Man to go for a ride, and Sid's becoming angrier by the minute, conditions quickly deteriorate. When Tracy suggests that maybe she should be the one to leave, Sara takes charge of the situation: "'No,' said Sara. 'Nobody's going anywhere.' In Sara's voice, the others heard something new: an adulthood ceremony taking place between syllables" (146). The authority with which Sara speaks lets everyone know that she is not just the daughter in this situation but also an adult. Her strength in trying to calm her parents and restore some kind of emotional order to what has transpired indicates that she is acting as an autonomous woman who knows how to deal with a volatile situation. The adulthood ceremony signifies that Sara has made the break from her parents, an act requiring emotional strength, an act that empowers her.

As Sara announces that she's leaving, she tells her parents that she loves them and steps away from the table toward Tracy. Sid warns his daughter that if she leaves, she should plan on never speaking to them again (147). Low Man tries to explain to Sid how useless that kind of threat is: "'These women don't need us. They never did'" (148). Unable to accept that his daughter chooses to disregard his parental and patriarchal authority, Sid resorts to physical intimidation. He chases after the two women, pushes Tracy into a wall, and takes Sara by the elbow, saying, "'You're coming with us'" (148). Estelle asks Low Man to help them, one of only two times that she speaks in the whole story, an example of how her voice is subsumed in a patriarchal marriage. Just as Low Man runs to their aid, Sid slaps his daughter twice, shouting, "'She's my daughter, she's mine'" (148). Sid punches Low, who falls to the floor, and Sid continues yelling ownership of his daughter, until Tracy slaps him: "Surprised, defeated, Sid dropped to the floor beside Low" (148). Low Man's final question to the parents emphasizes what should be important: "'What are you going to do when she's gone?'" (149).

Indeed, how will Sid and Estelle feel when they can never see their daughter again? Focusing on the love that families and friends have for one another, Alexie makes the point that the pain of not seeing loved ones ever again *should* be far greater than the discomfort of tolerating lifestyles different from their own. Tracy and Sara feel no guilt about their sexual orientation or their love for each other. Instead, they are proud of each other's accomplishments and do not hide in the closet. Both of these women are strong and powerful to confront the discrimination that they encounter, and their openness about their lifestyle and love for each other are a political statement about the rights of individuals to live their lives. Alexie's critique asks those who would shun gays and lesbians to examine the damage inflicted on families and friends when there is a lack of understanding, consideration, respect, and tolerance for those who are different.

Alexie presents a contemporary version of a peace party between warring factions: Indian/White, Christian/pagan, and heterosexual/homosexual. The parties meet at the dinner table, talk, fight, and part; however, there is no reconciliation, and no treaty is signed. The peace party, in one sense, is a failure. Alexie makes a case against those who try to control a woman and her sexual orientation. He also challenges the hero/coward opposition and makes a case for the antihero, Low Man, a Coeur d'Alene who does not meet the usual stereotype of the Indian warrior. In this story, the women are the contemporary warriors who win in a context of complementing each other.

When asked what people should know about Indians, Alexie answers by focusing on the political: "I think the primary thing that people need to know about Indians is that our identity is much less cultural now and much more political. That we really do exist as political entities and sovereign political nations. That's the most important thing for people to understand, that we are separate politically and economically. And should be" ("Dialogue" 6).

Alexie discusses the political aspect of tribal nations as sovereign entities. The same could be said on a microlevel about his strong female characters. They, too, are political sovereign entities who are strong, powerful, autonomous, contemporary female warriors, whether they are matriarchal mythic figures like Big Mom, college students and political activists like Marie Polatkin, teachers and wives like Grace Atwater, fry bread–making experts and nurturers-to-dying-people like Norma Many Horses, or lesbians like Tracy Johnson and Sara Polatkin. The value of these women's roles and work grows out of a context of gender complementarity; they are valued for who they are and what they give to relationships and the community within the context of specific tribal and intellectual sovereignties.

Alexie takes a more political position outside his writing and makes it his agenda within his writing, unlike Silko and Erdrich, who claim they do not want to focus on politics and instead want to let their writing speak for itself. That Alexie, a male author, is the one who makes public antipatriarchal statements, whereas usually women are perceived as doing this kind of criticizing, points out how men can comfortably critique patriarchy when they are securely grounded in a worldview of gender complementarity. This kind of behavior does not make men appear to be less masculine or more effeminate, merely as men who are comfortable with both sexes' equally contributing to the community in a balanced way. Just as women can perform what might appear to non-Natives as male-gendered behaviors, men can perform what might appear as female-gendered behaviors.

Also, Alexie's statements regarding the Spokane Tribe's assimilation into sexism, misogyny, and homophobia, characteristics of the U.S. patriarchal culture, are a way of critiquing the effects of colonization on Spokane Indians, but his writing constructs strong female characters as if the dynamics of gender complementarity have never vanished. His conscious construction of autonomous Native female characters is a political act of resistance and recovery of traditional tribal gender relations, a reconfiguration that results in powerful women.

CHAPTER 7

Conclusion: "Indian Women Were and Are Powerful"
Intellectual Sovereignty and the Strength of Female Warriors

The first Native American literature selections that I read as an undergraduate in a Survey of American Literature course were Zitkala-Ša's (Yankton Sioux) autobiographical essays in *American Indian Stories* and Leslie Marmon Silko's (Laguna Pueblo) "Lullaby." As did many non-Native female readers, I approached Native American literature with a white feminist sensibility that did not allow me to see or understand these female characters within their own tribal histories and cultures. I simply viewed them as exploited, oppressed, and marginalized women, who had suffered at the hands of the dominant mainstream society. Even in that context, however, I saw a certain determination in these Native characters that I attributed to their strength as women. I projected a definition onto them through my own non-Native lens of what a strong woman is—someone who resists patriarchy.

In addition to the lack of a clear understanding of how to see these female characters as subjects rather than objects, my instructor had no previous training in teaching Native American literatures. Therefore, my lack of appropriate critical theory resulted in a continuing colonization of the literature, seeing it through traditional European-American approaches. Since learning about the importance of tribal-specific histories and cultures to studying Native American literature, I now appreciate that gender relations are tribally constructed. Although gender complementarity is just one aspect to consider when examining literary Native characters, it provides a perspective in which to understand how these female characters can be powerful, autonomous, and valued for their contributions to the tribal community. The four authors whom I have examined in this discussion—Zitkala-Ša, Leslie Marmon Silko, Louise Erdrich (Ojibwe), and Sherman Alexie (Spokane/Coeur d'Alene)—consistently present Native women in this fashion. Furthermore, in looking at the tribes of the literary characters considered in this book—Yankton Sioux, Navajo, Ojibwe, and Spokane—I recognize that gender complementarity exists regardless of whether the tribe is matriarchal, patriarchal, or both. This idea that women are as important as men is a worldview that these writers share. In that sense, gender complementarity crosses tribal boundaries.

By claiming that I can better comprehend women in Native American literature, I do not presume that I can speak with personal authority for the Native authors, the female characters they have created, or the Native experience. However, I can say that I have better insights to "why" the literary Native women's experience includes the ability to move through their worlds with a solid knowledge of who they are and what they are capable of accomplishing. I have tried to avoid the pitfalls that American Indian studies scholar Devon A. Mihesuah (Oklahoma Choctaw) observes in feminist critics: "Numerous feminist scholars have expressed concern over the propensity of writers to ignore the heterogeneity among women, particularly among women of color. American Indian women are especially multifaceted, and with few exceptions this aspect is overlooked" (37). Zitkala-Ša, Silko, Erdrich, and Alexie do not overlook this aspect and illustrate through their constructions of female characters that "American Indian women are especially multifaceted."

Although "there has never been a unitary 'world-view' among tribes," the concept of gender complementarity, the idea that the roles of men and women complement each other in a balanced and equally valued fashion, has always existed: "In many cases Indian women did indeed have religious, political, and economic power—not more power than the men, but at least equal to what the men had" (Mihesuah 38, 44). Because culture is not static, however, the ways in which women respond to their own specific tribal circumstances vary. Ultimately, political ramifications for Native women in a context of gender complementarity result in sovereignty, power, strength, and autonomy, different consequences from those for white feminists, who usually are concerned with basic issues of inequality in a patriarchal culture.

In discussing the critical approaches of groups of women outside mainstream feminists, Toril Moi explains the benefit of considering their position:

> [B]y highlighting the different situations and often conflicting interests of specific groups of women, these critical approaches force white heterosexual

feminists to re-examine their own sometimes totalitarian conception of 'woman' as a homogeneous category. These 'marginal feminisms' ought to prevent white middle-class First-World feminists from defining their own preoccupations as universal female (or feminist) problems. In this respect, recent work on Third-World women has much to teach us. (86)

Moi's observations on the feminist approaches of groups of women outside the dominant culture support Mihesuah's position that the diversity of marginalized groups is not recognized. In their writings, Zitkala-Ša, Silko, Erdrich, and Alexie teach that among Native American tribes there are variations in worldviews about women's roles, status, and importance in the community. They clearly show that the conception of American Indian women is not homogeneous.

In Zitkala-Ša's personal correspondence with Carlos Montezuma (Yavapai), she emphasizes the importance of self-determination and tribal sovereignty, the idea that American Indians as sovereign nations should have the right to decide their own future without interference from the U.S. government: "If we would claim our full heritage we must be masters of our circumstances" (Montezuma). Zitkala-Ša exercises her intellectual sovereignty and autonomy in her speaking, writing, and political activism for American Indians, political issues involving men, women, and children, which set her apart from the traditional concerns of white feminists, who often are looking only at issues that deal with women's political status. "White feminists tend to focus on gender oppression and to overlook racial issues, thus alienating many Indian females," writes Mihesuah (40). She goes on to state, "Traditional Indian women have been more concerned about tribal or community survival than either gender oppression or individual advancement in economics, academia, or other facets of society" (40). Zitkala-Ša's concerns speak directly to the legal relationship between American Indians and the U.S. government, one that is dictated by established legal documents, treaties, and agreements. When she talks about "our full heritage," included in that tribal cultural and historical inheritance is the concept of gender complementarity, a political relationship in which there are balance and value accorded to both men and women.

In Silko's short story "Lullaby," she offers a Navajo setting of cultural and historical information that explains why the female protagonist, Ayah, has power that unnerves the non-Native characters in a local bar: "She felt satisfied that the men in the bar feared her. Maybe it was her face and the way she held her mouth with teeth clenched tight, like there was nothing anyone could do to her now" (*Storyteller* 48–49). Born into a Navajo culture that is matriarchal, matrilocal, and matrifocal, Ayah knows who she is, where she is from, and where she belongs. She has the power of intellectual sovereignty and the confidence that results from that kind of knowing.

Ayah's self-assurance, even in light of a history of cultural genocide, injustices suffered, and repression by the dominant culture, frightens the men outside her culture, who do not know how to deal with such a powerful woman. Ayah is a woman who feels empowered in her domestic sphere: "Numerous Indian women assert that they are not 'unfulfilled.' They refuse to be victims of gender oppression by taking charge of their lives, reveling in their roles and status as women who hold their tribes together" (Mihesuah 41). In Ayah's case, the oppression she endures is not that of the men in the bar but also that of losing her children to the dominant culture, but she does not allow this loss to overwhelm her, and instead her story ends on a note of survival and continuity.

In Erdrich's *The Blue Jay's Dance*, her nonfiction memoir about pregnancy, motherhood, and writing, she declares, "Women are strong, strong, terribly strong" (12). Her description of strong women, whether giving birth, living alone, being married, or being involved in political activism, saturates her writing. In fact, Mark Shechner argues that Erdrich views strong women and their capabilities as the glue that holds the community together:

> Erdrich's feminism, then, and her Native-Americanism go hand in hand, because what she shows us is the dynamism of a matriarchy, which, though it is a captive nation, is a society that can take care of its own. Whatever it is the men do and whatever power they may have, it is the women who define the moral life of the tribe and are the maintainers of the social order, which, though disorderly by white middle-class standards, has its own strict logic: a logic of care. (48–49)

Erdrich's female characters maintain the social order through their intellectual sovereignty, or as Shechner notes, their own "strict logic," and the dynamics of gender complementarity allow the women to share equally in creating the daily life of the community, balancing the roles and power of the men. In arguing that the value of Indian women is vastly underrated, Mihesuah stresses: "[I]t has not been only the men who were the catalysts for survival, adaptation, and development. Women have been just as crucial to the economic, social, religious, and political survival of tribes" (45). Erdrich's female characters are not underrated and attest to the strength of Ojibwe women who have been crucial to the survival of the tribe.

In the novel *Indian Killer*, Alexie characterizes Marie Polatkin as a contemporary female warrior, fighting with words, who challenges an arrogant white male professor when she says, "'I'm talking like a twentieth-century Indian woman. Hell, a twenty-first-century Indian'" (247). Marie is a contemporary Spokane Indian college student, but her embracing the dominant culture's educational system does not indicate that she breaks away from her tribal connections. On the contrary, Marie uses her education to further her social and political activism for urban Indians. She utilizes "the tools of the oppressors to overcome oppression, the struggle for equality against 'linguistic imperialism' and 'linguistic inequality'" (Pewewardy 32). She autonomously creates her own self-identification in Dr. Mather's classroom and does not allow the academy to determine who she is as an Indian woman. Marie can do this because in her worldview a woman's voice is as important and valued as any man's, and in this case, her opinion is more accurate than that of a cultural outsider, someone with no personal knowledge of Spokane Indians. Just as Marie chooses to behave independently of the dominant culture's expectations of her as an Indian woman, in their own ways so do Big Mom, Grace Atwater, and Norma Many Horses conduct themselves as autonomous Spokane Indian women. Their acts of self-determination demonstrate their intellectual sovereignty, power, and strength as contemporary female warriors.

Mihesuah makes clear why Native authors can portray accurate representations of Native women and what can be learned from reading their works: "Works written by culturally aware Indian women [and men] are derived from their consciousness, filled with experience and knowledge of tribal ritual. [...] Indeed, it is through their writings that we can learn that Indian women were and are powerful; they were and are as complex as their cultures are diverse. Their works are worth a look" (48). Through their cultural awareness, authors like Zitkala-Ša, Silko, Erdrich, and Alexie are able to depict powerful Indian women in the past and the present. With every action committed by their female characters, they resist the United States' patriarchal culture's colonized view of Indian women as inferior to men. Their writings not only defy erroneous images of Indian women but also recover in literature what they have always known to be true, that Indian women are powerful, in part, because of gender complementarity.

Notes

Chapter 1: Introduction: "Writing Is Different from Tribe to Tribe": Historical and Cultural Contexts

1. Throughout this book, I use the tribal affiliation with which people have self-identified. Although there might be a question of whether the people are enrolled members of a particular tribe, I do not address that issue.
2. In 1972, Michael Dorris founded the Native American Studies Program at Dartmouth College, and he taught there for fifteen years: <http://teacher.scholastic.com/authorsandbooks/authors/dorris/bio.htm>.

Chapter 3: "We Must Be Masters of Our Circumstances": Rhetorical Sovereignty as Political Resistance in the Life and Works of Zitkala-Ša

1. Simmons is Gertrude's family name, Bonnin is her married name, and Zitkala-Ša is her self-given Lakota name used for certain of her publications. Although she used both Bonnin and Zitkala-Ša for her publications, in order to minimize confusion and maintain consistency, the name Zitkala-Ša is used except when quoting a source that uses something else. I follow Doreen Rappaport's decision "to continue calling her Zitkala-Ša to reflect the fact that until the end of her life she worked to reassert her Indian identity." *The Flight of Red Bird: The Life of Zitkala-*Ša (New York: Puffin, 1997) introduction.
2. Biographical information for Zitkala-Ša has been compiled from the following: Dexter Fisher, foreword, *American Indian Stories*, by Zitkala-Ša (Lincoln: University of Nebraska Press, 1985), v–xx; P. Jane Hafen, "Zitkala-Ša (Gertrude Bonnin)," *Encyclopedia of North American Indians*, ed. Frederick E. Hoxie (Boston: Houghton, 1996), 708–10; Doreen Rappaport, *The Flight of Red Bird: The Life of Zitkala-*Ša (New York: Puffin, 1997); and Mary Young, "Gertrude Simmons Bonnin," *Notable American Women—1607–1950—A Biographical Dictionary*, ed. Edward T. James (Cambridge, MA: Belknap Press of Harvard University Press, 1971), 198–200.
3. On their book jackets, Joy Harjo spells *Muscogee* with a *c*, and Craig Womak spells *Muskogee* with a *k*. I honor their chosen spellings, so both are used in this discussion.
4. Although only one letter is noted in the works cited, each additional reference to a letter among the correspondence of Carlos Montezuma is noted by date within the body of the essay. Also, the source for the letters was not the actual microfilm edition of The Papers of Carlos Montezuma but typed transcripts of the letters.

Chapter 4: "The Men in the Bar Feared Her": The Power of Ayah in Leslie Marmon Silko's "Lullaby"

1. Leslie Marmon Silko, "Lullaby," *Storyteller* (New York: Arcade, 1981), 43. All quotations from "Lullaby" are taken from this edition and are referenced by page number in the text.
2. Silko's novel *Ceremony* (New York: Viking, 1997) deals in more detail with the issues of World War II veterans. Tayo, a Laguna Pueblo mixed-blood veteran, returns home to his reservation and has trouble dealing with the memories of his wartime experiences. Tayo suffers guilt due to a number of factors: he could not prevent the death of his cousin, Rocky,

with whom he enlisted and served in the Philippines; his uncle, Josiah, dies while he is away, and Josiah's cattle wander off; his Auntie Thelma will not let him forget that his mother was a prostitute and he is of mixed-blood heritage; and the drought from which New Mexico suffers must be due to his praying for the rain to cease while he was in the Philippines. Tayo's other veteran friends deal with their problems through alcohol, sexual promiscuity, violent acts, and braggadocio. Tayo has not found healing through the veterans' hospitals or the Laguna medicine man. He begins to recover when he visits a Navajo healer who believes that traditional practices must adapt and include modern techniques. Tayo begins to take responsibility for his own healing and reconnects with Laguna spirituality through Ts'eh, a female connected with Mount Taylor and the sacredness of the land.

3. Stephen J. Kunitz, and Jerrold E. Levy, et al., *Drinking Careers: A Twenty-Five-Year Study of Three Navajo Populations* (New Haven, CT: Yale University Press, 1994), 5. The authors argue that the results of their original study caused them to question the then-reigning explanation of abusive drinking by Indians, which Silko seems to suggest. Instead they argued: "As the livestock economy was destroyed by the government in the 1930s and as people were paid cash for the stock they had lost, beverage alcohol became easier to purchase. Moreover, during World War II many Navajos were in the army or employed off the reservation and learned to drink in those settings. After the war, roads improved, and motor vehicles became more available. The result was that alcohol was more accessible to more Navajos. From an item of high prestige available primarily to the wealthy and their dependents, by the mid-1960s—only a generation later—alcohol had become accessible to virtually everyone. Thus, more people could drink in the highly visible groups that had been one characteristic pattern of the traditional Navajo style" (3–4).

Chapter 5: "Women Are Strong, Strong, Terribly Strong": Female Intellectual Sovereignty in the Works of Louise Erdrich

1. Helen Hornbeck Tanner, "Ojibwa," *Encyclopedia of North American Indians*, ed. Frederick E. Hoxie (Boston: Houghton, 1996), 438–39. The Ojibwe are known by three names: Chippewa, Ojibwa, and Anishinaabe. Chippewa is the official tribal name recognized by the U.S. government, and it is considered to be a corruption of Ojibwa, a name found on seventeenth-century French maps and interpreted as "a reference either to the puckered toe of the Ojibwas' distinctive moccasins, or to their use of glyphs to inscribe historical and religious information as well as simple messages on birch bark or rock surfaces" (438). Tanner writes that Anishinaabe, a term meaning "First People," is the preferred name to identify themselves. Charles Phillip Whitedog (Ojibway) describes the differences and usage among the three names: "The name Chippewa is the 'official' name as recognized by the United States Government and is used on all treaties. As such, this name is often used when talking in an official matter, or informally to non-Indian people. [Ojibway] is the most popular and the most proper as it was given by our enemies. We use this when talking with other Indian people or someone more familiar than the above 'Chippewa.' It has many different spellings: Ojibway, Odjibwa, Odjibwe, Ojibwag, Ochipoy, Tschipeway, Chepeways, Achipoes and others. There is some controversy over its real meaning, but suffice it to say it means 'to pucker.' There are some that believe it is due to our puckered seam moccasins that were sewn that way to keep the snow out. There is another meaning too, but I won't go into that here. [Anishinabeg] is the word that we call ourselves. Generally, it is reserved for Anishinabe people to refer to themselves, although there are some that would rather be known by this name. Actually, the Anishinabe are also people that live in our creation stories. They are the original people and were very weak." Erdrich uses the three names interchangeably, so all three are used with variations in spelling throughout this chapter. Charles Phillip Whitedog, "Re: Chippewa/Ojibwa," Online posting, August 9, 1995, Native-L, September 17, 1999 <http://nativenet.uthscsa.edu/archive/nl/9508/0088.html>.

2. Biographical information for Louise Erdrich has been compiled mainly from the following: Peter G. Beidler, "Louise Erdrich," *Native American Writers of the United States*, ed. Kenneth M. Roemer, Dictionary of Literary Biography Ser., vol. 175 (Detroit: Gale Research, 1997),

84–100; and P. Jane Hafen, "Louise Erdrich" *Concise Dictionary of Literary Biography Supplement: Modern Writers, 1900–1998*, ed. Tracy Bitanti (Detroit: Gale Research, 1998) 44–55.
3. Pauline rejects her gender in giving birth to her baby and adopts asexuality as a novice at the convent. As a Catholic nun, she contrasts to Agnes DeWitt in *The Last Report on the Miracles at Little No Horse*, who as Sister Cecilia and Father Damien Modeste does not forsake her sexuality.
4. Dorris has said that he did not name a specific tribe in *A Yellow Raft in Blue Water* because he wanted it to be generic: "It's clearly Pacific Northwest. It's clearly set, for anybody who delves deep enough to look into it, on Rocky Boys or Fort Belknap. I mean if you look at the geography and where the Bearpaws *[sic]* are and where the town Havre is, there is no doubt." The Fort Belknap Reservation is home to the Gros Ventre and Assiniboine, and the Rocky Boys Reservation is home to the Chippewa Cree. Therefore, Christine Taylor is an Indian connected to one of these reservations. Interview with Daniel Bourne, *Artful Dodge* 28/29, College of Wooster, October 25, 1995, June 2, 2001 <http://www.wooster.edu/ArtfulDodge/Dorris.html>.
5. Alan Velie, "The Trickster Novel," *Narrative Chance: Postmodern Discourse on Native American Indian Literatures*, ed. Gerald Vizenor (Albuquerque: University of New Mexico Press, 1989), 122. Velie writes, "Gerry Nanapush is clearly a modern avatar of the trickster. Not only is he the consummate player of tricks (his miraculous escapes, for instance), but Nanapush is the name of the Chippewa Trickster Hare" (122). For more information on the tribal trickster Naanabozho, see Gerald Vizenor, ed. and interp., *Summer in the Spring: Anishinaabe Lyric Poems and Stories, New Edition* (Normal: University of Oklahoma Press, 1993). Erdrich does not develop Fleur's mythical identity beyond her midwife capacities in *Love Medicine*, but in her novel *Tracks*, Fleur's trickster characteristics are evident in the implication that her footprints change into an animal's, in her card-playing abilities, and in the joke she plays on loggers in the forest.
6. Vizenor, *Summer*, 80. Louise Erdrich uses this same symbol in *Tracks* when Lazarre and Clarence cut off Margaret's (Rushes Bear's) braids (115), "an event that started baldness in the Pillager women" (109).
7. In Erdrich's essay "A Time for Human Rights on Native Ground," published on December 29, 2000, in *The New York Times*, she argues for the release of Leonard Peltier, imprisoned for the 1973 murders of two Federal Bureau of Investigation (FBI) agents, Jack Coler and Ronald Williams. She describes the Indians, some of whom were American Indian Movement (AIM) members, who attended the trial at the federal court building in Fargo, North Dakota, in 1977: "Now, here were my friends dressed in flamboyant vest, beads and black hats hung with eagle feathers." She goes on to note, "The court system had been influenced, as had I, by the black hats and the feathers and the aura of paranoia. Only to me, these things were attractive. To others, the mood at the back of the courtroom and the drum beating in the street outside were threatening." Erdrich describes the AIM activists in *Love Medicine* in similar fashion. Louise Erdrich, "A Time for Human Rights on Native Ground," *New York Times on the Web* December 29, 2000, June 7, 2001 <http://nytimes.qpass.com/qpass-archives/>.
8. Francis Paul Prucha, *The Great Father: The United States Government and the American Indians* (Lincoln: University of Nebraska Press, 1984), 233. In *Tracks* Erdrich describes in more detail Lulu's haircut and the punishment that Lulu endured at the boarding school: "[her] braids were cut, [her] hair in a thick ragged bowl [. . .] [her] knees were scabbed from the punishment of scrubbing long sidewalks, and knobbed from kneeling hours on broomsticks" (226).
9. Erdrich, "A Time for Human Rights on Native Ground." Gerry Nanapush was hiding out on Pine Ridge Reservation when it was "overrun with federal agents and armored vehicles. Weapons were stashed everywhere and easy to acquire. Gerry got himself a weapon. Two men tried to arrest him. Gerry would not go along, and when he started to run and the shooting started, Gerry shot and killed a clean-shaven man with dark hair and light eyes, a state trooper, a man whose picture was printed in all the papers" (*Love* 210–11). Erdrich draws on details of the Leonard Peltier trial, and on the basis of her political stance, she creates a sympathetic cultural hero in Gerry Nanapush.
10. Chapter 15, "Redford's Luck," in *The Bingo Palace* is a reworking, different characters, same plot line, of Erdrich's short story "American Horse," *Earth Power Coming: An Anthology of*

Native American Fiction, ed. Simon Ortiz (Tsaile, AZ: Navajo Community College Press, 1984), 59–72.

Chapter 6: "'I'm Talking Like a Twentieth-Century Indian Woman'": Contemporary Female Warriors in the Works of Sherman Alexie

1. Biographical information for Sherman Alexie has been compiled mainly from the following: Sherman Alexie, interview with Tomson Highway, "Spokane Words: Tomson Highway Raps with Sherman Alexie," *Aboriginal Voices* 4.1, October 28, 1996, October 14, 2000 <http://www.aboriginalvoices.com/1997/04-01/sherman_alexie.html>; Susan B. Brill, "Sherman Alexie," *Native American Writers of the United States*, ed. Kenneth M. Roemer, Dictionary of Literary Biography Ser., vol. 175 (Detroit: Gale Research, 1997) 3–10; Lynn Cline, "About Sherman Alexie: A Profile," *Ploughshares* 26.4 (Winter 2000–1), 197–202; *Native American Authors Project*, Internet Public Library, June 2, 2001 <http://www.ipl.org/cgi/ref/native/browse.pl/A1>; Rani—FallsApart Webgirl, *The Official Sherman Alexie Site* 31 May 2001 <http://fallsapart.com/biography.html>.
2. Sherman Alexie is married to Diane, who is of Hidatsa, Ho Chunk, and Pottawatomi descent, and they have two young sons.
3. Sources do not cite specific numbers for the Indian dead and wounded except to note, "casualties for the Indians were high." <http://hometown.aol.com/Gibson0817/cadind.htm>.
4. The question of Indian authenticity is a complicated issue that I do not address here, but suffice it to say that there are various federal, state, tribal, and cultural definitions used to determine who is an Indian, and they carry different degrees of validity depending on who makes the judgment. For more information, see M. Annette Jaimes, "Federal Indian Identification Policy: A Usurpation of Indigenous Sovereignty in North America," *The State of Native America: Genocide, Colonization, and Resistance*, ed. M. Annette Jaimes, Race and Resistance Series (Boston: South End, 1992), 123–138.
5. Alexie writes, "Roman Gabriel Fury was named after an obscure professional football quarterback named Roman Gabriel—a man with his own kind of fury and the rumor of Indian blood—who'd toiled for the Los Angeles Rams in the early seventies" (*Toughest* 158–59). In addition to this historical fact, there are classical and biblical allusions for Roman's name. Gabriel is one of the archangels and messenger of God. He is the interpreter of Daniel's vision and announces the births of John the Baptist and Jesus Christ (Dan. 8.16; 9.21; Luke 1.19, 26). In Christian eschatology, Gabriel's trumpet will announce the Day of Judgment; in Islamic tradition, Gabriel dictated the Koran to Mohammed. Fury alludes to Erinyes, also known as the Furies from the Latin, Furiae, which are the primitive avenging spirits called upon to punish crimes, especially those committed against one's kin. They were merciless. In artistic representations, they look stern and fierce, but not ugly; are winged; and may carry or be encircled by snakes. Grace Atwater's name suggests the Old Testament usage of "favor" in the expression "found grace in the eyes or sight" (Gen. 6.8), and in the New Testament usage the name Grace evokes "the unmerited and abundant gift of God's love and favor to man," particularly made effective in Jesus Christ for the Christian. Grace also alludes to the Graces, the three daughters of Zeus, Euphrosyne (Mirth), Aglaia (Splendor), and Thalia (Good Cheer); the embodiment of charm and beauty, they give life its grace and loveliness. Alexie also includes an allusion to Sisyphus, king of Corinth, who was punished in Tartarus by being compelled to roll a huge stone up a hill. No sooner had he pushed it to the summit then it rolled down again. Thus Sisyphus's labor never ended. When asked whether he ever considers writing about other types of people besides Native Americans, Alexie answers: "That sort of question assumes that Indians have limited lives, or that there are only nine kinds of Indians. Every moment that's ever happened in Shakespeare happens in my tiny little reservation, every day. Writing about Indians and being an Indian actually makes me original and eccentric" (Barnes & Noble.com). In using classical and biblical allusions in a story that takes place on the Spokane Reservation, Alexie shows that the lives of Spokane Indians are as varied and

complex, "original and eccentric," as the lives of any other characters in the canon of Western literature. Barnes & Noble.com, Online Chat with Sherman Alexie, *Chats & Events*, May 1, 2000, October 14, 2000 <http://www.barnesandnoble.com/co.../transcript.asp?userid=24L2DFWCYO&eventId=218>. For more information on the classical allusions, see Abraham H. Lass, David Kiremidjian, and Ruth M. Goldstein, *The Dictionary of Classical, Biblical, and Literary Allusions*, 1987 (New York: Fawcett Gold Medal, 1989).

Bibliography

Albers, Patricia, and Beatrice Medicine (Standing Rock Sioux), eds. *The Hidden Half: Studies of Plains Indian Women*. Lanham, MD: University Press of America, 1983.
Alexie, Sherman (Spokane/Coeur d'Alene). Exclusive Interview. *Indian Killer*. Audiocassette. Original recording: Emerald City Productions, Seattle, WA. Recording engineer Jason Webley. San Bruno, CA: Audio Literature, 1996.
―――. *Indian Killer*. New York: Atlantic Monthly, 1996.
―――. Interview with Bernadette Chato. "Book-of-the-Month: *Reservation Blues.*" *Native America Calling*. Prod. Harlan McKosato (Sac & Fox/Ioway). KUNM 89.9 FM Albuquerque, NM. 26 June 1995. 2 June 2001 American Indian Radio on Satellite (AIROS) <http://www.airos.org/>.
―――. Interview with Harlan McKosato (Sac & Fox/Ioway). "Book-of-the-Month: *The Toughest Indian in the World.*" *Native America Calling*. Prod. Harlan McKosato. KUNM 89.9 FM Albuquerque, NM. 30 May 2000. 2 June 2001 American Indian Radio on Satellite (AIROS) <http://www.airos.org//>.
―――. Interview with Jennifer Niessen. "Local Filmmaker Sherman Alexie." *KPLU News. Public NewsRoom. KLUP.ORG NPR*. 2 Feb. 2002. 12 Mar. 2003 <http://www.publicbroadcasting.net/kplu/news.newsmain?action=article&ARTICLE_ID=330357>.
―――. Interview with Juliette Torrez. "Juliette Torrez Goes Long Distance with Sherman Alexie." *About the Human Internet: Poetry: Contemporary*. 31 Aug. 199. 6 Nov. 2000 <http://poetry.about.com/arts/poetry/library/weekly/aa083199.htm?terms=alexie>.
―――. Interview with Tomson Highway (Cree). "Spokane Words: Tomson Highway Raps with Sherman Alexie." *Aboriginal Voices* 4.1. 28 Oct. 1996. 14 Oct. 2000 <http://www.aboriginalvoices.com/1997/04-01/sherman_alexie.html>.
―――. *The Lone Ranger and Tonto Fistfight in Heaven*. New York: Harper, 1994.
―――. *One Stick Song*. Brooklyn: Hanging Loose, 2000.
―――. *Reservation Blues*. 1995. New York: Warner, 1996.
―――. "Some of My Best Friends." *Los Angeles Times*. 23 Jan. 2000. 1 Feb. 2000. <http://www.latimes.com>.
―――. *The Toughest Indian in the World*. New York: Atlantic Monthly, 2000.
Allen, Paula Gunn (Laguna Pueblo/Sioux). *The Sacred Hoop: Recovering the Feminine in American Indian Traditions*. Boston: Beacon, 1992.
―――. *Studies in American Indian Literature: Critical Essays and Course Designs*. New York: MLA, 1995.
"American Indian Languages." *FunkandWagnalls.com*. Encyclopedia. 4 May 2001 <http://www.fwkc.com/encyclopedia/low/articles/a/a001001440f.html>.
Arnold, Ellen. "Listening to the Spirits: An Interview with Leslie Marmon Silko." *Studies in American Indian Literature* 10.3 (Fall 1998): 1–33.
Asikinack, William (Anishinabe). "Anishinabe (Ojibway) Legends through Anishinabe Eyes." *Contemporary Native American Cultural Issues: Proceedings from the Native American Studies Conference at Lake Superior State University*, October 16–17, 1987. Ed. Thomas E. Schirer. Sault Ste. Marie: Lake Superior State University Press, 1988, 3–12.
Assuras, Thalia. "Sending Smoke Signals." *CBS Sunday Morning News*. 6 Dec. 1998. 6 Dec. 1998 <http://klas.cbsnow.com/prdl/now/display?p_who=KLAS&p_section=3400>.
Bacon, Katie. "An Emissary of the Between-World: A Conversation with Louise Erdrich: Whose Stories Occur in the 'Margin Where Cultures Mix and Collide.'" *Atlantic Unbound* 17 Jan. 2001. 7pp. 9 Feb. 2001 <http://www.theatlantic.com/unbound/interviews/int2001-01-17.htm>.
Bailey, Garrick, and Roberta Glenn Bailey. *A History of the Navajos: The Reservation Years*. Santa Fe: School of American Research, 1986.
Ballantine, Betty, and Ian Ballantine, ed. *The Native Americans: An Illustrated History*. Atlanta: Turner, 1993.

Baraga, Frederic. *A Dictionary of the Otchipwe Language.* Minneapolis: Ross & Haines, 1966.
Barnes, Kim. "A Leslie Marmon Silko Interview." *Journal of Ethnic Studies* 13 (Winter 1986): 83–105.
Barnes & Noble.com. Online Chat with Sherman Alexie. *Chats & Events.* 1 May 2000. 14 Oct. 2000 <http://www.barnesandnoble.com/co... / transcript.asp?userid=24L2DFWCYO&eventId=218>.
Bataille, Gretchen M., ed. Introduction. *Native American Women: A Biographical Dictionary.* Ed. Asst. Laurie Lisa. New York: Garland, 1993, xi–xvi.
Bataille, Gretchen M., and Kathleen Mullen Sands. *American Indian Women: Telling Their Lives.* Lincoln: University of Nebraska Press, 1984.
Beidler, Peter G. "Louise Erdrich." Roemer 84–100.
Bellante, John, and Carl Bellante. "Sherman Alexie: Literary Rebel." *The Bloomsbury Review* 14.3 (May/June 1994): 14+.
Bernstein, Alison. "A Mixed Record: The Political Enfranchisement of American Indian Women during the Indian New Deal." *Journal of the West* 23.3 (1984): 13–20.
Bevis, William. "Native American Novels: Homing In." *Critical Perspectives on Native American Fiction.* Ed. Richard F. Fleck. Washington, D.C.: Three Continents, 1993, 15–45.
Blicksilver, Edith. "Traditionalism vs. Modernity: Leslie Silko on American Indian Women." *Southwest Review* 64.2 (Spring 1979): 149–60.
Bloom, Harold, ed. *Native American Women Writers.* Philadelphia: Chelsea, 1998.
Bonnin, Gertrude Simmons (See Zitkala-Ša) (Yankton Sioux). "Address by Mrs. Gertrude Bonnin, Secretary-Treasurer." *The American Indian Magazine* 7 (1919): 153–57.
———. "Indian Woman in Capital to Fight Growing Use of Peyote Drug by Indians." *Washington Times* [Washington, D.C.]. 17 Feb. 1918. Gertrude Bonnin Collection. Archives and Manuscripts, Brigham Young University, Provo, UT.
———. "A Year's Experience in Community Service Work among the Ute Tribe of Indians." *The American Indian Magazine* 4 (1916): 307–10.
Bonnin, Gertrude, Charles H. Fabens, and Matthew K. Sniffen. *Oklahoma's Poor Rich Indians: An Orgy of Graft and Exploitation of the Five Civilized Tribes—Legalized Robbery.* Philadelphia: Office of the Indian Rights Association, 1924.
Boos, Florence. "An Interview with Leslie Marmon Silko." *Speaking of the Short Story: Interviews with Contemporary Writers.* Ed. Farhat Iftekharuddin, Mary Rohrberger, and Maurice Lee. Jackson: University Press of Mississippi, 1997, 237–47.
Brill, Susan B. "Sherman Alexie." Roemer 3–10.
Bruchac, Joseph (Abenaki). "A Living Tree with Many Roots: An Introduction to Native North American Literature." *Native North American Literature: Biographical and Critical Information on Native Writers and Orators from the United States and Canada from Historical Times to the Present.* Ed. Janet Witalec. Detroit: Gale Research, 1994, xxxix–xlv.
Buford, Bill. "The Talk of the Town: Comment." *The New Yorker* 21, 28 June 1999, 65+.
Catt, Catherine M. "Ancient Myth in Modern America: The Trickster in the Fiction of Louise Erdrich." *The Platte Valley Review* 19.1 (Winter 1991): 71–81.
Champagne, Duane (Chippewa). "American Indian Studies Is for Everyone." Mihesuah 181–89.
Chavkin, Allan, and Nancy Feyl Chavkin, eds. *Conversations with Louise Erdrich and Michael Dorris.* Jackson: University Press of Mississippi, 1994.
Clements, William M., and Kenneth M. Roemer. "Leslie Marmon Silko." Roemer 276–90.
Cline, Lynn. "About Sherman Alexie: A Profile." *Ploughshares* 26.4 (Winter 2000–1): 197–202.
Coleman, Michael C. "Motivations of Indian Children at Missionary and U.S. Government Schools." *Montana: The Magazine of History* Winter 1990, 30–45.
Coltelli, Laura. *Winged Words: American Indian Writers Speak.* 1990. Lincoln: University of Nebraska Press, 1992.
Cook-Lynn, Elizabeth (Crow Creek Sioux). "American Indian Intellectualism and the New Indian Story." Mihesuah 111–38.
———. *Why I Can't Read Wallace Stegner and Other Essays: A Tribal Voice.* Madison: University of Wisconsin Press, 1996.
Cox, James. "Muting White Noise: The Subversion of Popular Culture Narratives of Conquest in Sherman Alexie's Fiction." *Studies in American Indian Literatures* 9.4 (Winter 1997): 52–70.
Culler, Jonathan. *Literary Theory: A Very Short Introduction.* Oxford: Oxford University Press, 1997.

Danielson, Linda L. "*Storyteller:* Grandmother Spider's Web." *Journal of the Southwest* 30.3 (Autumn 1988): 325–55.
Deloria, Philip J. (Standing Rock Sioux). "The Twentieth Century and Beyond: Termination." Ballantine and Ballantine 421–29.
Deloria, Vine, Jr. (Standing Rock Sioux). *Custer Died for Your Sins: An Indian Manifesto.* Norman: University of Oklahoma Press, 1988.
―――. *Singing for a Spirit: A Portrait of the Dakota Sioux.* Santa Fe: Clear Light, 2000.
"A Dialogue on Race with President Clinton." Host Jim Lehrer. *Online NewsHour.* PBS. 9 July 1998. Transcript. 31 May 2001 <http://www.pbs.org/newshour/bb/race_relations/OneAmerica/transcript.html>.
Donovan, Kathleen M. *Feminist Readings of Native American Literature: Coming to Voice.* Tucson: University of Arizona Press, 1998.
Dorris, Michael (Modoc). "Native American Literature in an Ethnohistorical Context." *Paper Trail.* New York: HarperCollins, 1994, 232–54.
―――. *A Yellow Raft in Blue Water.* New York: Warner, 1988.
Drury, Clifford M. *Nine Years with the Spokane Indians: The Diary, 1838–1848, of Elkanah Walker.* Glendale: Arthur H. Clark, 1976.
Emerson, Gloria J. "Navajo Education." Ortiz 659–71.
Erdrich, Louise (Ojibwe). *The Beet Queen.* 1986. New York: HarperFlamingo, 1998.
―――. *The Bingo Palace.* New York: HarperPerennial, 1995.
―――. *The Birchbark House.* New York: Hyperion, 1999.
―――. *The Blue Jay's Dance: A Birth Year.* New York: HarperPerennial, 1996.
―――. Interview with Harlan McKosato (Sac & Fox/Ioway). "Book-of-the-Month: *The Last Report on the Miracles at Little No Horse.*" *Native America Calling.* Prod. Harlan McKosato. KUNM 89.9 FM Albuquerque, NM. 29 May 2001. 29 May 2001. American Indian Radio on Satellite (AIROS) <http://www.airos.org/>.
―――. *The Last Report on the Miracles at Little No Horse.* New York: HarperCollins, 2001.
―――. *Love Medicine: New and Expanded Version.* New York: HarperPerennial, 1993.
―――. "The Names of Women." *Granta* 41 (1992): 132–38. Rpt. in *Language: Readings in Language and Culture.* Ed. Virginia P. Clark, Paul A. Eschholz, and Alfred F. Rosa. 6th ed. New York: St. Martin's, 1998, 392–96.
―――. *Tales of Burning Love.* 1996. New York: HarperPerennial, 1997.
―――. "A Time for Human Rights on Native Ground." *New York Times on the Web.* 29 Dec. 2000. 7 June 2001 <http://nytimes.qpass.com/qpass-archives/>.
―――. *Tracks.* 1988. New York: Harper & Row-Perennial, 1989.
Evans, Charlene Taylor. "Mother-Daughter Relationships as Epistemological Structures: Leslie Marmon Silko's *Almanac of the Dead* and *Storyteller.*" *Women of Color: Mother-Daughter Relationships in 20th-Century Literature.* Ed. Elizabeth Brown-Guillory. Austin: University of Texas Press, 1996, 172–87.
Evans, Sara M. *Born for Liberty: A History of Women in America.* New York: Free-Macmillan, 1989.
Evers, Larry, ed. *Between Sacred Mountains: Navajo Stories and Lessons from the Land.* Vol. 11 Sun Tracks: An American Indian Literary Series. Tucson: Sun Tracks and University of Arizona Press, 1984.
"The Evolution of Gunships." *Helicopter History Site.* 10 Feb. 2000 <http://www.helis.com/types/gunship.htm>.
Fisher, Dexter, ed. "Stories and Their Tellers—a Conversation with Leslie Marmon Silko." *The Third Woman: Minority Women Writers of the United States.* Boston: Houghton, 1980. 18–23.
―――. "The Transformation of Tradition: A Study of Zitkala-Ša and Mourning Dove, Two Transitional American Indian Writers." *Critical Essays on American Literature.* Ed. Andrew Wiget. Boston: Hall, 1985, 202–11.
―――. "Zitkala-Ša: The Evolution of a Writer." Foreword. *American Indian Stories.* By Zitkala-Ša. Lincoln: University of Nebraska Press, 1985. v–xx. Rpt. of "Zitkala-Ša: The Evolution of a Writer." *American Indian Quarterly* 5.3 (August 1979): 229–38.
Fitzgerald, James, and John Hudak. "Interview: Leslie Silko, Storyteller." *Persona* (1980): 21–38.
Flavin, Louise. "Louise Erdrich's *Love Medicine:* Loving over Time and Distance." *Critique: Studies in Contemporary Fiction* 31.1 (Fall 1989): 55–64.
Forbes, Jack D. "Basic Concepts for Understanding History and Culture." Lobo and Talbot 28–40.

Freire, Paulo. *The Pedagogy of the Oppressed.* Trans. Myra Bergman Ramos. New York: Herder & Herder, 1970.
Graulich, Melody, ed. "Remember the Stories." Introduction. *"Yellow Woman"/Leslie Marmon Silko.* Women Writers Texts and Contexts Series. New Brunswick, NJ: Rutgers University Press, 1993, 3–25.
Green, Rayna (Cherokee). "Review Essay: Native American Women." *Signs: Journal of Women in Culture and Society* 6.2 (Winter 1980): 248–67.
Hafen, P. Jane (Taos Pueblo). Introduction. *Dreams and Thunder: Stories, Poems, and The Sun Dance Opera by Zitkala-Ša.* Ed. P. J. Hafen. Lincoln: University of Nebraska Press, 2001.
———. "Louise Erdrich." *Concise Dictionary of Literary Biography Supplement: Modern Writers, 1900–1998.* Ed. Tracy Bitanti. Detroit: Gale Research, 1998, 44–55.
———. "Pan-Indianism and Tribal Sovereignties in *House Made of Dawn* and *The Names.*" *Western American Literature* 34.1 (Spring 1999): 6–23.
———. "Rock and Roll, Redskins, and Blues in Sherman Alexie's Work." *Studies in American Indian Literatures* 2nd ser. 9.4 (Winter 1997): 71–78.
———. "Zitkala-Ša (Gertrude Bonnin)." Hoxie 708–10.
Harjo, Joy (Muscogee Creek), and Gloria Bird (Spokane), eds. Introduction. *Reinventing the Enemy's Language: Contemporary Native Women's Writings of North America.* New York: Norton, 1997, 19–31.
Hernandez, Inés (Nimipu). Foreword. *Growing up Native American.* Ed. and Intro. Patricia Riley. New York: Avon, 1993, 7–16.
Hertzberg, Hazel W. *The Search for an American Identity: Modern Pan-Indian Movements.* Syracuse: Syracuse University Press, 1971.
"History of the Spokane." *Spokane Tribe.* 2 June 2001 <http://www.spokanetribe.com/>.
Horr, David Agee, comp. and ed. *Pueblo Indians.* V. *Commission Findings on the Pueblo Indians.* A Garland Series: American Indian Ethnohistory: Indians of the Southwest. New York: Garland, 1974.
Hoxie, Frederick E., ed. *Encyclopedia of North American Indians.* Boston: Houghton, 1996.
Indian Reservations: A State and Federal Handbook. Comp. The Confederation of American Indians, New York, N.Y. Jefferson NC: McFarland, 1986.
"Indian Welfare Work Will Be Undertaken." *General Federation News* [Fayetteville, Arkansas]. August 1921, 1+.
Iverson, Peter. *Diné: A History of the Navajos.* Albuquerque: University of New Mexico Press, 2002.
Jaffe-Notier, Tamara J. "Sherman Alexie." *The Door Magazine* March/April 2001, 8–12.
Jahner, Elaine M. "Leslie Marmon Silko." *Dictionary of Native American Literature.* Ed. Andrew Wiget. New York: Garland, 1994, 499–511.
Jaimes, M. Annette (Juaneño/Yaqui). "Federal Indian Identification Policy: A Usurpation of Indigenous Sovereignty in North America." Jaimes 123–38.
———, ed. *The State of Native America: Genocide, Colonization, and Resistance.* Race and Resistance Series. Boston: South End, 1992.
Jaimes, M. Annette (Juaneño/Yaqui), and Theresa Halsey (Standing Rock Sioux). "American Indian Women: At the Center of Indigenous Resistance in Contemporary North America." Jaimes 311–44.
Johnson, David L., and Raymond Wilson. "Gertrude Simmons Bonnin, 1876–1938: 'Americanize the First Americans.'" *American Indian Quarterly* 12.1 (1988): 27–40.
Jorgensen, Karen. "White Shadows: The Use of Doppelgangers in Sherman Alexie's *Reservation Blues.*" *Studies in American Indian Literatures* 2nd ser. 9.4 (Winter 1997): 19–25.
Klein, Laura F., and Lillian A. Ackerman, eds. *Women and Power in Native North America.* Norman: University of Oklahoma Press, 1995.
Kunitz, Stephen J., Jerrold E. Levy, et al. *Career Drinkers: A Twenty-five-year Study of Three Navajo Populations.* New Haven, CT: Yale University Press, 1994.
Landes, Ruth. *The Ojibwa Woman.* New York: Columbia University Press, 1938. Intro. Sally Cole. Lincoln: University of Nebraska Press, 1997.
Lass, Abraham H., David Kiremidjian, and Ruth M. Goldstein. *The Dictionary of Classical, Biblical, and Literary Allusions.* New York: Fawcett Gold Medal, 1989.
Leitch, Barbara A. *A Concise Dictionary of Indian Tribes of North America.* Algonac, MI: Reference, 1979.
Lobo, Susan, and Steve Talbot, eds. *Native American Voices: A Reader.* New York: Longman, 1998.

Louise Erdrich and Michael Dorris. Writers Talk: Ideas of Our Time. Interviewer Paul Bailey. Northbrook, IL: Anthony Roland Collection of Films on Art. Videotape. ICA Video, 1989.
Lukens, Margo. "Zitkala-Ša (Gertrude Simmons Bonnin). Roemer 331–36.
Lyons, Scott Richard (Ojibwe/Mdewakanton Dakota). "Rhetorical Sovereignty: What Do American Indians Want from Writing?" *The Journal of the Conference on College Composition and Communication* 51.3 (February 2000): 447–68.
Maristuen-Rodakowski, Julie. "The Turtle Mountain Reservation in North Dakota: Its History as Depicted in Louise Erdrich's Love Medicine and *The Beet Queen.*" *American Indian Culture and Research Journal* 12.3 (1988): 33–48. Rpt. in *Louise Erdrich's* Love Medicine: *A Case Book.* Ed. Hertha D. Wong. New York: Oxford University Press, 2000, 13–26.
McAllester, David P., and Douglas F. Mitchell. "Navajo Music." Ortiz 605–23.
McFarland, Ron. "Sherman Alexie's Polemical Stories." *Studies in American Indian Literatures* 2nd ser. 9.4 (Winter 1997): 27–38.
Medicine, Beatrice (Standing Rock Sioux). "'Warrior Women'—Sex Role Alternatives for Plains Indian Women." Albers and Medicine 267–80.
Mihesuah, Devon M. (Oklahoma Choctaw). "Commonality of Difference: American Indian Women and History." Mihesuah 37–54.
———, ed. *Natives and Academics: Research and Writing about American Indians.* Lincoln: University of Nebraska Press, 1998.
Moi, Toril. *Sexual/Textual Politics: Feminist Literary Theory.* London: Methuen, 1985.
Montezuma, Carlos (Yavapai). Letter to Gertrude Simmons. 20 Feb. 1901. Carlos Montezuma Papers. Division of Archives and Manuscripts, State Historical Society of Wisconsin.
Moyers, Bill. "Louise Erdrich and Michael Dorris." *A World of Ideas.* New York: Doubleday, 1989, 460–69. Rpt. in *Conversations with Louise Erdrich and Michael Dorris.* Ed. Allan Chavkin, and Nancy Feyl Chavkin. Jackson: University Press of Mississippi, 1994, 138–50.
Nabokov, Peter. "The Closing in." Ballantine and Ballantine 359–69.
Noriega, Jorge (Mestizo). "American Indian Education in the United States: Indoctrination for Subordination to Colonialism." Jaimes 371–402.
Odem, Mary E. *Delinquent Daughters: Protecting and Policing Adolescent Female Sexuality in the United States, 1885–1920.* Chapel Hill: University of North Carolina Press, 1995.
Opler, Morris E. "The Apachean Culture Pattern and Its Origins." Ortiz 368–92.
Ortiz, Alfonso (San Juan Pueblo), ed. *The Southwest.* Vol. 10. *Handbook of North American Indians.* 17 vols. to date. Gen. Ed. William C. Sturtevant. Washington, D.C.: Smithsonian Institution, 1978–.
Pellerin, Simone. "An Epitome of Erdrich's Art: 'The Names of Women.'" *European Review of Native American Studies* 11.1 (1997): 35–38.
Perry, Donna. "Leslie Marmon Silko." *Backtalk: Women Writers Speak out.* New Brunswick, NJ: Rutgers University Press, 1993, 313–40.
Pewewardy, Cornel (Comanche-Kiowa). "'I' Is for Indigenous." *MultiCultural Review* 10.2 (June 2001): 30–33.
Picotte, Agnes M. (Lakota Sioux). Foreword. *Old Indian Legends: Retold by Zitkala-Ša.* Boston: Ginn, 1901. Lincoln: University of Nebraska Press, 1985, xi–xviii.
Prucha, Francis Paul. *The Great Father: The United States Government and the American Indians.* Vols. I and II, Unabr. ed. Lincoln: University of Nebraska Press, 1995.
Purdy, John. "Crossroads: A Conversation with Sherman Alexie." *Studies in American Indian Literatures* 2nd ser. 9.4 (Winter 1997): 1–18.
Rani—FallsApart Webgirl. *The Official Sherman Alexie Site.* 31 May 2001 <http://fallsapart.com/biography.html>.
Rappaport, Doreen. *The Flight of Red Bird: The Life of Zitkala-Ša / Re-created from the Writings of Zitkala-Ša and the Research of Doreen Rappaport.* New York: Puffin-Penguin, 1999.
Rich, Adrienne. *Of Woman Born: Motherhood as Experience and Institution.* New York: Norton, 1995.
Roemer, Kenneth M., ed. Introduction. *Native American Writers of the Untied States.* Dictionary of Literary Biography Ser. Vol. 175. Detroit: Gale Research, 1997, xi–xxi.
Roessel, Ruth (Navajo). "Navajo Arts and Crafts." Ortiz 592–604.
Rosen, Kenneth, ed. *The Man to Send Rain Clouds: Contemporary Stories by American Indians.* New York: Viking, 1974.
Ruiz, Vicki L., and Ellen Carol DuBois, eds. *Unequal Sisters: A Multicultural Reader in U. S. Women's History.* New York: Routledge, 1994.

Ruoff, A. LaVonne Brown. *Introduction to American Indian Literatures: An Introduction, Bibliographic Review, and Selected Bibliography.* New York: MLA, 1990.
———. "Ritual and Renewal: Keres Traditions in the Short Fiction of Leslie Silko." *MELUS* 5.4 (1978): 2–17.
Ruppert, James. "Mediation and Multiple Narrative in *Love Medicine*." *North Dakota Quarterly* 59.4 (Spring 1991): 229–42.
———. *Mediation in Contemporary Native American Fiction.* Norman: University Oklahoma Press, 1995.
Ryan, Kiernan, ed. *New Historicism and Cultural Materialism: A Reader.* New York: St. Martin's, 1996.
Salyer, Gregory. *Leslie Marmon Silko.* Twayne's United States Authors Series No. 692. New York: Twayne, 1997.
Sands, Kathleen M. "Preface: A Symposium Issue." *American Indian Quarterly* 5 (1979): 1–5.
Schumacher, Michael. "A Marriage of Minds." *Writer's Digest* June 1991, 28+.
Seasons of a Navajo. Prod. KAET, Tempe, AZ. 1985. Videocassette. PBS VIDEO, 1988.
Seyersted, Per. *Leslie Marmon Silko.* Boise State University Western Writers Series, No. 45. Boise, ID: Boise State University Press, 1980.
———. "Two Interviews with Leslie Marmon Silko." *American Studies in Scandinavia* 13 (1981): 17–33.
Shechner, Mark. "American Realisms, American Realities." *Neo-Realism in Contemporary American Fiction.* Ed. Kristiann Versluys. Postmodern Studies 5. Amsterdam: Rodopi, 1992, 27–50.
Shepardson, Mary. "The Gender Status of Navajo Women." Klein and Ackerman 159–76.
"Sherman Alexie." *Native American Authors Project.* Internet Public Library. 2 June 2001 <http://www.ipl.org/cgi/ref/native/browse.pl/A1>.
Sherman Bulletin 10.14. Riverside, CA: Sherman Institute Student Press, 4 Apr. 1917.
Sherwood, Robert (Spokane). Telephone Interview. 18 Apr. 1996.
Silberman, Robert. "Opening the Text: *Love Medicine* and the Return of the Native American Woman." *Narrative Chance: Postmodern Discourse on Native American Indian Literatures* (1989). Ed. Gerald Vizenor. Norman: University of Oklahoma Press, 1993, 101–20.
Silko, Leslie Marmon. *Ceremony.* New York: Viking, 1977.
———. Foreword. *A Circle of Nations: Voices and Visions of American Indians.* Ed. John Gattuso. Hillsboro, OR: Beyond Words, 1993, 4–7.
———. Foreword. *Border Towns of the Navajo Nation.* By Aaron Yava. Alamo, CA: Holmgangers, 1975.
———. *Laguna Woman.* Greenfield Center, NY: Greenfield Review Press, 1974.
———. "An Old-Time Indian Attack in Two Parts." *Yardbird Reader* 5 (1976): 77–84.
———. *Storyteller.* New York: Arcade, 1981.
———. *Yellow Woman and a Beauty of the Spirit: Essays on Native American Life Today.* New York: Simon & Schuster, 1996.
Simmons, Gertrude (See Zitkala-Ša) (Yankton Sioux). "Side by Side." *The Earlhamite* 2.12 (16 Mar. 1896): 177–79.
Smith, Joan. "Young Once, Indian Forever." Lobo and Talbot 400–6.
Smith, Linda Tuhiwai (Ngati Awa/Ngati Porou). *Decolonizing Methodologies: Research and Indigenous Peoples.* London: Zed; Dunedin: University of Otago Press, 1999.
Spack, Ruth. *America's Second Tongue: American Indian Education and the Ownership of English, 1860–1900.* Lincoln: University of Nebraska Press, 2002.
Spivak, Gayatri Chakravorty. *The Post-Colonial Critic: Interviews, Strategies, Dialogues.* Ed. Sarah Harasym. New York: Routledge, 1990.
Stout, Mary. "The Literature of Politics." *Coyote Was Here: Essays on Contemporary Native American Literary and Political Mobilization.* Ed. Bo Scholer. Arhus, Denmark: Seklos, 1984, 70–78.
Strom, Karen M. "Lakota/Nakota/Dakota." 1995. 4 Feb. 2001. <http://www.hanksville.org/daniel/lakota/Lakkota.html>.
Tanner, Helen Hornbeck. "Ojibwa." Hoxie 438–39.
Thorpe, Dagmar (Sac & Fox). "The Spirit of the People Has Awakened and Is Enjoying Creation Through Us: An Interview with Jeanette Armstrong, Okanagan." *Native Americas.* Ithaca, NY: Awe:kon, 1995. Rpt. in Lobo and Talbot 235–39.

Tobert, Natalie, and Fiona Pitt. "The Southwest." *Native American Myths and Legends*. Ed. Colin F. Taylor. New York: Smithmark, 1994, 26-39.
Tohe, Laura (Diné). "There Is No Word for Feminism in My Language." *Wicazo Sa Review* 15.2 (Fall 2000): 103-10.
Trennert, Robert. "Educating Indian Girls at Nonreservation Boarding Schools, 1878-1920." *Western Historical Quarterly* 13.3 (July 1982): 271-90. Rpt. in Ruiz and DuBois 224-37.
Trout, Lawana, ed. *Native American Literature: An Anthology*. Lincolnwood: NTC/Contemporary, 1999.
Tsosie, Rebecca (Pascua Yaqui). "Changing Women: The Crosscurrents of American Indian Feminine Identity." *American Indian Culture and Research Journal* 12.1 (1988): 1-37. Rpt. in Ruiz and DuBois 508-30.
University of Nebraska Press Online. *Indigenous American Women: Decolonization, Empowerment, Activism* by Devon Abbott Mihesuah. 11 Mar. 2003 <http://www.nebraskapress.unl.edu/bookinfo/4338.html>.
Velie, Alan. "The Trickster Novel." *Narrative Chance: Postmodern Discourse on Native American Indian Literatures*. Ed. Gerald Vizenor. Albuquerque: University of New Mexico Press, 1989, 121-39.
"Vietnam—the Helicopter War." *Drew's World of Choppers*. 10 Feb. 2000 <http://www.slick-net.com/vthw/index.phtml>.
Vizenor, Gerald (Ojibwe), ed. and interp. *Summer in the Spring: Anishinaabe Lyric Poems and Stories, New Edition*. Norman: University of Oklahoma Press, 1993.
Waldman, Carl. *Encyclopedia of Native American Tribes*. New York: Facts on File, 1988.
Warrior, Robert Allen (Osage). *Tribal Secrets: Recovering American Indian Intellectual Traditions*. Minneapolis: University of Minnesota Press, 1995.
Wexler, Laura. "Tender Violence: Literary Eavesdropping, Domestic Fiction, and Educational Reform." *The Yale Journal of Criticism* 5.1 (1991): 151-87.
Whitedog, Charles Phillip (Ojibway). "Re: Chippewa/Ojibwa." Online posting. 9 Aug. 1995. Native-L. 17 Sept. 1999 <http://nativenet.uthscsa.edu/archive/nl/9508/0088.html>.
Willard, William (Cherokee). "The First Amendment, Anglo-Conformity and American Indian Religious Freedom." *Wicazo Sa Review* 7.1 (1991): 25-41.
———. "Zitkala-Ša: A Woman Who Would Be Heard!" *Wicazo Sa Review* 1.1 (1985) 11-16.
Wilson, Angela Cavender (Wahpetonwan Dakota). "American Indian History or Non-Indian Perceptions of American Indian History?" Mihesuah 23-26.
Witherspoon, Gary. *Language and Art in the Navajo Universe*. Ann Arbor: University of Michigan Press, 1977.
———. "Language and Reality in Navajo World View." Ortiz 570-78.
———. *Navajo Kinship and Marriage*. Chicago: University of Chicago Press, 1975.
———. "Navajo Social Organization." Ortiz 524-35.
Womack, Craig S. (Muskogee Creek/Cherokee). *Red on Red: Native American Literary Separatism*. Minneapolis: University of Minnesota Press, 1999.
Wub-e-ke-niew (Ojibwe). *We Have the Right to Exist: A Translation of Aboriginal Indigenous Thought: The First Book Ever Published from an Ahnishinahbaeotjibway Perspective*. New York: Black Thistle, 1995.
Wynecoop, David C. *Children of the Sun: A History of the Spokane Indians*. Wellpinit, WA: David C. Wynecoop, 1969.
Yellow Bird, Michael (Sahnish/Hidatsa). "What We Want to Be Called: Indigenous People's Perspectives on Racial and Ethnic Identity Labels." *American Indian Quarterly* 23.2 (Spring 1999): 1-21.
Young, Mary E. "Bonnin, Gertrude Simmons," *Notable American Women—1607-1950—a Biographical Dictionary*. Ed. Edward T. James. Cambridge, MA: Belknap Press of Harvard University Press, 1971.
Zitkala-Ša (See Gertrude Simmons Bonnin) (Yankton Sioux). *American Indian Stories*. Lincoln: University of Nebraska Press, 1985.
———. *Old Indian Legends: Retold by Zitkala-Ša*. Boston: Ginn, 1901. Lincoln: University of Nebraska Press, 1985.

Index

Ackerman, Lillian F., 6, 24
Albers, Patricia, 25, 30
Alexie, Sherman (Spokane/Coeur d'Alene), 1–6, 12–15, 26, 133–69, 172–75
 "Approximate Size of My Favorite Tumor, The," 4, 140, 155–64
 Business of Fancydancing, The, 134–35, 138
 First Indian on the Moon, 135
 "Indian Country," 165–69
 Indian Killer, 3, 135, 140, 143–50, 152, 174–75
 I Would Steal Horses, 135
 Lone Ranger and Tonto Fistfight in Heaven, The, 135, 138–41, 145, 155–64
 Man Who Loves Salmon, The, 135
 Mourning Songs for the Cedar Flute I Have Yet to Learn to Play, 135
 Old Shirts and New Skins, 135
 One Stick Song, 135, 145, 149
 Reservation Blues, 3, 135, 137, 139–43, 145, 152, 155
 "Saint Junior," 4, 137, 151–55
 Smoke Signals: The Screenplay, 135
 Summer of Black Widows, The, 135
 Ten Little Indians, 135
 Toughest Indian in the World, The, 135, 137–38, 148, 151–52, 154–55, 165–69
 Water Flowing Home, 135
Allen, Paula Gunn (Laguna Pueblo/Sioux), 9, 11, 19, 24, 31–32, 40, 113, 117, 156, 164
American Indian Movement (AIM), 22, 110
Apess, William (Pequot), 37
Armstrong, Jeanette (Okanagan), 124
Arnold, Ellen, 61
Asikinak, William (Anishinabe), 107
Assuras, Thalia, 164

Bacon, Katie, 91
Bailey, Garrick, 57, 65–66
Bailey, Roberta Glenn, 57, 65–66
Barnes, Kim, 64
Bataille, Gretchen, 19, 24
Beidler, Peter, 91

Bellante, Carl, 133–34
Bellante, John, 133–34
Bernstein, Alison, 28
Bevis, William, 109, 111, 122
Bird, Gloria (Spokane), 6
Blicksilver, Edith, 78
Bloom, Harold, 39
boarding school, 13, 36, 38–39, 40, 45–46, 77–78, 90
Bonnin, Gertrude Simmons (Yankton Sioux), *See* Zitkala-Ša
Bonnin, Raymond T. (Yankton Sioux), 3, 30
Boos, Florence, 73
Brill, Susan, 135, 144
Bruchac, Joseph (Abenaki), 5–6, 18–19
Buford, Bill, 133

Callahan, S. Alice (Muscogee), 37
Carlisle Indian Industrial School, 29, 43
Catholicism, 3, 92–94, 98, 110, 125, 127, 131, 142, 145, 151
Catt, Catherine M., 106–07
Champagne, Duane (Chippewa), 150
Changing Woman, 3, 69–70
Chato, Bernadette, 133–34, 138, 140–41, 145
Chavkin, Allan, 104–05
Chavkin, Nancy Feyl, 104–05
Christianity, 3, 39–40, 43, 86, 90, 116, 127, 130, 167
Clements, William M., 53, 59–60
Cline, Lynn, 135
Coleman, Michael, 39
colonialism, 10, 15, 152–53, 164–65
colonial legacy, 25–26
colonization, 2–3, 10, 12, 32, 86, 169, 171
Coltelli, Laura, 9, 90–91, 100, 165
Cook-Lynn, Elizabeth (Crow Creek Sioux), 21, 64–65, 150
Cox, James, 140
Culler, Jonathan, 11–12
cultural context, 1, 6, 9, 11–12, 24–26, 93, 156, 165
cultural genocide, 90
culture, 2, 4–15, 18–19, 21, 23, 26, 28, 30, 32–33, 35–36, 39–40, 43, 53, 55–57,

59–62, 64–65, 67–68, 70–71, 75–79, 81–82, 84–85, 92–93, 98–99, 104–05, 114, 118–20, 122, 125, 133–34, 137–38, 140–42, 144–46, 148–50, 152, 154, 156–58, 161, 164–69, 171–75; sentimental culture, 49, 51

Danielson, Linda L., 82
Deloria, Vine, Jr. (Standing Rock Sioux), 8, 18, 27–28, 31, 72, 83, 153–54, 164
Donovan, Kathleen, 23
Dorris, Michael (Modoc), 1, 8–9, 18, 20, 90, 97, 100–1, 104
  Yellow Raft in Blue Water, A, 97, 100–1
Drury, Clifford M., 136

Earlham College, 29, 36, 38
economics, 3, 56, 66, 68, 80, 123, 125, 149, 161, 172–74
education, 3–4, 29–30, 34–36, 39, 45–48, 78, 91, 106, 114, 116, 134, 138, 143–46, 149, 151–54, 174
Emerson, Gloria J., 78
Erdrich, Louise (Ojibwe), 1–4, 6, 9, 12, 14–15, 17, 19–20, 26, 89–131, 134, 137, 140–41, 165, 169, 172–75
  Antelope Wife, The, 90
  Baptism by Desire, 90
  Beet Queen, The, 90, 97, 99–100
  Bingo Palace, The, 4, 26, 90, 114–25
  Birchbark House, The, 4, 89–90, 94–96, 109, 130, 141
  Blue Jay's Dance: A Birth Year, The, 92, 103, 113, 174
  Crown of Columbus, The, 90
  Grandmother Pigeon, 90
  Jacklight, 90
  Last Report on the Miracles at Little No Horse, The, 3, 89–91, 110, 120, 125–30
  Love Medicine, 4, 20, 89–90, 97, 101–14, 123
  Master Butchers Singing Club, The, 90
  "Names of Women, The," 92
  Range Eternal, The, 90
  Route Two, 90
  "Scales," 90
  Tales of Burning Love, 90, 94
  "Time for Human Rights on Native Ground, A," 179 n

Tracks, 89–90, 96–99, 106
"World's Greatest Fisherman, The" 90
Evans, Charlene Taylor, 69
Evans, Sara M., 40
Evers, Larry, 56

Fabens, Charles H., 29, 47–49
Father Sky, 3, 85
feminism, 1, 17, 21–23, 55, 86, 171–74
  feminist theory, 6
Fisher, Dexter, 8, 19, 30, 42, 54–55
Fitzgerald, James, 57, 59
Flavin, Louise, 105
Forbes, Jack D., 74, 77
Freire, Paulo, 145–46

gender complementarity, 1–6, 11–14, 16–17, 20–21, 23–26, 28, 32, 40, 42, 44, 47–48, 51, 55, 57, 63–64, 80, 86, 89, 92, 94, 96–97, 100, 110–11, 114, 116, 119, 121, 123, 125–128, 130–131, 140–43, 145, 151–52, 156, 159, 161, 163, 167, 169, 171–75
General Allotment Act, 93
General Federation of Women's Clubs (GFWC), 29, 30, 40–43, 45, 47, 51
Graulich, Melody, 20, 54–55
Green, Rayna (Cherokee), 2, 18–19

Hafen, P. Jane (Taos Pueblo), 39, 43, 138, 142–43
Halsey, Theresa (Standing Rock Sioux), 12, 22, 24
Hanson, William, 30
Harjo, Joy (Muscogee Creek), 6, 35, 86
Hernandez, Inéz (Nimipu), 15
Hertzberg, Hazel W., 29, 41–44
Highway, Tomson (Cree), 137, 149
historical context, 1, 6, 11–12, 24–25, 93, 150
history, 2, 6–11, 18, 21, 23, 36, 55, 57, 59–60, 62–65, 73, 76, 78, 90–93, 110, 118, 123, 133, 136–43, 150, 152, 156–57, 161, 165, 173–74
Horr, David Agee, 57–58
Hudak, John, 57, 59

Indian:
  nomenclature, 15
Indian Rights Association, 30, 44, 47
Indian Welfare Committee, 30, 47
Iverson, Peter, 21, 66

Jaffe-Notier, Tamara J., 141
Jahner, Elaine, 83
Jaimes, M. Annette (Juaneño/Yaqui), 12, 22, 24
Johnson, David L., 39
Jorgensen, Karen, 142, 152

Klein, Laura F., 6, 24
Kluckhohn, Clyde, 65
Krupat, Arnold, 20
Kunitz, Stephen J., 74

Landes, Ruth, 93–96, 108
Leighton, Dorothea, 65
Leitch, Barbara A., 136–37
Levy, Jerrold E., 74
Lincoln, Kenneth, 53
Lukens, Margo, 39
Lyons, Scott Richard (Ojibwe/Mdewakanton Dakota), 8, 34–35, 51

Maristuen-Rodakowski, Julie, 92–93
marriage, 4–5, 64, 80, 86, 134, 136, 151, 153, 155–56, 158, 161–65, 167–68
matriarchy, 4, 64, 133, 136–37, 141, 151, 169, 172–74
    matrilineal society, 55, 64, 68, 80, 136–37
Matthews, John Joseph (Osage), 8
McAllester, David P., 67
McCloud, Janet (Tulalip), 22
McKosato, Harlan (Sac & Fox/Ioway), 98, 136
McNickle, Darcy (Salish/Kootenai), 111
Means, Lorelei DeCora (Minneconjou Lakota), 22
mediation, 5, 30, 40, 43, 51, 56–57, 71
Medicine, Beatrice (Standing Rock Sioux), 25, 30, 33–34
Merriam Commission, 30
Mihesuah, Devon (Oklahoma Choctaw), 21–22, 172–75
Mitchell, Douglas F., 67
Mohawk, John (Seneca), 19
Moi, Toril, 172–73
Momaday, N. Scott (Kiowa), 18, 53–54, 111
Montezuma, Carols (Yavapai), 3, 30, 44–45, 48, 51, 173
Mother Earth, 3, 85
Moyers, Bill, 165

National Council of American Indians (NCAI), 3, 30, 44
Native American Church, 40, 42–43
Native spirituality, 3, 20, 37, 67, 141–42, 147
new historicism, 11–12
Niessen, Jennifer, 135

Odem, Mary E., 49
Opler, Morris E., 73
Ortiz, Simon J. (Acoma Pueblo), 18
Owen, Louis (Choctaw/Cherokee), 20

Pan-Indianism, 29–30, 32, 42–44
patriarchy, 4–6, 13–14, 133–34, 136, 141, 145–46, 168–69, 171–72, 175
Pellerin, Simone, 92
Perry, Donna, 81, 83
Pewewardy, Cornel (Comanche-Kiowa), 175
peyote, 40–44
Picotte, Agnes M. (Lakota Sioux), 36
Pitt, Fiona, 66
Pocahontas, 2, 146
politics, 91, 150–51, 163–65, 167–69, 173
    political action, 23, 75
    political activism, 3, 55, 173–74
    political agenda, 54–55, 57, 69, 82, 86
    political empowerment, 5–6, 24, 172
    political ramifications of gender complementarity, 1, 6, 11–14, 23, 55, 172
    political roles, 21, 53, 174
Prucha, Francis Paul, 36, 51, 138
Purdy, John, 149

Rappaport, Doreen, 36, 38
Red Power Movement, 22
Rich, Adrienne, 100
Roemer, Kenneth M., 53, 59–60
Roessel, Ruth (Navajo), 66, 68
Ronnow, Gretchen, 20
Rosen, Kenneth, 57
Ruoff, A LaVonne, 63, 85
Ruppert, James, 5, 105, 107, 110–11
Ryan, Kiernan, 11

Sacajawea, 2
Salyer, Gregory, 10
Sands, Kathleen Mullen, 19, 60
Santee School, 29
Schumacher, Michael, 91
Sekaquaptewa, Helen (Hopi), 19

Seyersted, Per, 54, 56
Shanley, Kathryn (Assiniboine), 21
Shechner, Mark, 174
Shepardson, Mary, 64, 70, 74, 79–80, 82
Sherwood, Robert, 137
Silberman, Robert, 20
Silko, Leslie Marmon (Laguna Pueblo), 1–4, 6, 8, 12–15, 18–20, 26, 53–87, 111, 134, 169, 171–75
   Almanac of the Dead, 54
   "Border Patrol State, The," 56, 82
   Ceremony, 54, 62, 82
   "Fences against Freedom," 55
   Laguna Woman, 59
   "Language and Literature from a Pueblo Perspective," 56
   "Lullaby," 3–4, 13, 53–55, 57–58, 61–65, 67–87, 173–74
   "Old-Time Indian Attack Conducted in Two Parts, An," 60
   "Storyteller," 54, 63
   Storyteller, 61, 63, 69
   "Yellow Woman," 62–63
   "*Yellow Woman*"/*Leslie Marmon Silko*, 20, 55, 56
Smith, Joan, 77
Smith, Linda Tuhiwai (Ngati Awa/Ngati Porou), 7
Sniffen, Matthew K., 29, 47–49
Society of the American Indian (SAI), 30
sovereignty, 3–10, 13–15, 44, 114, 116, 119, 120, 142–44, 150, 173
   intellectual, 4–6, 8, 14, 89, 94, 96–98, 102, 108–11, 114–25, 131, 143–44, 146, 149, 153–54, 156, 164, 171, 173–75
   rhetorical, 8, 13, 27, 34–35, 51
Spack, Ruth, 33
Spivak, Gayatri Chakravorty, 23
Stout, Mary, 29
Strom, Karen M., 27
survival humor, 14, 63, 82–83, 133, 151, 155–65

Tanner, Helen Hornbeck, 92–93
Thorpe, Dagmar (Sac & Fox), 124
Tobert, Natalie, 66
Tohe, Laura (Diné), 22, 26, 55, 68–70, 75, 83–84, 86
Torrez, Juliette, 140
Trennert, Robert, 40

Trout, Lawana, 72
Tsosie, Rebecca (Pascua Yaqui), 11–12, 25, 31

Velie, Alan R., 53, 106
Vizenor, Gerald (Ojibwe), 20, 53, 106, 108–9

Waldman, Carl, 138
Warrior, Robert Allen (Osage), 7–8, 94, 115–16, 125, 144–45
warriors, 2, 31, 139
   female, 2, 14–15, 33–34, 81, 133, 159, 168–69, 171, 174–75
Welch, James (Blackfeet/Gros Ventre), 18, 53, 111
Wexler, Laura, 48–49
White's Manual Labor Institute, 29, 36
Willard, William, 41–42
Wilson, Angela Cavender (Wahpetonwan Dakota), 150
Wilson, Raymond, 39
Winnemucca, Sarah (Paiute), 18
Witherspoon, Gary, 66–67, 73–75, 79
Womack, Craig (Muskogee Creek/Cherokee), 9–10, 147, 150
Wub-e-ke-niew (Ojibwe), 115–16
Wynecoop, David C., 136

Yazzie, Ray, 56–57
Yellow Bird, Michael (Sahnish/Hidatsa), 15
Yellow Woman, 20

Zitkala-Ša (Yankton Sioux), 1–3, 5–6, 12–15, 18–19, 26–51, 171–73, 175
   "Address by Mrs. Gertrude Bonnin, Secretary-Treasurer," 32
   American Indian Stories, 18, 29
   "Impressions of an Indian Childhood," 31, 46
   "Indian Teacher among Indians, An," 46–47
   "Indian Welfare," 45
   "Indian Woman in Capital to Fight Growing Use of Peyote Drug by Indians," 41
   Oklahoma's Poor Rich Indians: An Orgy of Graft and Exploitation of the Five Civilized Tribes—Legalized Robbery? 14, 20, 29, 47–51

Old Indian Legends, 29, 35–36
"School Days of an Indian Girl, The," 38–39, 45
"Side by Side," 36–38
Sun Dance Opera, The, 30

"Toad and the Boy, The," 35–36
"Warrior's Daughter, A," 33–34
"Year's Experience in Community Service Work among the Ute Tribe of Indians, A," 32

For Product Safety Concerns and Information please contact our EU
representative GPSR@taylorandfrancis.com
Taylor & Francis Verlag GmbH, Kaufingerstraße 24, 80331 München, Germany

www.ingramcontent.com/pod-product-compliance
Lightning Source LLC
Chambersburg PA
CBHW051059230426
43667CB00013B/2369